Louis Kahn
Essential Texts

EDITED BY

ROBERT TWOMBLY

W. W. NORTON & COMPANY

New York • London

PAGE 2: Indian Institute of Management (1962–74),
Ahmedabad, India, wall fenestration system.

PHOTO CREDITS

Louis I. Kahn Collection, University of Pennsylvania and the Pennsylvania
Historical and Museum Commission: 2, 81, 83, 84 top and bottom, 85 top, 86,
88, 89 top and bottom, 90, 91 top and bottom (Photo: Craig Kuhner), 94, 95.

Marshall Keyers Collection, Architectural Archives, University of Pennsylvania:
82, 92, 93.

George Pohl Collection, Architectural Archives, University of Pennsylvania: 85
bottom, 96.

Architectural Archives, University of Pennsylvania, gift of the First Unitarian
Church of Rochester: 86-87.

For information about permission to reproduce
selections from this book, write to
Permissions, W. W. Norton & Company, Inc.,
500 Fifth Avenue, New York, NY 10110

Manufacturing by Maple-Vail Book Manufacturing Group
Book design by Gilda Hannah
Production Manager: Ben Reynolds

Library of Congress Cataloging-in-Publication Data

Kahn, Louis I., 1901-1974
      Louis Kahn: essential texts / [edited] by Robert Twombly.
          p. cm.
Includes bibliographical references and index.
ISBN 0-393-73113-8 (pbk.)
          1. Architecture. I. Twombly, Robert C. II. Title.

NA2560.K24 2003
720—dc21   2003048726

W. W. Norton & Company, Inc., 500 Fifth Avenue,
New York, N.Y. 10110
www.wwnorton.com

W. W. Norton & Company Ltd., Castle House,
75/76 Wells St., London W1T 3QT

0 9 8 7 6 5 4

Contents

Preface and Acknowledgments

This book grew out of a fascination with Louis Kahn that snuck up on me without my realizing it. I had first visited the Richards Laboratories in Philadelphia years ago but only later noticed some of its subtleties: how ground-hugging windows lighting below-grade workspaces also turn the lawn into an eye-level meadow and how narrow corner fenestration slots, some ivy-covered, delicately link indoors and out. Joseph Keating, former student now architect, introduced me to Temple Beth-El Synagogue in Chappaqua, New York, an underknown Kahn building flooded with light by means quite different than those employed at Phillips Exeter Academy Library in New Hampshire, which I initially saw when my son David decided to have a bit of fun under the guise of attending summer school. When I took students to Kahn's two museums at Yale University, I found it difficult to extract them, and myself, from the Mellon Center for British Art, so magnetically does its interior attract. By then I was already hooked, of course.

The students in my seminar on Kahn—I had to do something about my addiction—were simultaneously drawn to and troubled by his work. They were drawn, for example, to his brilliant lighting arrangements at the Kimbell Art Museum in Fort Worth but troubled by its cramped auditorium; drawn to the beautiful stairwells at both Yale museums but troubled by their façades; drawn to the sheer virtuosity of Phillips Exeter's atrium (in a library everyone wished was on our campus) but troubled by what they regarded as a misreading of student social life at Eleanor Donnelley Erdman Hall at Bryn Mawr College in Pennsylvania (a dormitory no one wanted to live in); drawn, finally, to Kahn's brick and concrete work and joinery but troubled by his sometimes dark, claustrophobic entrances. The students wrestled long, hard, and seriously with Kahn, seeing him in the end as a kind of flawed genius. I have not made up my mind about that yet, but I certainly thank them for their stimulating analyses and insightful observations in class and on site.

Thanks also to George Ranalli, Dean of the City College School of Architecture, Urban Design, and Landscape Architecture, and to Lance Jay Brown, Chair of the same, the former for getting me on the faculty, the latter for allowing me to teach pretty much what I please. My other dean, James F. Watts of Humanities and Art, also had a hand in my institutional relocation, enabling me to offer seminars on Kahn rather than surveys of American history. I have decided to postpone retirement.

William Whitaker, Collections Manager of the Architectural Archives, University of Pennsylvania, and Laura Stroffolino, research assistant there, were immensely helpful, making my stay in Philadelphia almost but not quite pleasant enough for me to reconsider what W. C. Fields said about it. Nancy Green, Casey Ruble, and others at W. W. Norton & Company were enthusiastic about this book and eminently professional in its editing and production.

Jeanne Chase, Research Professor at the Ecole des Hautes Etudes en Sciences Sociales in Paris offered excellent editorial advice and a hugely significant suggestion that greatly improved the introduction, which also benefited from a close reading and an equally important suggestion from City College of New York Professor Ravi Kalia. In thanking them, I in no way absolve myself of responsibility for any remaining gaffes.

Kahn is a difficult read but worth the effort. This volume contains a selection of his essential texts, several previously unpublished. Students thought it a good idea to have such a volume at hand. I think they were right.

ROBERT TWOMBLY
Professor of Architectural History

Introduction
Kahn's Search

• •

Louis Kahn rarely discussed buildings other than his own except for a few from long ago of which he often spoke. A favorite was the Pantheon, for him a spiritual place unfettered by time, location, or programmatic demand, a place in which to transcend everyday life by pondering those eternal truths, which for Kahn included humanity's omnipresent urge to better understand and thus improve itself. When he visited the Pantheon he detected basic, irreducible principles of architecture serving basic, irreducible verities of human existence—a sense of wonder, the love of beauty, of perfection, the search for the divine—that he believed had always been and would always be. His compulsive discussion of his own work was less an indication of self-absorption than of his relentless search for timeless principles.

Nor did he often speak of work by his contemporaries, many of whom—especially Le Corbusier—he admired. A notable exception was the 1947–50 Mexico City residence designed by Luis Barragan, who had left his garden terrain "as he found it," Kahn reported in l967, except for adding a watercourse resembling "a mountain stream in light" whose "silvery" tone was enhanced by trickling into a "rhinoceros gray black stone" basin. Subtleties of natural light and color were not much appreciated by modernist architects at mid-twentieth century; nor were architects of that era apt to ruminate about the spiritual qualities of historical design—religious structures excepted, of course—that captivated him so. Considerable philosophical and artistic differences separated him from them. Although he rarely argued with his peers, on those infrequent occasions when he criticized them, he discussed buildings architecturally, not designers personally. That, too, distanced him from some of his best-known colleagues.

By and large, what Kahn thought to be of primary importance—the past and the innate characteristics of materials, color, water, light, and nature itself—were of secondary importance for his contemporaries, who would probably have demurred at his contention that monumentality in architecture derived from its "spiritual quality," meaning that *all* architecture was potentially monumental.

Kahn's idiosyncratic use of certain words has caused confusion. Monumentality did not mean to him what it meant to others: big, important, lavish buildings dominating their surroundings. This understanding of monumentality was an aspect of nineteenth-century eclecticism—along with flamboyant ornament, potpourris of color and materials, and forms reproduced from history—that modernists rejected. Using new technologies and materials to express the "machine age," they developed "a new architecture for a new era," and if not one but several styles were born under the rubric "modernism," its disparate practitioners were more likely to look for inspiration from science and contemporary life than from the natural world and the past.

Louis Kahn was not such an architect. Trained during the 1920s in the Beaux-Arts methods of Paul Cret, his mentor at the University of Pennsylvania, but immersed during the 1930s and 1940s in modernist circles—especially from 1941 to 1947 as a partner of Philadelphia architect Oscar Stonorov—Kahn gave allegiance to neither the Beaux-Arts nor modernist approaches but drew from both what seemed important.

From the Beaux-Arts tradition he took the concept of hierarchical, centralized spatial organization and of the priority of plan: Allow the program to suggest a general scheme by arranging philosophical and material essentials in what he came to call a "form-drawing," from which elevations and façade compositions would eventually emerge. Frank Lloyd Wright (certainly no modernist) would have agreed, claiming as he did that the problem with Le Corbusier (modernist par excellence) was that he thought first of elevation and façade composition and later manipulated the plan to fit. Accurate or not (Wright cared little for accuracy when belittling "inferior" architects like Le Corbusier), he nevertheless shared Kahn's belief that enclosed space (to both of them a building's reason for being), not the enclosure itself, was architecture's essence.

From modernism Kahn learned about materials like reinforced concrete and technologies like truss-framing, about decorative minimalism ("the joint is the beginning of ornament," he insisted), about the visual clarity of simple forms and basic geometries. From modernist ideas he derived his lifelong insistence on forthrightly revealing how a building was made, in the end surpassing most of his peers at turning structure and the visible residues of construction technologies into art. Perhaps most significantly, however, Kahn took from modernism the concept of interpenetrating spaces, not of the so-called free plan that risked devolving into a single room housing competing functions but by developing instead an interdependency of hierarchically arranged "servant" and "served" spaces in which functions of lesser and greater importance, though sharing a common mega-space, were nonetheless distinguishable by variations in scale, lighting, floor level, or materials.

The subtleties of Kahn's architecture—including its obvious though understated constructive quality, its palpable if intangible spiritual content, and its structured yet flowing arrangements of space—have confounded some observers, some of whom consider him a modernist (perhaps its last master), others of whom say he rebelled against it (perhaps as the first postmodernist). Neither view is entirely true or false but both miss a fundamental point. The point about Kahn is his search.

What he was searching for is difficult to say—perfection, truth, essence, order, harmony, serenity, perhaps more or less than these. But ultimately his search was more metaphysical, more psychological or existential, than it was architectural. Architecture was his means of reaching for greater profundity. He never found what he was looking for—not the whole of it anyway—but he knew that that was as it should be.

His search, which was also a struggle, resembled that of John Coltrane, the great jazz saxophonist of the 1950s and 1960s, Kahn's artistic contemporary. Coltrane's signature song was Richard Rogers's and Oscar Hammerstein's "My Favorite Things," a mundane, mindless ditty he recorded at least six times from 1960 to 1967 and played at countless clubs and concerts. Over the years his performances grew longer and more complex, from fifteen minutes to almost an hour, with no two versions very much alike. The melody virtually disappeared into improvisational explorations of his own emotions, his creative potential, and of musical forms and structures.

But absence of melody did not did not mean lawlessness, for Coltrane was bound by the inviolable constants of key, time, harmonics, and rhythm patterns from which he could not stray during his solos lest he and his group lapse into musical anarchy. Bound by immutable laws akin to those governing Kahn in architecture—only so much concrete can be poured in a day, bearing arches must be buttressed, sun must be screened in hot climates—Coltrane nevertheless refused to acknowledge limits on his own capacity to search for new forms of self-expression, for the ultimate self-expression, not knowing what that might be, knowing only that more and better were possible. He never found what he was looking for—never reached his nirvana—but knew he never would. And this very knowledge, far from discouraging him, gave him strength, because he fully understood that creativity and growth derived from the journey, not from arrival. To arrive, in a sense, was to die. Kahn knew this, too.

Kahn's journey became apparent, at least in print, around 1955. In a brief statement that came to be called "Order Is" published that year in *Perspecta*, the Yale University magazine of architecture, Kahn wrote that "Order is intangible/It is a level of creative consciousness/forever becoming higher in level/The higher the order the more diversity in design," adding, "From what the space wants to be the unfamiliar may be revealed to the architect/From order he will derive creative force and power of self-criticism/to give form to this unfamiliar."

Important Kahnian tenets can be extrapolated from these passages (when read in light of other texts in this volume): Prior to humanity's awareness of it, the universe was a coherent, self-regulating entity awaiting discovery. Humankind's additions to and modifications of that preexisting order often damaged it, so that the architect's charge is a kind of restoration effort requiring him to incorporate his understanding of the eternal in every design, as did the Pantheon's makers, hence its everlasting appeal. "What the space wants to be" is itself—that is, it wants to assume its rightful place in and be a proper manifestation of the eternal order of things. In sum, Kahn set himself the task of finding and designing "ideal types"—structures to house "Unitarianness" or "librariness," for example—that would at the same time accommodate the requirements of the particular and unique congregation or library at hand. In that sense he was a kind of modern-day Platonist. Kahn's search as a designer and thinker involved determining what a particular building "wanted to be" in light of what the nature of that kind of building "had always been." His was an intellectual and spiritual journey he knew was endless because eternal order could never be fully grasped.

Kahn's life journey began in 1901 on the Baltic Sea island of Ösel in Estonia. In 1904 his parents took him to Philadelphia, where he was schooled and received his bachelor of architecture diploma in 1924. During the next two decades he worked with several local architects including Cret, took a year-long European tour (1928–29), was appointed to the city planning commission, the New Deal Resettlement Administration, and the United States Housing Authority. After passing the Pennsylvania licensing examination in 1935, he opened his own office, but in the depths of the Depression found it necessary to associate with established firms, George Howe's from 1941 to 1942 and also Oscar Stonorov's, with the latter designing a range of buildings including public and private housing.

His association with Stonorov ended in 1947 when Kahn became visiting and later chief critic of design at the Yale School of Architecture. He took a year off from those responsibilities in 1950–51 to tour Greek and Egyptian ruins from his post as architect in residence at the American Academy in Rome. After his return, while maintaining a Philadelphia office, he commuted to New Haven until 1955 when he was appointed professor of architecture at the University of Pennsylvania. In 1966 he was named Paul Philippe Cret Professor of Architecture in tribute both to him and to his mentor, a position he held until he died in 1974.

Before joining the Penn faculty he had designed, on his own or in collaboration, more than a hundred buildings dating from 1925. Of these, forty-three were built. Structures like the 1948–54 addition to the Philadelphia Psychiatric Hospital and the Mill Creek public housing development (first phase, 1951–56) in Philadelphia, along with other built and unbuilt projects, as well as his work for planning and housing authorities, generated critical acclaim and professional visibility. But it was his 1951–53 extension of the Yale University Art Gallery that put him on the architectural map. Kahn did not become famous until he was over fifty years old, at just the moment that he began to lecture and publish essays with increasing regularity.

During his remaining twenty-four years, Kahn lectured, was interviewed, appeared at panel discussions or open forums, and issued statements to the press at least 138 times, not counting repeat performances of speeches (of which there were many, though never quite alike) and brief remarks that found their way into print. Kahn published a handful of essays, but he liked public speaking better, regardless of whether the occasion called for a formal lecture or, as was much more often the case, seemingly improvised, off-the-cuff remarks. He frequently illustrated his talks with slides, but he preferred standing at a blackboard, drawing in chalk with both hands simultaneously. He enjoyed taking questions from the audience.

All this was not as casual as it may have appeared, however. Even a seemingly spontaneous talk was ordinarily accompanied by a typescript that was usually the result of multiple drafts and occasionally further edited by hand. This is not to say he preferred to read the text or was reluctant to depart from it. But it does reveal his meticulous preparation no matter how the presentation ultimately played out. When he repeated a speech to a second or third audience, he rewrote it yet again: The two versions of "Silence and Light" reproduced here, for example, address similar issues but in significantly different ways. The same is true of "Law and Rule in Architecture."

Constant revision might suggest dissatisfaction—with not finding exactly the right words to convey his meaning, not expressing himself with sufficient clarity, with not, in short, achieving presentational perfection. Nevertheless, Kahn invariably spoke enthusiastically, with obvious pleasure, invariably using the subject at hand as an entrée into his ongoing investigation of architecture's eternal truths. He may have been displeased with his inability to make his words coincide perfectly with his thoughts, but his manifest delight in trying suggests a certain satisfaction in knowing that intellectually and as a designer he was making progress.

Parallels with his design procedure are striking. Of the approximately 106 commissions Kahn received from 1951 until his death, some thirty-six were realized (including a handful posthumously), a rather small percentage for an architect of his standing. He devoted a great deal of time to these designs. The average duration from receipt of a commission to completion of construction was six years, on projects ranging from a few weeks devoted to a 1955 kitchen remodeling in Philadelphia to thirteen years on the vast Indian Institute of Management complex (1962–74) in Ahmedabad.

He also labored long and hard on what was never built—for instance, off and on for twelve years (1961–72) on the Mikvah Israel Synagogue in Philadelphia; for nine years (1966–74) on the Altgar office tower in Kansas City; and for eight (1967–74) on the Hurva Synagogue in Jerusalem. A proper if relatively unimportant conclusion to draw from these figures is that it took Kahn an unusually long time to design what would probably not be constructed. But more important is this: Built or not, most Kahn designs were rethought, reworked, and reconceived, in short, agonized over with the same care and determination he devoted to his speeches. In either case it is impossible to know if or to what extent he was pleased with the outcome, assuming, that is, that he measured the outcome against some elusive standard of perfection or completeness he could sense but not necessarily explain. The speculation here is that he was generally pleased with what he had done but felt he might have done better, which in part suggests why he had such difficulty letting go of whatever he drew or wrote.

There were occasions on which clients almost literally had to tear Kahn away from his plans because they, but not he, were satisfied and wanted to start construction. Kahn also was known to keep working on projects his clients had decided not to build, to offer to continue without additional compensation because he was not completely happy with what he had done even though the clients were, or to tender his services without charge—or at reduced fee—simply because he was especially excited by the problem. (It has been reported that he died heavily in debt; in some instances he failed to vigorously pursue money owed him—$40,000 for his unbuilt 1968–74 Palazzo dei Congressi in Venice, for example—perhaps in the misplaced hope that if he were particularly accommodating he could somehow convince his clients to change their minds and build anyway.)

Kahn struggled longer and harder and at times for less remuneration than most other designers of his stature, not because he was slow or doubted his abilities, but because he wanted his work to be perfect. But there was something else: As simple and naïve as it may sound, making money was not Kahn's primary motivation. Nor was it pursuit of fame or ego gratification, of which he already had plenty. His primary motivation resided in a sensibility foreign to most architects then and now but fundamental to him. This is how he put it: Because architecture is "completely insatiable" and "can never be satisfied," every one of his buildings was merely "an offering" to it (see selection 13).

One might make an offering to the insatiable in the vain hope of appeasing it, lightening its burden, getting it off one's back. Or one might make the offering in an attempt to approach it, gain access to the sanctuary where its deepest secrets are kept. With Kahn it was the latter, and his words about architecture were every bit as sincere an offering to it as his designs were, for the two were inseparable, a gift from the servant to the master/muse he served. The offerings assembled here represent his essential thinking as it evolved and should be read not only for content but also for the manner in which content is conveyed, because the form of Kahn's talks is a function of their substance. What he said is sometimes difficult to grasp because of its abstractness, which has everything to do with the way in which he said it. These texts are difficult, but close reading of them yields substantial rewards.

There are certain things to be aware of in reading Louis Kahn, the first of which is his language. Certain words and phrases, being distillations of broad concepts, recur in these texts, and as time passed and his concepts broadened or new ones assumed priority, those words and phrases occasionally took on additional meaning or were substituted one for another. The headnotes attempt to define those concepts and to clarify their transformations, to explain the shifting relationships among "form" and "design," "law" and "rule," for example, or between "institutions" and "availabilities." Kahn did not necessarily use words in the same way as other people, or mean the same things by them. "Silence" and "light" are but two of many that in his thinking carried much greater significance (bordering on the metaphysical) than their dictionary definitions allow, but which can nevertheless be understood through careful consideration.

And then there are Kahnian aphorisms—"what a building wants to be," "the plan is a society of rooms," "what will be has always been," and many more—that when repeated by others ad nauseam appear, like a holy script reduced to glib slogans, to be empty, even silly, clichés. But Kahn knew what his words and phrases meant even if he had trouble explaining them to others.

His unusual terminology and phraseology probably forced audiences to listen closely. But it is unlikely that he was trying to be difficult. Resorting to obscurity as a means of securing attention is as apt to backfire as speaking so softly that listeners strain to hear. And Kahn desperately wanted to be heard. Even with an enormous workload— seventeen substantial commissions in progress the year he died—he was hard-pressed to refuse any of the lecture invitations that flooded his office. Given the heavy demands on his time he probably spoke more often than was prudent. But he was unable to stop, and people were obviously pleased that he did not because they flocked to hear him, especially architecture students, opaque prose notwithstanding.

Kahn's tortured language was neither a misdirected strategy not a lack of verbal command. It was another manifestation of the same questioning process that drove him to refer incessantly in reformulated lectures to his redesigned projects, as well as another indication of his consuming struggle to achieve perfect clarity of thought and its expression. At the root of the problem was the fact that far from being a systematic or analytical thinker, Kahn was in reality an instinctive and intuitive sensor of things he could not completely fathom and thus not clearly convey to others.

But there was something more: A lecture for Kahn was a kind of dialogue between recapitulation and invention. Which meant that in style but not substance his talks were mostly improvisational. Just as John Coltrane explored "his" song, "My Favorite Things," over and again, each time deriving from it something new, so too Louis Kahn reinvestigated his own design and literary themes, stretching their limits. For both Coltrane and Kahn, reexamining one's own work fundamentally meant reexploring one's own self. And just as Coltrane's music was incomprehensible to many, so too were Kahn's ideas. This did not prevent people from crowding in to hear them, however. Louis Kahn was unable to communicate in simple, unvarnished prose (and for that matter, grammatical construction) partly because of his struggle to put into words what he could only sense, and partly because he lived so intensely in an architectural universe so personal that even the most perceptive of his colleagues and listeners had trouble gaining access.

If Kahn was something of an intellectual hermit, it was because he believed that the knowledge and wisdom a person accumulated during the course of life originated from within, and had always been inside that person, awaiting discovery. His continual reformulation in word and design of what he had often said and drawn was nothing less than a search for the ultimate "more" and "better"—for those traces of eternal order—he knew existed somewhere within himself, and that could be tapped but would never be completely accessible. Nirvana was not to be had.

Failure to reach it did not discourage him, however. He knew he had achieved a great deal—that he had marked architecture indelibly, in fact—despite never attaining that ultimate more and better. Observers knew it too: Kahn was, for example, an acknowledged master at bringing natural light deep into buildings and, conversely, at keeping the sun at bay when conditions required it. The ways he toplit the First Unitarian Church (1959–69) in Rochester, New York, the Phillips Exeter Academy Library (1965–72) in Exeter, New Hampshire, the Temple Beth-El Synagogue (1966–72) in Chappaqua, New York, and the Yale Center for British Art (1969–74) in New Haven, Connecticut, were variations on a system of his own invention for guiding baffled light to its proper destination. The perforated walls at the Indian Institute of Management and at Sher-e-Bangla Nagar (1962–83), the capital complex of Bangladesh in Dhaka, were variations on another of his systems, this one for preventing harsh light from entering at all. At Dhaka, at the Salk Institute for Biological Studies (1959–65) in La Jolla, California, and inside Kahn's two New Haven art museums are exquisitely poured concrete wall surfaces, as beautiful in design and execution as the brickwork at Phillips Exeter and the First Unitarian Church. And when it came to creating compelling spaces, including partially enclosed exterior spaces like those at the Salk Institute, Kahn had few rivals. He could hardly have been discouraged by all he had accomplished.

Not reaching nirvana drove him onward, in fact, because he understood that the pleasure and meaning of life was in the search. Kahn ended one of his last speeches, in 1973 at Pratt Institute in Brooklyn, by noting that when all was said and done the architect's job was to make an "offering of man to [the] next man." That, to him, was "joy." "If you don't feel joy in what you're doing," he told the assembled students, "then you're not really operating." You will probably experience great frustration as architects, "but really," he concluded, surely referring to himself, "joy will prevail."

NOTE: The texts reproduced here from the Kahn archives are as he left them—incorporating his hand-written amendments of typescripts—with the following exceptions: Typos, spelling, and certain punctuation have been corrected, and spelling and punctuation made to conform to standard American practice. Phrases such as "thank you" and "next slide" have been deleted. Words enclosed in brackets indicate stenographic omissions or misunderstandings of the text. (When stenographers or tape recorders were available to capture Kahn's deviations from prepared manuscripts, he sometimes requested transcriptions in order to have an accurate record of what he actually said, especially if publication was anticipated.) Ellipsis marks indicate the removal of confusing repetitions, except in selection 6, where they indicate pauses in Kahn's presentation.

Introduction: Kahn's Search

1   Monumentality (1944)

Implicit in Louis Kahn's first major essay as a sole author is a critique of modernism's poverty of form and variety, which he associated with neglect of the past. He chided his contemporaries for failing to examine, for example, the "magnificent variations" with which medieval builders had adorned cathedrals in their "search for clarity of purpose" based on "love of perfection." Defining monumentality as "the spiritual quality of architecture" that Kahn knew could not be achieved simply by copying historical forms, he called on young, creative minds to study the new materials and construction processes World War II had generated, so that architecture might return to those "basic principles" that in the past had been the "common characteristics of its greatness."

As Kahn matured he gradually and without fanfare dissociated himself from the conventional modernist forms of his early design work. Seeds of his fully developed philosophy are apparent in this contribution to Paul Zucker's *New Architecture and City Planning: A Symposium.*

Gold is a beautiful material. It belongs to the sculptor.

M onumentality in architecture may be defined as a quality, a spiritual quality inherent in a structure which conveys the feeling of its eternity, that it cannot be added to or changed. We feel

From Paul Zucker, ed., *New Architecture and City Planning: A Symposium.* (Freeport, N.Y.: Books for Libraries Press, 1944)

that quality in the Parthenon, the recognized architectural symbol of Greek civilization.

Some argue that we are living in an unbalanced state of relativity which cannot be expressed with a single intensity of purpose. It is for that reason, I feel, that many of our confrères do not believe we are psychologically constituted to convey a quality of monumentality to our buildings.

But have we yet given full architectural expression to such social monuments as the school, the community or culture center? What stimulus, what movement, what social or political phenomenon shall we yet experience? What event or philosophy shall give rise to a will to commemorate its imprint on our civilization? What effect would such forces have on our architecture?

Science has given to the architect its explorations into new combinations of materials capable of great resistance to the forces of gravity and wind.

Recent experiments and philosophers of painting, sculpture and architecture have instilled new courage and spirit in the work of their fellow artists.

Monumentality is enigmatic. It cannot be intentionally created. Neither the finest material nor the most advanced technology need enter a work of monumental character for the same reason that the finest ink was not required to draw up the Magna Carta.

However, our architectural monuments indicate a striving for structural perfection which has contributed in great part to their impressiveness, clarity of form and logical scale.

Stimulated and guided by knowledge we shall go far to develop the forms indigenous to our new materials and methods. It is, therefore, the concern of this paper to touch briefly on the broader horizons which science and skill have revealed to the architect and engineer and sketch the faint outlines of possible structural concepts and expressions they suggest.

No architect can rebuild a cathedral of another epoch embodying the desires, the aspirations, the love and hate of the people whose heritage it became. Therefore the images we have before us of monumental structures of the past cannot live again with the same intensity and meaning. Their faithful duplication is unreconcilable. But we dare not discard the lessons these buildings teach for they have the common characteristics of greatness upon which the buildings of our future must, in one sense or another, rely.

In Greek architecture engineering concerned itself fundamentally with materials in compression. Each stone or part forming the structural members was made to bear with accuracy on each other to avoid tensile action stone is incapable of enduring.

The great cathedral builders regarded the members of the structural skeleton with the same love of perfection and search for clarity of purpose. Out of periods of inexperience and fear when they erected over-massive core-filled veneered walls, grew a courageous theory of a stone over stone vault skeleton producing a downward and outward thrust, which forces were conducted to a column or a wall provided with the added characteristic of the buttress which together took this combination of action. The buttress allowed lighter walls between the thrust points and these curtain walls were logically developed for the use of large glass windows. This structural concept, derived from earlier and cruder theories, gave birth to magnificent variations in the attempts to attain loftier heights and greater spans creating a spiritually emotional environment unsurpassed. The influence of the Roman vault, the dome, the arch, has etched itself in deep furrows across the pages of architectural history. Through Romanesque, Gothic, Renaissance and today, its basic forms and structural ideas have been felt. They will continue to reappear but with added powers made possible by our technology and engineering skill.

The engineer of the latter part of the nineteenth century developed from basic principles the formulas of the handbook. Demands of enormous building quantity and speed developed the handbook engineer who used its contents, more or less forgetting basic principles. Now we hear about continuity in structures, not a new word but recently an all important word in engineering which promises to relegate the handbook to the archives.

The I-beam is an engineering accomplishment deriving its shape from an analysis of the stresses involved in its use. It is designed so that the greater proportion of the area of cross section is concentrated as far as possible from the center of gravity. The shape adapted itself to ease of rolling and under test it was found that even the fillets, an aid in the rolling process, helped convey the stresses from one section to another in continuity.

Safety factors were adopted to cover possible inconsistencies in the composition of the material of manufacture. Large scale machinery and equipment needed in its fabrication led to standardization.

The combination of safety factors (ignorance factor as one engineer termed it) and standardization narrowed the practice of engineering to the section of members from handbooks recommending sections much heavier than calculations would require and further limited the field of engineering expression stifling the creation of the more graceful forms which the stress diagrams indicated. For example, the common practice of using an I-beam as a cantilever has no relation to the stress diagram which shows that the required depth of material from the supporting end outward may decrease appreciably.

Joint construction in common practice treats every joint as a hinge which makes connections to columns and other members complex and ugly.

To attain greater strength with economy, a finer expression in the structural solution of the principle of concentrating the area of cross section away from the center of gravity is the tubular form since the greater the moment of inertia the greater the strength.

A bar of a certain area of cross section rolled into a tube of the same area of cross section (consequently of a larger diameter) would possess a strength enormously greater than the bar.

The tubular member is not new, but its wide use has been retarded by technological limitations in the construction of joints. Up until very recently welding has been outlawed by the building codes. In some cases, where it was permitted, it was required to make loading tests for every joint.

Structure designs must discard the present moment coefficients and evolve new calculations based on the effect of continuity in structures. The structural efficiency of rigid connection, in which the sheer value and the resisting moment is at least equal to the values of the supporting member, is obtained by the welding of such connections. The column becomes part of the beam and takes on added duties not usually calculated for columns.

The engineer and architect must then go back to basic principles, must keep abreast with and consult the scientist for new knowledge, redevelop his judgment of the behavior of structures and acquire a new sense of form derived from design rather than piece together parts of convenient fabrication.

Riveted I-beam plate and angle construction is complex and graceless. Welding has opened the doors to vast accomplishments in pure engineering which allows forms of greater strength and efficiency to be used. The choice of structural forms are limitless even for given problems and therefore the aesthetic philosophy of the individual can be satisfied by his particular composition of plates, angles and tubular forms accomplishing the same answer to the challenge of the forces of gravity and wind.

The ribs, vaults, domes, buttresses come back again only to enclose space in a more generous, far simpler way and in the hands of our present masters of building in a more emotionally stirring way. From stone, the part has become smaller and cannot be seen by the naked eye. It is now the molecular composition of the metal observed and tested by the scientist through spectroscopy or by photoelastic recordings. His finding may go to the architect and engineer in the more elemental form of the formula, but by that means it shall have become an instrumental part of the builder's palette to be used without prejudice or fear. That is the modern way.

Gothic architecture relying on basically simple construction formulas derived from experience and the material available, could only go so far. Beauvais cathedral, its builders trying to reach greater spans and height, collapsed.

The compressive stress of stone is measured in hundreds of pounds.

While not only the compressive, but also the bending and tensile stress of steel is measured in thousands of pounds.

Beauvais cathedral needed the steel we have. It needed the knowledge we have.

Glass would have revealed the sky and become a part of the enclosed space framed by an interplay of exposed tubular ribs, plates and columns of a stainless metal formed true and faired into a continuous flow of lines expressive of their stress patterns. Each member would have been welded to the next to create a continuous structural unity worthy of being exposed because its engineering gives no resistance to the laws of beauty having its own aesthetic life. The metal would have now been aged into a friendly material protected from deterioration by its intrinsic composition.

This generation is looking forward to its duty and benefit to build for the masses with its problems of housing and health.

It is aware of our outmoded cities.

It accepts the airship as a vital need.

Factories have adopted horizontal assembly and shifting population has required the transformation of large tracts of virgin territory at least temporarily for complete human living.

The building of a complete permanent town was attempted and almost built for the workers at Willow Run.

The nation has adopted the beginnings of social reform.

War production may become normal production on the same scale accepted as sound economics.

Still untried but pledged stand the noble principles of the Atlantic Charter.[1]

In the days we look forward to must then the cathedral, the culture center, the legislative palace, world island—the seat of the congress of nations, the palace of labor and industry, the monuments to commemorate the achievements and aspirations of our time, be built to

---

1. The Atlantic Charter, jointly issued on August 14, 1941, by Winston Churchill and Franklin Delano Roosevelt, was an informal statement of World War II objectives adopted in principle on January 1, 1942, by twenty-six "United Nations" in a formal "Declaration."

resemble Chartres, Crystal Palace, Palazzo Strozzi, or the Taj Mahal? War engineering achievements in concrete, steel and wood are showing the signs of maturity appropriate to guide the minds entrusted with the conception of buildings of such high purpose. The giant major skeleton of the structure can assert its right to be seen. It need no longer be clothed for eye appeal. Marble and woods feel at ease in its presence. New wall products of transparent, translucent and opaque material with exciting textures and color are suspended or otherwise fastened to the more delicate forms of the minor members. Slabs of paintings articulate the circulation in the vast sheltered space. Sculpture graces its interior.

Outstanding masters of building design indicated the direction an architect may take to unravel and translate into simple terms the complexity of modern requirements. They have restated the meaning of a wall, a post, a beam, a roof and a window and their interrelation in space. They had to be restated when we recall the conglomerations that style-copying tortured these elements into.

Efforts towards a comprehensive architecture will help to develop these elements and refine their meaning. A wall dividing interior space is not the same wall dividing the outside from the interior. Masonry shall always function as retaining and garden walls. It may be used for exterior walls for its decorative qualities, but be supplemented by interior slabs designed to meet more directly the challenge of the elements.

Structural ingenuity may eliminate the interior post, but as long as it must exist its place is reserved and its independence respected in the planning of space.

Structural problems center about the roof. The permanence and beauty of its surfaces is a major problem confronting science. The surfacing of the domes, vaults and arches appearing as part of the exterior contours of the building may be an integral part of the structural design. Stainless metal, concrete or structural plastics, structural glass in light panes, or great reinforced glass castings may be the choice for domes and vaults, depending on the requirements, the climate and the desired effect. The surfacing of flat roofs should be given equally serious consideration whether it is planned for use or not.

The citizens of a metropolitan area of a city and their representatives have formulated a program for a culture center endorsed by the national educational center. The citizens' committee collaborated with the architect and his staff of engineers. Costs were not discussed. Time was not "of the essence." Its progress was the concern of many.

From above we see the noble outlines of the building. Much taller buildings some distance from the site do not impress us with the same feeling of receptiveness. Its site is a prominent elevation in the outlying countryside framed by dark forests defining the interior of broad strokes in land architecture.

On the ground the first reaction comes from the gigantic sculptural forms of the skeleton frame. This backbone of the architect's central idea successfully challenges the forces which during its design challenged to destroy it. To solve the more minute complexities of the entire organism, its creator had drawn his conclusions and made his decisions from the influences of many people and things around him.

The plan does not begin nor end with the space he has enveloped, but from the adjoining delicate ground sculpture it stretches beyond to the rolling contours and vegetation of the surrounding land and continues farther out to the distant hills.

The immediate ground sculpture disciplines his mind in shaping it into stronger geometric planes and cubes to satisfy his desire for terraces and pools, steps and approaches. The landscape designer countered or accentuated these planes with again geometric and free forms interwoven with the lacy leaf patterns of the deciduous tree.

The plans reveal that the vast spans shelter smaller areas designed for specific use, which are divided from the whole by panels of glass, insulated slabs, and marble. These partitions are free of the structure and related only to the circulation pattern. The ground plan seems continuous. The great lobby is a part of the amphitheater which dips down to the stage. The light comes from above through an undulating series of prismatic glass domes.

Ahead, some distance from the entrance, is a great mural of brilliant color. As we approach it the forms clearly defined from a distance seem to divide into forms of their own, each with its own color power, clear and uncluttered.

To one side is the community museum of sculpture, painting and crafts. It exhibits the work of the younger men and women attending the vocational and art academies. Here they are accepted because their talents can be judged by those who have themselves been instructed in the basic principles underlying the use of a material. The emotional adaptations are left for the exhibitor himself to evaluate by contact, comparison and experience.

Sculpture shows the tendency to define form and construction. Marble and stone is carved as of old. Castings in new alloys and plastics are favorite methods of obtaining permanency. Solids are interwoven with sheets and tubes of metal. The subject matter exhibited has no bounds. With the new materials and tools, chemical tints, and with manufacture at the artist's disposal, his work becomes alive with ideas. Metal sprays and texture guns, with fine adjustments have also become the instruments of the sculptor, painter and craftsman. One of the younger men had cast within a large, irregular cube of transparent plastic other forms and objects of brilliant color. A sphere, planes at various angles, copper wire in free lines are seen through the plastic.

From these experiments in form the architect will eventually learn to choose appropriate embellishments for his structures. So far he has omitted them. His judgment leads him to freestanding forms in space.

Some of the younger artists are influenced by the works of an older sculptor who has developed a theory of scale in relation to space. He has argued that as the size of the structural work is increased the monolithic character of smaller work does not apply. He chose for large work a small consistent part or module of a definite shape, a cube, a prism, or a sphere which he used to construct block over block, with delicate adjustments to the effect of light and shadow, the overall form. His work seen from great distances retains a texturally vibrant quality produced by these numerous blocks and the action of the sun upon them.

Before we can feel the new spirit which must envelop the days to come we must prepare ourselves to use intelligently the knowledge derived from all sources. Nostalgic yearning for the ways of the past will find but few ineffectual supporters.

Steel, the lighter metals, concrete, glass, laminated woods, asbestos, rubber, and plastics, are emerging [as] the prime building materials of today. Riveting is being replaced by welding, reinforced concrete is emerging from infancy with prestressed reinforced concrete, vibration and controlled mixing, promising to aid in its ultimate refinement. Laminated wood is rapidly replacing lumber and is equally friendly to the eye, and plastics are so vast in their potentialities that already numerous journals and periodicals devoted solely to their many outlets are read with interest and hope. The untested characteristics of these materials are being analyzed, old formulas are being discarded. New alloys of steel, shatter-proof and thermal glass and synthetics of innumerable types, together with the material already mentioned, make up the new palette of the designer.

To what extent progress in building will be retarded by ownership patterns, dogmas, style consciousness, precedent, untested building materials, arbitrary standards, outmoded laws and regulations, untrained workmen and artless craftsmen, is speculation. But the findings of science and their application have taken large steps recently in the development of war materials which point to upset normally controlled progress and raise our hopes to the optimistic level.

Standardization, prefabrication, controlled experiments and tests, and specialization are not monsters to be avoided by the delicate sensitiveness of the artist. They are merely the modern means of controlling vast potentialities of materials for living, by chemistry, physics, engineering, production and assembly, which lead to the necessary knowledge the artist must have to expel fear in their use, broaden his creative instinct, give him new courage and thereby lead him to the adventures of unexplored places. His work will then be part of his age and will afford delight and service for his contemporaries.

I do not wish to imply that monumentality can be attained scientifically or that the work of the architect reaches its greatest service to humanity by his peculiar genius to guide a concept towards a monumentality. I merely defend, because I admire, the architect who possesses the will to grow with the many angles of our development. For such a man finds himself far ahead of his fellow workers.

2 An Approach to Architectural Education (1956)

● ●

Prompted by 1950s redevelopment of central Philadelphia, Kahn and his University of Pennsylvania colleague Robert Le Ricolais assigned their students the problem of designing a skyscraper without space-consuming columns. Aside from the obvious maximizing of floor area and natural light, the objective was to express the not-so-obvious "crushing down forces" of great height and the lateral "side forces" of wind. Students were to develop a structural system that, screening against sun and bracing against wind, was also its own façade. Kahn saw the architect not "as a designer of exteriors and selector of tasteful finish materials" but "as a master coordinator-builder"—a latter-day medieval master—whose structural systems and façade art were inseparable, one and the same. This essay was published in the University of Pennsylvania's magazine, *Pennsylvania Triangle*.

The center of Philadelphia is being given new life by the developments around Independence Mall and Penn Center. The completion of the Vine Street Expressway, the planning and the eventual completion of the Lombard Street and Delaware Avenue Expressways will frame the area with new traffic rivers eliminating the necessity for through traffic and freeing all the street-ways for a new order of movement.

● ●

From *Pennsylvania Triangle*, v. 42 (January 1956): 28–32. Reprinted with the permission of the Dean of the Graduate School of Fine Arts, University of Pennsylvania.

This order of movement with its system of municipal garages integrated with the entrances from the expressways will mark the gateways to the center. These gateways together with commercial garages on the interior and the assignment of most streets for parking should satisfy the motorist's objective of a place to stop for shopping, recreation and business. Public transportation and pedestrian ways would belong to a separate system of movement on other streets. Zoning for land use will grow naturally out of the street zoning for movement. Architecture will tend to relate to the street character.

The Triangle Redevelopment Area of which Penn Center is a part and the area along the river south of it to Walnut and east to 20th may be considered as the site for the greater recreation, culture and civic center of the city.

The redevelopment of this area, the Mall and other areas in relation to the new movement and garage system is the subject of many possible studies in Architecture and environment.

Tower Buildings are likely to become gigantic space structures consolidating many uses in one complex, in order to economize in the services of communication—sanitation, heating and air conditioning. This consolidation will tend also to free the ground for the reestablishment of plant life and the parking of vehicles.

Tower design is a timely problem for students in Architecture preparing for an approach to the study of these future buildings. Though circumstances may change the location and nature of the centers of redevelopment, an approach to design through a comprehension of order reflecting the nature and spirit of what a space or a street wants to be could lead to an architecture of cities.

The office tower is built essentially for investment. The fixed cost and the calculated financial return is the program handed the architect. His problem therefore is to build on a specific lot so much space for so much money. The efficiency of the plan is measured by the amount of usable space both near and away from natural light in proportion to the amount of space given over to services and corridors.

Little time elapses from the real estate transaction to the finished drawings.

The financial scheme must be put into effect immediately.

More or less the tower (or slab) results from an assembly of competitive materials and techniques unsympathetic to integration and to development into an expressive and inspiring architecture. Any experienced builder or promoter feels he knows enough to bring together such responsible engineers, technicians and material men to result in an intelligent assembly of a physically functioning office building without the aid of an "expensive" architect. Consequently the average promoter, though he must employ an architect, does not regard him as a master coordinator-builder but rather as a designer of exteriors and selector of tasteful finish materials. His fee is whittled down accordingly and it is not uncommon for the architect to accept part of his fee in promotion stock.

The "treatment" of the façade is recognized by all interested and responsible as belonging solely to the architect. Sometimes the promoter interferes and insists on a horizontal motive against the wishes of the architect who may feel a vertical tendency. The facade is regarded as an enclosure playing no part in the structural conception of the building. This is intellectualized into a standardization of function—as a skin. The architect has much fun and uses much money making sketches of all possible "treatments."

But the face is no casual matter of structure in a building hundreds of feet high.

As the face to the sun, to the wind and the rain it can well be conceived as the beginning of the structure able to break up or receive the rays of the sun or become a buttress against the force of wind and thus becoming an integral part of the conception contributing in the development of a higher order of construction.

The many storied trabeated construction with columns of essentially the same dimensions as the building rises and elevator spaces in high proportion to the usable space seem to negate the competitive objectives of more space for less money and cannot be accepted by the questioning mind of the architect as solved.

The conception of a straight tower or slab of equal dimension from base to roof though possible to construct does not express the crushing down forces and upsetting side forces acting on it.

The mind sees a building of a construction growing from a base crossing its members as it rises against the forces of wind. Gravity and wind and the logic of space in proportion to its service suggest a tower pyramidal in form.

Robert Le Ricolais with a few developed remarks introduced the spirit and logic of space construction. His grasp of architecture, as a life molded by conditions governed by ever resourceful laws, he applied full of life to each problem and had the effect of action and delight.

A TOWER

A single office tower of 800,000 square feet of rentable space to be built on the plot opposite Pennsylvania Suburban Station Building in Penn Center, Philadelphia.

It was intended that this exercise in design express an approach to the problems of space distribution and space needs of circulation and services and the construction character of a sun controlled building rising against gravity and wind.

This problem was conducted by the studio of Kahn, Le Ricolais, Deam and Vreeland. The studio is indebted to Mr. James King of the Otis Elevator Company for the two lectures he conducted on elevators; to Mr. Leonard Weger for his lecture on mechanical services; to Mr. Willo Von Moltke of the City Planning Commission for information on the site.

The studio grouped four students to a team in seven teams. Each team discussed their problems with the faculty as a unit. Emphasis was placed on approach to design through a comprehension of order. Examples of contemporary construction on the site and elsewhere were discussed to point out the many problems which are to be solved and those which are generally considered unresolved as architecture.

Reasonable deviation from the program was allowed to encourage a fuller expression of possibilities. That grade B space is considered less desirable by present investment standards was not emphasized. Favor was given to exploring the possibilities inherent in a chosen construction and a space and service order natural to the growth of a vertical building. This attitude of allowing more interior areas than usually considered practical turned the mind away from well known examples and gave freedom, interest and intellectual means to aid discussion, especially since conclusive solutions were not expected.

Special areas not requiring daylight such as meeting rooms, exhibition and display space, work rooms and light industry were discussed and thought economical and complementary spaces to offices.

Before its construction an undertaking like a large tower has much of its space committed to corporations and other organizations requiring large uninterrupted floor space. The lower stories containing these larger interior areas may also be developed as a vertical expansion of shopping near the street, a department store, or for any other commercial use not requiring natural light.

Towers are usually built with less usable space on the lower levels where the greatest concentration of elevators exist, the usable space increasing as the number of elevators decrease.

Broader space use on the lower levels where more elevators exist seems compatible with the whole economy logic of tower.

Elevator shafts, redistributed away from the central core space may suggest a system of construction in which the broad elevator shafts become the major interior columns of the building.

Talk at the Conclusion of the Otterlo Congress (1959)

• •

The Congrès Internationale de l'Architecture Moderne (CIAM), an association of prominent practitioners around the world, met periodically from 1928 to 1959 to discuss a variety of issues, including their profession's social obligations, town planning, post–World World II reconstruction, and the nature of modern architecture itself. Kahn's informal talk at the group's last meeting—in Otterlo, the Netherlands—touched on key concepts that had begun to characterize his thinking: "existence-will," or what anything, especially a building, "wants to be"; the ancient "beginnings" of the social "institutions" (education and religion, for example) for which architects designed and that when clustered form a city; the relationship between space and light; and the "hierarchy" of "servant" and "served" spaces. His remarks were published in Oscar Newman's *New Frontiers in Architecture: CIAM '59 in Otterlo.*

I have had the good fortune to observe the plans and work of the men here, and have seen that almost everyone started with the solution of the problem, given the conditions upon which design was made. But I think I may say freely that very few started with a kind of sense of realization of the problem and then inserted design as its natural extension—a circumstantial thing, because I really do believe

• •

From Oscar Newman, ed., *New Frontiers in Architecture: CIAM '59 in Otterlo.* (New York: Universe Books, 1961).

that design is a circumstantial thing. I believe that a man must realize something before he has the stimulation within himself to design something. I believe that there are many in our profession who rely entirely upon the actual design and very little on the way of thought as to what a thing wants to be, before they try to develop the design— the solution of the problem.

Design is very comparable to a musical composition, for a composer has a sense of music before he composes. I would say that if a dish fell in Mozart's kitchen he would know the difference between the noise of it and the music of it. Another man would run with the noise of it and make a career out of it, because it is different. But Mozart would choose the difference and say, "Yes, dissonance awards to music," and he would have discovered something else in the realm of music. He would compose from this realization—that the falling dish had a meaning in music—where another person would take the noise only and think that he could make a career of it.

I might talk a little about realizations, because realizations are to me a finer part of us than, say, thought. Knowledge is a servant of thought and thought is a satellite of feeling.

If one was to ask, "What is feeling?", I think you could say that it is the residue of our mental evolution, and that in this residue was an ingredient which is thought. And this ingredient somehow was a spirit in itself, and one time it said to feeling, "Look, I have served you well, I have helped you to become man, and now I want to go out for myself. I want to be a satellite, I want you to consider me as something independent of you. I will come back to you, I must." Thought goes independently and deals with other thoughts of other men, and from it comes a postulate. But still a postulate must say to feeling, "How am I doing?" It must!

Now realization, I think, is thought and feeling together. Because feeling itself is completely unable to act, and thought also is unable to act, but thought and feeling combined create a kind of realization. This realization can be said to be a sense of order; a sense of the nature of sense.

Often when one says order, one means orderliness, and that is not what I mean at all. I do not mean orderliness because orderliness has to do with design but has nothing to do with order. Orderliness is nothing tangible about order, it is simply a state of comprehension about existence, and about a sense of a sense of existence. From it you can get a sense of the existence-will of something. The existence-will, let us say, of a form, of a need, which one feels. The existence-will of this need can be sensed through a realization. From the realization you get much richness of design—design comes easily. This is the reason why I mention Mozart again. Mozart could lose his composition and rewrite it verbatim after he had lost it, because he did not deal with his design per se. It had a very definite order-sense about it which made the design something that could be easily varied but still be the same. Now I said that what a thing wants to be is the most important act of an object. It is for the architect to derive from the very nature of things —from his realizations—what a thing wants to be.

In the center of a very large city, maybe I cannot use Amsterdam as an example as it is a city of a different nature, but certainly in Paris, Rome, New York, in Philadelphia or in any other large city, the street in the middle of the town wants to be a building; it does not want to be just a street, and that is realization. If you think of it only as a street, then it never can occur to you that the construction of it is anything but a leftover thing in which you use the meanest ways of making it, because you will not see it.

But if you think of it as being that which it really wants to be—and that is a building—you will not have to dig it up every time a pipe goes bad. You will have a place for these things. You will have a place for walking under, you will have a place for other things, and it will occur to you what this building is which is called a street, and then you will realize that you are actually walking on or riding on the roof of this building. That is a very important thing to realize about a street in the middle of a town, because it is really a contour, it is really a level, and it really is a building.

The same is true of an auditorium. An auditorium wants to be a thing—it wants to be an instrument. It cannot be any old instrument, because acoustically it is true that a large auditorium has a different tempo, a different sound from a small auditorium. No matter how much you try, you cannot make a really large auditorium unless you use artificial means to create a tonality which is other than the actual tonality of the volume which you are encompassing. I don't agree with solutions which say, "I shall build a form and then I will correct it acoustically." This, I would say, is sheer design. I accuse design for such approaches because designers invariably start with square wheels and eventually have to use round ones. But they discard the square wheels to be different. Also they start with short-necked giraffes. The giraffe cries out to have a long neck. But no, the designer says, "I do not want it." So he makes the giraffe with a small neck. Eventually, of course, it turns out "for practical reasons, damn it!" that a giraffe has to have a long neck, and so it is. But a man who watches his realizations does not care what a giraffe looks like. As a matter of fact if you think of it, a giraffe is a pretty ridiculous animal; from the standpoint of design it does not make any sense. But in the same way, a porcupine comes to the Order of Things and says, "I want to be a porcupine," and the Order says, "My God, what an idea. Whoever dreamed up this ugly thing." "Oh!" he says, "but I still want to be a porcupine." And Order says, "Well I have really not much to do with this." And this is true. Nature is not concerned with form, only man is concerned with form. It makes it according to circumstances. If it meets the order of things in the nature of things, it will make any form that answers to the very nature of things. That is why we have what we call such peculiar-looking animals. Because there is a certain existence-will in this kind of thing which produces itself into this kind of animal and nature is not concerned about form— but we are. So, therefore, the existence-will of something, an auditorium, a street, a school, will be the thing which makes the form. Think of a school for a minute. A school. What is the existence-will of a school?

If you get a program from a school-board, the first thing it will say, in our country, is that it must have a nine-foot fence around it—wire fence—and that it must have stainless-steel doors and the corridors must be no less than nine feet wide, and that all its classrooms must be well ventilated and have good light and all be a certain size. They will give you many things which will help the practitioner make a pretty good profit out of his commission by following the rule of rules. But this is not an architect at work. An architect thinks of a school possibly as being a realm of spaces within which it is well to learn. I think schools, for instance, have now gotten away from the original spark or the existence-will or seed of "school."

Think of a man under a tree, talking to a few people about a realization he had—a teacher. He did not know he was a teacher, and those who listened to him did not consider themselves pupils or students. They were just there, and they liked the experience of being in the presence of one who had a realization—a sense of order. This is the way it began. But around such a man there was a need that also grew. You felt that his existence also had a need content. Around him were people who realized that they would like to send their children to this man too—that it was nice to know, to realize—the things he realized. So, therefore, a need was automatically felt for this thing, for this phenomenon, for this seed, for this beginning, which is called "teacher" and "student."

Every city is made up of institutions. If you were to consider the making of a city you would have to consider the organization of the institutions. But you have got to review those institutions and really know what those institutions are. The institution of learning must have in its mind—must have in its sense—the realm of spaces which are good for learning, and not a program which says that you must have so many of this, or so many of that, but a realm of spaces which you feel is sympathetic to learning. So, therefore, you may go into a space which may be a Pantheon-like space. You would name it absolutely nothing—it would just be a good place to arrive in which you say "school"—from which may come other spaces: small or large, some with light above, some with light below, some big spaces made for many people, some small spaces for a few people, some small spaces for many people and some big spaces for only a few people, some seminal spaces, spaces to meet in some other ways, never naming any more of them either "classroom" or "auditorium" or "seminal" or anything, just realizing that there is a sense to the realm of spaces where it is good to learn. That is all you have to know. The program is nothing. The program is a hindrance. You must answer the program.

The economic thing is not the budgetary thing. The economic thing is to build what I have just described. The budgetary thing is the program which is based on another program, which is based on yet another program, all of which are stupid, and you simply have nothing but a struggle to produce that which should cost much more than what the budget allows, and you can never express the real thing. Now if you create the realm of spaces you are also feeling the institution—you are making the institution alive—that which you call part of the city.

You were talking about urbanism. Well, I would like to add this one point, that urbanism is a study of [the] institution of housing, the institution of movement, the institution of schools, the institution of anything you like. You see, they are all institutions really because around them somehow there must be an idea—a need must have been established.

Now, if this is what a school is—a realm of spaces where it is good to learn—then it is the occupation of the architect to change the program, to make the program alive to the very existence-will which started the school.

The spirit of the start is the most marvelous moment at any time for anything. Because in the start lies the seed for all things that must follow. A thing is unable to start unless it can contain all that ever can come from it. That is the characteristic of a beginning, otherwise it is no beginning—it is a false beginning.

Now therefore, that moment under a tree was the beginning of the institution of "school" which has gone completely haywire because it has been handled by too many men who assumed a feeling for it, but who have long lost the meaning of it, and the architect must constantly be there to revive the existence-will sense of this thing.

Now you take in our country, a city-hall. You go by it but it is really a place you don't participate in any more. There is no assembly held there. It is a place where the mayor does not want to be. It is a place where you pay fees and taxes, but everything it does not represent, represents it. Participation—the original existence-will, that which made city-hall a city-hall, a village green, a place for getting together (and participation was the most important part of it) does not exist any more.

Suppose you wanted to meet here, upholding certain cultural, social, or other interests of our democracy; you now have no place to meet. The city-hall which was the place to meet is now something else. It must be again a realm of space where people should meet— where fountains play. When Picasso comes to Philadelphia, he should not have to go to the Sheraton Hotel, which he has to do now, you see. There is simply no place you can take him. Here in Europe you are very fortunate in having much more of a sense of this than we have in our country. I merely bring this out because it comes as a ready kind of example.

Now take the institution "house." A house has to answer, I think, three important things: it has to answer "house," symbolically house, it has to answer "a house" which is the problem. A house is a circumstantial house. It indicates how much money you have. It means who your client is. It means where it is or how many rooms it has. It means a lot of things. But the architect lies in his ability to make house, not a house. That is what architecture really is. "A house" can be the professional, but the architect lies in "house" itself—symbolically "house." He has to find somehow a realm of spaces where it is good to live. Sometimes he must find it with very little space, but essentially that is his job and he must do it so, he does not name the rooms, bedrooms and living-rooms and kitchens, he has got to do it in such a way that it is obvious because of the way they are served, that these things are there and that they are there rightfully and they want to be there. It is a realm of spaces really, which you call "house." Then there is one thing that the architect can do nothing about, and that is "home." A "home" has to do with the people in it, and it is not his business, except that he must prepare this realm to make it suitable for "home." But these three characteristics—or rather I would say aspects—of house, must be there.

Now one can go wrong. I will give you an example which I think is significant. If I were to describe a chapel for a university, a university as one where there is nothing partisan, nothing denominational. M.I.T. Chapel,[1] for instance, is a chapel which is done with immediate calling on the ingredients of a chapel: stained-glass, ornamental work, and all the paraphernalia which you must need to make a chapel. Actually they are a very minor consideration in a chapel. I would say that it comes from a kind of personal ritual. If I were a student of architecture and I got a good criticism from my professors— a criticism which gave me a sense of dedication to my work, a good criticism—then I would be happy, really happy, and I would go by the chapel and wink at it. I wouldn't have to go in, it wouldn't be necessary, nor would I wink at the gymnasium—I would wink at the chapel. So, what is a chapel really? A chapel, to me, is a space which one can be in, but it must have excess of space around it, so that you don't have to go in. That means, it must have an ambulatory, so that you don't have to go into the chapel; and the ambulatory must have an arcade outside, so that you don't have to go into the ambulatory; and the object outside is a garden, so that you don't have to go into the arcade; and the garden has a wall, so that you can be outside of it or inside of it.

The essential thing, you see, is that the chapel is a personal ritual, and that it is not a set ritual, and it is from this that you get the form. The form is derived from this, and not from changing, modifying, making modern that which was already set for you as a chapel.

Now, existence-will then, of trying to grasp the realm of spaces or defining the character of space which is good for a space, is, I tell you from the little that I have had a chance to develop it, the most delightful, most fulfilling experience of all. How to do it is infinitely less important than what to do, for it gives you the means to do it. You can hire anybody to do it. Even those who are untrained in how to do it

1. Eero Saarinen's interdenominational chapel (1954–55) at the Massachusetts Institute of Technology, Cambridge.

will find by whatever means they can how to do it, if they would only know what to do. Of course you will make many mistakes if you don't know how to do it and I think that the horrible ones may affect even what you do. But essentially this is the role of the architect, and if you think of planning, it is certainly this.

Now, in the planning aspect of it—since we are talking about urbanism—I have made a few observations. When I think of a street, I don't think of a street per se, and I don't dismiss it. I stop when I think of a street and I say, "A street? What is a street? Must I assume that a street is a street?" No. A street is either a stream or it's a river or it's a dock. It is something which is different in characteristic depending on the order of movement which I can sense.

In our streets today there is a new order of movement. The order of movement is not a horse and carriage movement, but our streets are still horse and carriage streets. The only difference is that we don't have hitching-posts in the streets, we have gasoline pumps. But the streets are quite the same. Nowadays if you go through the streets of Paris, you don't have the same sense of going through the streets that you had before. You are constantly watching for your life, and not watching the environment of the street.

The meaning of street: There is a type of character, of movement, of go (as Smithson has pointed out[2]), which is a definitely deliberate thing and a kind of place (which is a much better word than I could ever think of) for this street. It is a sort of an arrival, sort of a place where—well, it's a place—that is the right word for it. And it's still the same street, only now you're redefining it. You are giving it a new life by redefining it. Then you place those services next to these things, so that you don't have them haphazardly develop—like a garage here or there—which tends to destroy the imagery of a city.

The original imageries of cities based on defense, were all based on the order of defense. All the walls, and all the details were made, not by the architect but by the order of defense. It was circumstantially

2. Kahn refers to English architects Peter and Alison Smithson's "deck streets" or "streets in the air"—raised plazas on which pedestrians could safely go about their various activities unencumbered by vehicular traffic.

that particular design because it was on a mountainside, or because it had a certain kind of stone, or it had a river close by. Those were circumstances that made one city look different from another. But the order of defense made very stark decisions as to what, when, or where, to defend yourself. It was inconceivable to have a city which did not account for this aspect.

It is also inconceivable today for a city not to have an order of movement; to define every element of movement for what it does, so that one can make form around it. It is a form making thing. I believe that zoning should start with streets, not with buildings. If you zone streets, as Smithson did in his project—give it its use in other words—then you are giving automatically the use of environments and buildings.

In other words, the common activity you can have in a street depends on the movement, and it depends on the design of this movement. In the design of this movement are also buildings. It isn't only just a street.

Then there are the buildings which make you stop. The buildings which you call garages, but which I call gateways. I call them places which really are monumental structures, which simply are wound-up streets. It is the street come to a conclusion. These are the sculpture— the image of a city that you come to now. You can have them very close. You can have them farther away. But you are entering a series of defined forms which are derived out of the order of movement, which is a very positive beginning for a city.

Now I saw one project, and I don't mean to point this out as being an example of any kind, but I noticed one project where buildings were placed next to an old town very regularly around the periphery. They were grouped at the entrance points so that one could see them. I did not like this. I would like to place a gate at the entrance. But I would not like to use people, upon people, upon people, upon people as a symbol for an entrance to a town. No. These should be placed somewhere else. Because an apartment building only wants to be a house, but it can't be a house, so it must be a house upon a house, upon a house, upon a house, upon a house. When you build a house, upon a house, upon a house, it must still satisfy house. Therefore, as a gateway, it seems to be the wrong element to enter that part of the city. What you should have is a gate, and it belongs to the order of movement, and does not belong to apartment buildings which are not part of the order of movement. An apartment building is a thing you arrive at—but it is not part of the movement. Therefore, if you have this conception of movement first then the entire design would change. The design would not be the way you have made it—not made movements out of people and toilets going up, and up, and up. It wouldn't be so.

Speaking about spaces, I said that architecture was the thoughtful making of spaces. I think that could be said in many ways. I have often thought about whether it was a full definition, and it really is not. However, for the moment, if we think of spaces, what are architectural spaces?

I think an architectural space is one in which it is evident how it is made; you will see the columns, you must see the beams, or you must see the walls, the doors, or the domes in the very space which is called a space.

If you try to think of points from which we can reach points of departure in architecture, we can very easily state that a space in architecture is one in which it is evident how it is made, and that the introduction of a column or any device for making a roof is already thought of from the standpoint of light, and no space is really an architectural space unless it has natural light. Artificial light does not light a space in architecture, because it must have the feeling in it of the time of day and season of the year—the nuances of this is incomparable with the single moment of an electric bulb. It is ridiculous to think that an electric bulb can do what the sun can do or the seasons can do. And this is what gives you a real sense of space architecturally—it is natural light. Then, at night, it becomes a totally different space. And almost a realization of this tells you that you should not have your electric lights where the sun comes in, because it is so ridiculous to try to imitate it. Why not make it entirely different? Have your chandeliers doing all sorts of gay things about being night.

I have seen theories about putting lights where the daylight comes in but how ridiculous it is really to follow this when you think in terms of spaces being served by the sun—by the light of the day—it's so marvelous.

The making of spaces is the making of light at the same time. When the light is destroyed, the rhythm is destroyed, and the music is destroyed, and music is terribly important to architecture.

There is a side thing I should mention before I forget it. I think that music is more akin to architecture than either sculpture or painting. If you think of music, it is very, very close to architecture, and I think personally, that every architect should learn to write music. It is wonderful to realize that when a man writes music he is not enthralled by the beauty of what he sees as a kind of writing—he is enthralled by what he hears. The musician hears what he writes—he doesn't see it. The architect comes over and looks at his drawings and says: "Oh, isn't it wonderful! I think I'll make a blow-up of it and put it in my living room!" To the musician his writing means something beyond itself—it means sound, it means organization of sound. An architect must be able to read the life that comes into his works through his plans. His realm of spaces is analogous to a sheet of music. His columns and his beams and his walls should be almost assumed. You must say that in this interior space I must have light. Because I have made a space therefore I must have light. I must assume that it must be some kind of order. I am looking for something. I am looking for the space-making of this in my plan. I think a sheet of music and an architectural plan are the same thing.

Every space must have its own definition for what it does, and from that will grow the exterior, the interior, the feeling of spaces, the feeling of arrival. All these things indicate themselves once we think of them as being a realm of spaces—a hierarchy of spaces—and not just simply a feeling. It is just not enough to say: "I feel this should be larger here and bulge out here," and so forth. This you can also do—it is absolutely all right to do it—but it must have an internal kind of structure which permits you to do it, just as the musician has his formal structure and discipline which permits him to play on almost any instrument. It depends on his genius. In the same way, and I think some of you are familiar with my personal way of saying that spaces must be distinguished. The serving areas of a space and the spaces which are served, are two different things. It is very likely that a plan starts this way, and the architect says: "Oh, don't touch this!" The client says: "I need an office, I need a toilet, I need a closet, I need a few things in here," and the architect says: "Oh, don't do this, this is a wonderful thing on a podium and you cannot touch it," and the client says: "But I need it!" And the architect says: "Put it down in the cellar. You can't have it around here. This is really very important and everything depends on it." Actually this is where the architect goes wrong. This is a very limited man at work, because what he could probably come out with may actually be better, and he will get the spaces he needs, and will have contained elements which can serve those spaces.

The architect must find a way in which the serving areas of a space can be there, and still not destroy his spaces. He must find a new column, he must find a new way of making those things work, and still not lose his building on a podium. But you cannot think of it as being one problem, and the other things as being another problem.

Actually, these are wonderful revelations because modern space is really not different from Renaissance space. In many ways it is not. We still want domes, we still want walls, we still want arches, arcades, and loggias of all kinds. We want all these things and, with that belief, need them. But they are not the same in character because a space today demands different things. If I build a dome it does not have to talk back to me. It must be quiet. A Renaissance dome can talk back to me, and it's alright, but not a modern one. So therefore, something in the fabric of making this thing is already the ingredient of making it not speak back to you.

Another characteristic of this dome is that it must have temperature control. I must want it warm when it is cold out, and cool when it is warm out. This is a very definite demand of modern society. If we don't have it radically so, it certainly will gradually become so by the pressures and fury of business, or whatever it is that will make you do it.

Talk at the Otterlo Congress

49

There is another thing—light must also be there. If you see all these things only after you have made a great form—suppose you got the right engineer, let's say Candela or Nervi[3] to do the building for you—and then you said, "Now, how shall we light it?" Then you're wrong. Or if you then said "How shall we breathe in this place?" you are also wrong. In the very fabric of making it must already be the servants that serve the very things I've talked about—its timbre, its light, and its temperature-control; the fabric of the construction must already be the container of these servants.

I spoke before about "beginnings." I should like to go back to that now and talk more about it. I should like to talk of the Renaissance, and of Giotto in particular.

Giotto was a wonderful painter. But why was he wonderful? Because he painted the skies black in the daytime, and painted dogs that couldn't run and birds that couldn't fly, and people who were larger than buildings—because he was a painter. He was not an architect, he was not a sculptor.

The prerogatives of the painter allow him—the very fact that he can draw in this way allows him—to do that very thing. The extent of his fantasy is within his realm, definitely within his realm.

But Giotto also satisfied the need by being true to the allegory, let us say, of St. Francis in this case. So he found that St. Francis kept the right company in the painting. People understood it. The combination of both the beautiful sense of the rights of the painter that Giotto very thoroughly understood—felt—combined the life of St. Francis with the mystical atmosphere which was necessary to bring it to a religious sense, of nobility, of sacrifice, of things which are religious.

Chagall, a lesser painter, also felt the same kind of freedom. Modern painters have the same freedom. I do think, however, that modern painters have not as yet established a form.

Giotto did establish a form because others followed him immediately. The artists immediately sensed that they had a life to begin with from what Giotto had set up as the prerogatives of the painter. But

3. Architect-engineers Felix Candela and Pier Luigi Nervi of Spain and Italy, respectively.

modern painters have not indicated a form. Now I mean not necessarily form as it finally is, I mean really preform. Preform is archaic form. In the preform actually exists more life, more of the story that can come after, than anyone who walks from it and nibbles at it can ever attain. In the preform—in the beginning, in the first form—lies more power than in anything that follows. And I believe that there is much to be gained by this thought if it comes through your minds, not only through mine, in what it can mean to you, because I am really worried about the beautiful things that exist around us today.

I can worry about the Seagram Tower.[4] She is a beautiful bronze lady but she is all corseted inside. She wears corsets from the first to the fifteenth story, but you can't see the corsets. She is a beautiful bronze lady, but she is not true. She is not that shape on the inside.

Now the preform may be a protoform. It may not be a beautiful thing in the eyes of the beholder, but to the artist it is a beautiful thing. It is the form before beauty as we know it, sets in.

Think of sculpture for a minute! The Greeks in their archaic sculpture (and of course in the sculpture that later followed too, but not so much as in the archaic sculpture) symbolized aspects of man by indicating images of man. The torso was really an ever-serving servant—it did not have lung trouble—it was an ever serving thing. The arms were ever capable. The eyes could not see, but could see forever.

It was this aspect which you catch very definitely. The helmet of the archaic warrior was more heraldic than it was useful. He could not go to battle with this thing—he would be knocked on the head in no time. He couldn't walk with it. But that wasn't the point. The sculptor realized he was indicating, symbolizing, something constantly. That was the important aspect—that sculpture knew that it was not indicating man at all.

Later, sculpture thought that it would perfect—"Look how ugly the lady's arms are, and look how disproportionate this torso is!" They misinterpreted the spirit—which is the beginning, from which sculp-

4. Mies van der Rohe's Seagram Building (1954–58) in New York with its disguised wind-bracing system.

ture actually began—which was the symbolizing of aspects of realizations in man. Using man because he was very concerned about it.

Now, how to do it in architecture? Well, I tried to explain, by saying what a space was, what a thing wants to be. There are new problems, tremendous new problems today, which have not been touched by the architect because he is thinking about exterior forms. He is thinking of all kinds of extraneous things before he arrives at a kind of realization of what a space really wants to be.

If you could only have the opportunity, where you can express more than just a single space or two or three, or a simple composition, like the campus of a university, some such thing as this which is a symphony really.

What is a campus of a university? Let's talk about it a little. It is really a realm of spaces which may be connected by ways of walking, and the walking is a protected kind of walking (it seems logical that it is protected). You consider it as high spaces together with low spaces, and various spaces where people can sort of find the place where they can do what they want to do.

In the few university buildings I have done, I came to several realizations with regard to space in that sense. I simply said, in a university building which was a laboratory for medical people, that the air you breathe should never come in contact with the air you throw away. That's all. Then I said that a scientist is like an artist—he is like an architect: He does not like to work as they do at M.I.T., in corridors with names on them. He likes to work in a kind of studio. A place which he can call his own, or with his confrères, working on a problem. He feels it very well if his space is a dead-end of some kind, or a traffic way, or a place you would build a tunnel, or a place you take the elevator, or where the duct-shafts are, and that you have limited the space, so that he cannot ever succeed in experimenting because his space is always being taken away from him by utilities which are in the way.

In the Medical Research Building at Pennsylvania,[5] I developed

5. Kahn discusses his Alfred Newton Richards Medical Research and Biology buildings

Talk at the Otterlo Congress

characteristics within the studio itself where you can get darkness and light, not by pulling shades, but by simply characterizing the building so that there are natural places where darkness exists, and natural places where light exists.

Now in the art gallery at Yale University—and I'll criticize my own gallery freely—I only came to a very slight conclusion there about order. The realization there was something which was not fully understood by me; had it been, the design would probably have been different. Though, I must say that it has certain aspects which are very good still. If I were to build a gallery now, I would really be more concerned about building spaces which are not used freely by the director as he wants. Rather I would give him spaces that were there and had certain inherent characteristics. Then the visitor, because of the nature of the space, would perceive a certain object in quite a different way. The director would be fitted out with such a variety of ways of getting light, from above, from below, from little slits, or from whatever he wanted, so that he felt that here was really a realm of spaces where one could show things in various aspects.

I would say that dark spaces are also very essential. But to be true to the argument that an architectural space must have natural light, I would say that it must be dark, but that there must be an opening big enough, so that light can come in and tell you how dark it really is— that's how important it is to have natural light in an architectural space.

In discussing Giotto and the prerogatives of a painter I mentioned realm. I should like to elaborate on what I mean by realm. The realm of architecture is a realm within which all other things are. In the realm of architecture there is sculpture, there is painting, there is physics, there is nursing—everything is in it. But the emphasis is on architecture. Architecture is the king of this realm. It is the reason for its existence altogether. And I think you know this realm best when you can touch the walls of its limits—when you know you've reached

(1957–65) at the University of Pennsylvania, Philadelphia, and his Yale University Art Gallery extension (1951–53), New Haven, Connecticut.

Talk at the Otterlo Congress   53 the point where, when you go across the wall, you are in a different realm. When you are able to touch the limits of it—not the limitations, but the limits, knowing how far you can go—I think at that point you really understand the realm.

When I went to school, we had a reference library divided into various architectural periods: Egyptian, Greek, Roman, Gothic and so on, and this was my realm of architecture. If I had a cemetery to design, nothing could be better than a walk up to the Egyptian area where I could find what I needed. That was just the kind of life I led, and it was most delightful; I looked through the books and saw wonderful examples I could follow. Now when I got through with school, I walked around the realm and I came to a little village, and this village was very unfamiliar. There was nothing here that I had seen before. But through this unfamiliarity—from this unfamiliar thing—I realized what architecture was. Not right then, because I was then dealing with answers, but Le Corbusier raised the question for me, and the question is infinitely more powerful than the answer. So through the question—the power of it—the real thing was brought out.

As one person remarked, "A good question is greater than the most brilliant answer," and that is true. A good question is one that touches realization; it touches order, whereas an answer is very fragmentary in comparison to it. I never really got to architecture by simply taking convenient things; it was through the unfamiliar that I learned and realized what architecture really was.

I think that striving to not be afraid when you are confronted with the unfamiliar is a wonderful thing. It is something we can recognize in your CIAM meetings. I find, however, that you occupy so much time in explaining the circumstantial aspects of your problem; you spend so much time in talking about contours, and about design, and about all these things, all of which are terrifically important but are not really the essence of it. Because if you are making an auditorium, you are dealing with people who are to hear. The main thing about the auditorium is that you must hear and that it must have a certain tonality in order to hear properly. Therefore, your first concern is: What do you realize about an auditorium? If you must make it out of icecubes, that is the next thing because you are building it in Iceland. But that is incidental, that is circumstantial; the design is circumstantial. What material you use is circumstantial; it is a design problem; it is a practical absolute problem. The design is the making of your composition, so that you can play the music. That is all very important. It is the imagery. It is the first thing you see. It is the tangible thing.

The realization of what is an auditorium is absolutely beyond the problem of whether it is in the Sudan, or in Rio de Janeiro. Therefore, your getting to the essence of what you are trying to do in creating what it wants to be, should be the first concern—should be the first act—of an architect explaining his project to another architect, and not all the circumstantial things, the amount of money you had, and the difficulties of regulations and so forth. I think that it is the circumstantial things which show with what brilliance you have attacked the problems of design with which you were confronted. But those are design problems; they are not problems in my opinion of the real essence of architecture today. The present is not a time of style whatsoever, it is a time of groping—a time of discovery. It is a time, you might say, of realization. Our problems are all new, our spatial demands are new, and it is a time, therefore, more concerned with trying to create better institutions from those we already have established. Our institutions are very much down. They are not good institutions now, because the spaces which must serve them are antiquated. We must find the realm of spaces which can now serve these institutions well. To think about what a school should be, and what those other things should be, is terribly important. To establish the right kind of budget, the right kind of approach to what really should be provided for these things, should be the concern and the preoccupation of CIAM in the expression of your problems.

The group that was talking just the other day (Ed. note: discussion on Lovett's work[6]) came to a point where there was a kind of—a sort of feeling of—tension about this very issue. It was about the issue of the approach to the problem—of realizations about things. The cli-

6. Wendell H. Lovett of Bellevue, Washington, residence on Mercer Island, Puget Sound.

mate of discussion should be such that people can go back home with a feeling that they owe nothing to anybody; because actually a man who discovers things that belong to the nature of things does not own these things. The designs belong to him but the realizations do not. If you copy Corbusier's designs you are somewhat of a thief. But if you take that which is in essence architectural from him, you take it very freely, because it does not belong to him either. It belongs to the realm of architecture. The fact that he discovered it is a very fortunate thing for us, but it does not belong to him. In the same way, music does not belong to Mozart, but his compositions do.

I would like to conclude here, but first I mean to show my appreciation to Aldo[7] who simply talked about a door. I think it is a wonderful thing to review the aspects of architecture from that sense. The mere fact that one can get to be totally preoccupied with this sort of thing is wonderful, because from it can grow many wonderful things; it could lead a man to realizations which go far beyond the problems of a door or a gateway.

I think it is not just the preoccupation with the little things, about whether you will put toilets here or there, or whether you have so much opening in the wall, it is a much broader thing, it is a climate within which these things can develop well, which means it must have a framework.

A city has a framework which is based on movement. The movement must also include a place to stop, where the pedestrian begins, which means there is a square; there is a place where he can stop. But it is not the same square as the European square is now. It is not the same in duplicate, because it is somehow a different thing. We are really walking on wheels, and as such it becomes quite different because you can now bypass a city; you can simply say: "I'll go somewhere else."

I think that cities will become greater as time goes on, but there won't be as many of them, as I think that a city cannot produce enough of the power, which you call city, in small places. I believe also

7. Dutch architect Aldo van Eyck.

that shopping centers in our country are not shopping centers—they are buying centers, that is all they are—and they can never develop into shopping centers, that is too wonderful a thing. They are devices for buying, that's all. They are as stupid as anything when the cars are away. They look like some of the abandoned American West. You see nothing and more nothing in most of them. Well, now I think I would like questions.

DISCUSSION

QUESTION: You mentioned the Seagram Building in your talk. Would you elaborate on it further?

KAHN: The Seagram Building is, I think, one of the really beautiful buildings of the world today. It stands there, a tall and marvelous looking building but it does not tell the true story of the architecture; it is a facile thing. It is stillborn on a sort of podium. As it stands now, the only thing left for some architects to do, who are jealous of it, is to make it out of silver, so that it will not cost 88 dollars per square foot, but 200 dollars per square foot.

However, the building is not honest, because the wind forces are not being expressed. Hidden in the building are great forces which offset the wind. The building, though, does not express the fact that these forces are in play. The force of gravity is nothing, you can easily calculate that. But the wind stresses are not so easily calculated, and there is a great form making thing about them.

If this building expressed the force of wind, I am sure that when an ordinary man passed by he would look at it, more than he does now, even if it were done brutally. He would stop to think of it, of how it was done, and how it works, whereas he gives the present building far less thought. What we have here is another example of the short-necked giraffe approach. It is forcing a thing into a preconceived notion as to what it might look like. With the other approach you simply allow it to look like what it wants to be; as nature does with the porcupine—you let it tell you something about it; about the forces of truth from which you can derive a way of life. So it is important that these forms do come out.

Another thing is that I feel strongly that a building should not be considered as having no ending. I believe that an ending, as a sawed-off thing, is an indication of our society; a kind of frustrated way of looking at things. But if you believe in architecture sufficiently, you must put an ending to a thing, so that it is evident that you are not going to build some more. Nobody is going to build above it anyway. You know you must end it, and it is a good thing to indicate it if you can feel what it should be.

QUESTION: Architects seem forever to be wrangling about originality and the use of other men's ideas. What are your opinions on this?

KAHN: I don't think that you should be limited by the fact that someone has sort of opened the door for you, not at all. But it must be an opened door which isn't going to lead to your saying, "Now how can I make it different, so I can open another door?"

There is such a thing as the phenomenon of the man who somehow can do the unfamiliar thing and that it be right. The unfamiliar thing, however, cannot exist without already feeling that you need it. You should feel the need of it, as I said about Giotto. Giotto actually brought people to a state of need for his paintings. And I think a work of art must have that quality of need. I would say that a work of art is like an axe. An axe is created by a man, not by society. But society leads him to produce the axe because there is a certain need for it. At first the axe was not perfect. It probably fell off the handle and you had trouble with lifting it. But society demanded that it be developed—it needed it.

Art is definitely something of that nature. Art is the making of meaningful form. It is very much a part of our life, and is actually the concrete product of religion—feeling at its greatest moment is religion. Not ritualistic religion. I mean religion from which we derive such feelings as nobility—that religion.

QUESTION: When you spoke of a gateway, with reference to our project for instance, a gateway is something that is open or closed, and my feeling is that I did not even want a gateway, that I just wanted it open and that the trees and garden are there as a kind of symbol of the gateway.

KAHN: When you say you did not want it, one must question this for a moment, because it is not what you want, it is what you sense is the order of things which tells you what to design. It is then you can say that you want this or that as a way of satisfying this realization which you must of course believe in. It cannot be something that is imposed on you—you believe in it. In other words, the realization you have about movement, which says, it must be open, so that you can come in easily, is what you believe in. I do not disagree with this being open, but in my opinion, you cannot come too suddenly to an entrance in our movement, in our time. In a horse and carriage movement you can, for it is a very incidental, slow-moving thing. It is very easy to contemplate an entrance through horse and carriage movement, but with a car it is a different kind of entrance, it is a much more deliberate, quick-moving, and demanding kind of entrance. You must see the entrance, and you must be prepared for it beforehand. Now, I don't say that your project is so big that it requires this kind of thought. I am only using it as an example, as I said, with all apology. I just did not think that a house was a proper gateway symbol. I did not mean a gateway with gates, I meant a gateway only as a kind of symbol. The distinction is that you realize that a gateway is necessary, and it is not the casual kind of thing you know about. When you are in a car you actually can lose your own entrance.

QUESTION: What do you feel about group work and partnership in architecture?

KAHN: Well, I think, that an act of architecture—not a professional performance in building a building, which is a different thing—cannot be done by more than one person. Whereas performing a building, doing a service and making it work, can be done by any number of people; by an organization as well. But that which has to do with making a space what it wants to be, that must be very jealously guarded by the man who does it. He cannot share this. It would be like asking two painters to paint one portrait. It is just impossible.

I think certain realizations can come through teamwork. The

cross-stimulization of one person working with another, and resulting in realizations, is very possible. But again, I think, that if an artist is an artist he has to guard very, very religiously his personal work. He cannot share his work with another. Those who are willing to share and work together should only be willing to do so for a certain period of time.

I have always had my apprehensions about partnerships because of the very fact that eventually one person or the other will try to claim ownership to that part which he cannot divulge from the other. If the partnership is really a significant thing, then its very hard to do. I think that the more the artist, the more it is one person.

I am one who does not believe that we should have a collaborator, sculptor or painter, in a team with the architect doing a building. I believe that an architect is entrusted with the making of spaces—the thoughtful making of spaces—and if he defines these spaces by the very way in which they are made, then in the fabric of the making, already exist all the places where painting and sculpture can exist—if it wants to exist. The sculptor or the painter can come in at that moment, if you like.

I am not saying that collaboration is impossible. I am just saying that I believe that the architect never allows himself to create spaces so defined that the painter is inscribed by the knowledge of where he should paint. The painter may very well come to the architect and say "Look I want to collaborate with you," and he knows very much what the architect is trying to do, and in this way can help him enormously. In most cases, however, the architect's work has not been concerned with the architecture. In order to make the painter understand what the architect is driving at, architects should produce architecture.

In connection with this let me talk a little about ornament. I feel that the beginning of ornament comes with the joint. The way things are made, the way they are put together, the way one thing comes to the other, is the place where ornament begins. It is the glory of the joint which is the beginning of ornament. The more a man knows the joint, the more he wants to show it. The more he wants to show the joint, the more he wants to show the distance. And if he wants to have it show the distance, he wants to exaggerate and caricature things which ordinarily are small. The beginning of ornament lies also in the challenge against the elements. The problems are there. Now, one can also apply ornament. There is no reason why one can't apply it. But one must apply it with humor, and know he is applying it. But one must satisfy the other things too. It isn't merely a question of saying: "I need ornament, because these things are too bulky and I'm going to put something on so that it has more life in it." This is meaningless, as we all know.

I don't really believe it is even bad to exaggerate a beam's action—to give it more the power of the effort. But I do believe that if exaggeration is employed in a little way, it loses itself. In other words a short span cannot afford to be exaggerated—it becomes ridiculous. However, the larger the span the more the column says to the beam, "I like you," and puts its arms out and becomes definitely something which can be developed, and the expression of the joint between the column and the beam will be the ornament.

4 Form and Design (1960)

Called "Structure and Form" when taped for a *Voice of America* radio lecture series on architecture, this talk was retitled for publication, first as "A Statement by Louis I. Kahn" for *Arts and Architecture* (February 1961), then definitively as "Form and Design" for *Architectural Design* (April 1961) and its several subsequent republications. Kahn repeated some of his CIAM remarks—as he was wont to do—but went on to distinguish between two key concepts that had recently jelled in his thinking and would be mainstays throughout the rest of his life: "form," which is immaterial and immeasurable, a Platonic-like ideal that preexists awareness and understanding of it (as in the concept "school"); and "design," which is material and measurable, an architect's interpretation of form in an actual construction (as in the elementary school across the street). When an architect grasps what the form is—that is, the defining and essential characteristics of the concept that make it different from every other form or concept—he can then create a design—the physical structure in which the form is manifest.

A young architect came to ask a question. "I dream of spaces full of wonder. Spaces that rise and envelop flowingly without beginning, without end, of a jointless material white and gold. When I place

•••

Original text from "Voice of America—Louis I. Kahn. Recorded November 19, 1960" folder, Box LIK 53, Louis I. Kahn Collection, University of Pennsylvania and Pennsylvania Historical and Museum Commission (hereafter cited as Kahn Collection).

the first line on paper to capture the dream, the dream becomes less."

This is a good question. I once learned that a good question is greater than the most brilliant answer.

This is a question of the unmeasurable and the measurable. Nature, physical nature, is measurable.

Feeling and dream has no measure, has no language, and everyone's dream is singular.

Everything that is made however obeys the laws of nature. The man is always greater than his works because he can never fully express his aspirations. For to express oneself in music or architecture is by the measurable means of composition or design. The first line on paper is already a measure of what cannot be expressed fully. The first line on paper is less.

"Then," said the young architect, "what should be the discipline, what should be the ritual that brings one closer to the psyche. For in this aura of no material and no language, I feel man truly is."

Turn to Feeling and away from Thought. In Feeling is the Psyche. Thought is Feeling and presence of Order. Order, the maker of all existence, has No Existence Will. I choose the word Order instead of knowledge because personal knowledge is too little to express Thought abstractly. This Will is in the Psyche.

All that we desire to create has its beginning in feeling alone. This is true for the scientist. It is true for the artist. But I warned that to remain in Feeling away from Thought means to make nothing.

Said the young architect: "To live and make nothing is intolerable. The dream has in it already the *will to be* and the desire to express this *will*. Thought is inseparable from Feeling. In what way then can Thought enter creation so that this psychic will can be more closely expressed? This is my next question."

When personal feeling transcends into Religion (not a religion but the essence religion) and Thought leads to Philosophy, the mind opens to realizations. Realization of what may be the *existence will* of, let us say, particular architectural spaces. Realization is the merging of Thought and Feeling at the closest rapport of the mind with the Psyche, the source of *what a thing wants to be.*

It is the beginning of Form. Form encompasses a harmony of systems, a sense of Order and that which characterizes one existence from another. Form has no shape or dimension. For example, in the differentiation of a spoon from spoon, spoon characterizes a form having two inseparable parts, the handle and the bowl. A spoon implies a specific design made of silver or wood, big or little, shallow or deep. Form is "what." Design is "how." Form is impersonal. Design belongs to the designer. Design is a circumstantial act, how much money there is available, the site, the client, the extent of knowledge. Form has nothing to do with circumstantial conditions. In architecture, it characterizes a harmony of spaces good for a certain activity of man.

Reflect then on what characterizes abstractly House, a house, home. House is the abstract characteristic of spaces good to live in. House is the form, in the mind of wonder it should be there without shape or dimension. *A* house is a conditional interpretation of these spaces. This is design. In my opinion the greatness of the architect depends on his powers of realization of that which is House, rather than his design of *a* house which is a circumstantial act. Home is the house and the occupants. Home becomes different with each occupant.

The client for whom a house is designed states the areas he needs. The architect creates spaces out of those required areas. It may also be said that this house created for the particular family must have the character of being good for another. The design in this way reflects its trueness to Form.

I think of school as an environment of spaces where it is good to learn. Schools began with a man under a tree who did not know he was a teacher discussing his realization with a few who did not know they were students. The students reflected on what was exchanged and how good it was to be in the presence of this man. They aspired that their sons also listen to such a man. Soon spaces were erected and the first schools became. The establishment of school was inevitable because it was part of the desires of man. Our vast systems of education, now vested in institutions, stem from these little schools but the spirit of their beginning is now forgotten. The rooms required by our institutions of learning are stereotype and uninspiring. The institute's required uniform classrooms, the locker-lined corridors and other so-called functional areas and devices, are certainly arranged in neat packages by the architect who follows closely the areas and budgetary limits as required by the school authorities. The schools are good to look at but are shallow in architecture because they do not reflect the spirit of the man under the tree. The entire system of schools that followed from the beginning would not have been possible if the beginning were not in harmony with the nature of man. It can also be said that the existence will of school was there even before the circumstances of the man under a tree.

That is why it is good for the mind to go back to the beginning because the beginning of any established activity of man is its most wonderful moment. For in it lies all its spirit and resourcefulness, from which we must constantly draw our inspirations of present needs. We can make our institutions great by giving them our sense of this inspiration in the architecture we offer them.

Reflect then on the meaning of school, *a* school, institution. The institution is the authority from whom we get their requirements of areas. A school or a specific design is what the institution expects of us. But School, the spirit school, the essence of the existence will, is what the architect should convey in his design. And I say he must, even if the design does not correspond to the budget. Thus the architect is distinguished from the mere designer. In School as a realm of spaces where it is good to learn, the lobby measured by the institute as so many square feet per student would become a generous Pantheon-like space where it is good to enter. The corridors would be transferred into classrooms belonging to the students themselves by making them much wider and provided with alcoves overlooking the gardens. They would become the places where boy meets girl, where the student discusses the work of the professor with his fellow-student. By allowing classroom time to these spaces instead of passage time from class to class, it would become a meeting connection and not merely a corridor, which means a place of possibilities in self-learning. It becomes the classroom belonging to the students. The classrooms should evoke their use by their space variety and not follow the usual soldier-like dimensional similarity, because one of the most wonderful spirits of this man under the tree is his recognition of the singularity of every man. A teacher or a student is not the same when he is with a few in an intimate room with a fireplace as in a large high room with many others. And must the cafeteria be in the basement, even though its use in time is little? Is not the relaxing moment of the meal also a part of learning?

As I write alone in my office, I feel differently about the very same things that I talked about only a few days ago to many at Yale. Space has power and gives mode.

This, with the singularity of every person, suggests a variety of spaces with a variety of the ways of natural light and orientation to compass and garden. Such spaces lend themselves to ideas in the curriculum, to better connection between teacher and student, and to vitality in the development of the institution.

The realization of what particularizes the domain of spaces good for school would lead an institution of learning to challenge the architect to awareness of what School *wants to be* which is the same as saying what is the form, School.

In the same spirit I should like to talk about a Unitarian Church.[1]

The very first day I talked before the congregation using a blackboard. From what I heard the minister speak about with men around I realized that the form aspect, the form realization of Unitarian activity was bound around that which is Question. Question eternal of why anything. I had to come to the realization of what existence will and what order of spaces were expressive of the Question.

I drew a diagram on the blackboard which I believe served as the Form drawing of the church and, of course, was not meant to be a suggested design.

I made a square center in which I placed a question mark. Let us say I meant it to be the sanctuary. This I encircled with an ambulatory for those who did not want to go into the sanctuary. Around the ambulatory I drew a corridor which belonged to an outer circle enclosing a

1. Kahn's First Unitarian Church and School (1959–69), Rochester, New York.

Form and Design

space, *the school*. It was clear that School which gives rise to Question became the wall which surrounds Question. This was the form expression of the church, not the design.

This puts me in mind of the meaning of Chapel in a university.

Is it the mosaics, stained glass, water effects and other known devices? Is it not the place of inspired ritual which could be expressed by a student who winked at chapel as he passed it after being given a sense of dedication to this work by a great teacher. He did not need to go in.

It may be expressed by a place which for the moment is left undescribed and has an ambulatory for the one who does not want to enter it. The ambulatory is surrounded by an arcade for the one who prefers not to go into the ambulatory. The arcade sits in the garden for the one who prefers not to enter the arcade. The garden has a wall and the student can be outside winking at it. The ritual is inspired and not set and is the basis of the form Chapel.

Back to the Unitarian Church. My first design solution which followed was a completely symmetrical square. The building provided for the schoolrooms around the periphery, the corners were punctuated by larger rooms. The space in the center of the square harbored the sanctuary and the ambulatory. This design closely resembled the diagram on the blackboard and everyone liked it until the particular interests of every committee member began to eat away at the rigid geometry. But the original premise still held of the school around the sanctuary.

It is the role of design to adjust to the circumstantial. At one stage of discussion with the members of the church committee a few insisted that the sanctuary be separated entirely from the school. I said fine, let's put it that way and I then put the auditorium in one place and connected it up with a very neat little connector to the school. Soon everyone realized that the coffee hour after the ceremony brought several related rooms next to the sanctuary, which when alone were too awkwardly self-satisfying and caused the duplication of these rooms in the separated school block. Also, the schoolrooms by separation lost their power to evoke their use for religious and intellectual purposes and, like a stream, they all came back around the sanctuary.

The final design does not correspond to the first design though the form held.

I want to talk about the difference between form and design, about realization, about the measurable and the unmeasurable aspects of our work and about the limits of our work.

Giotto was a great painter because he painted the skies black for the daytime and he painted birds that couldn't fly and dogs that couldn't run and he made men bigger than doorways because he was a painter. A painter has this prerogative. He doesn't have to answer to the problems of gravity, nor to the images as we know them in real life. As a painter he expresses a reaction to nature and he teaches us through his eyes and his reactions to the nature of man. A sculptor is one who modifies space with the objects expressive again of his reactions to nature. He does not create space. He modifies space. An architect creates space.

Architecture has limits.

When we touch the invisible walls of its limits then we know more about what is contained in them. A painter can paint square wheels on a cannon to express the futility of war. A sculptor can carve the same square wheels. But an architect must use round wheels. Though painting and sculpture play a beautiful role in the realm of architecture as architecture plays a beautiful role in the realms of painting and sculpture, one does not have the same discipline as the other.

One may say that architecture is the thoughtful making of spaces. It is, note, the filling of areas prescribed by the client. It is the creating of spaces that evoke a feeling of appropriate use.

To the musician a sheet of music is seeing from what he hears. A plan of a building should read like a harmony of spaces in light.

Even a space intended to be dark should have just enough light from some mysterious opening to tell us how dark it really is. Each space must be defined by its structure and the character of its natural light. Of course I am not speaking about minor areas which serve the major spaces. An architectural space must reveal the evidence of its making by the space itself. It cannot be a space when carved out of a greater structure meant for a greater space because the choice of a structure is synonymous with the light and which gives image to that space. Artificial light is a single tiny static moment in light and is the light of night and never can equal the nuances of mood created by the time of day and the wonder of the seasons.

A great building, in my opinion, must begin with the unmeasurable, must go through measurable means when it is being designed and in the end must be unmeasurable. The design, the making of things is a measurable act. In fact at that point, you are like physical nature itself because in physical nature everything is measurable, even that which is yet unmeasured, like the most distant stars which we can assume will be eventually measured.

But what is unmeasurable is the psychic spirit. The psyche is expressed by feeling and also thought and I believe will always be unmeasurable. I sense that the psychic Existence Will calls on nature to make what it wants to be. I think a rose wants to be a rose. Existence Will, *man*, becomes existence, through nature's law and evolution. The results are always less than the spirit of existence.

In the same way a building has to start in the unmeasurable aura and go through the measurable to be accomplished. It is the only way you can build, the only way you can get it into being is through the measurable. You must follow the laws but in the end when the building becomes part of living it evokes unmeasurable qualities. The design involving quantities of brick, method of construction, engineering is over and the spirit of its existence takes over.

Take the beautiful tower made of bronze that was erected in New York.[2] It is a bronze lady, incomparable in beauty, but you know she has corsets for fifteen stories because the wind bracing is not seen. That which makes it an object against the wind which can be beautifully expressed, just like nature expresses the difference between the moss

2. Mies van der Rohe's Seagram Building (1954–58), New York.

and the reed. The base of this building should be wider than the top, and the columns which are on top dancing like fairies, and the columns below growing like mad, don't have the same dimensions because they are not the same thing. This story if told from realization of form would make a tower more expressive of the forces. Even if it begins in its first attempts in design to be ugly it would be led to beauty by the statement of form.

I am doing a building in Africa, which is very close to the equator.[3] The glare is killing, everybody looks black against the sunlight. Light is a needed thing, but still an enemy. The relentless sun above, the siesta comes over you like thunder.

I saw many huts that the natives made.

There were no architects there.

I came back with multiple impressions of how clever was the man who solved the problems of sun, rain and wind.

I came to the realization that every window should have a free wall to face. This wall receiving the light of day would have bold opening to the sky. The glare is modified by the lighted wall and the view is not shut off. In this way the contrast made by separated patterns of glare which skylight grilles close to the window make is avoided. Another realization came from the effectiveness of the use of breeze for insulation by the making of a loose sun roof independently supported and separated from the rain roof by a head room of six feet. These designs of the window and wall and of the sun and rain roofs would tell the man on the street the way of life in Angola.

I am designing a unique research laboratory in San Diego, California.[4]

This is how the program started.

The director, a famous man, heard me speak in Pittsburgh. He came to Philadelphia to see the building I had designed for the University of

---

3. The unbuilt United States Consulate and Residence (1959–62), Luanda, Angola.
4. Salk Institute for Biological Studies (1959–65), La Jolla, California. Kahn repeatedly mislocated this building in San Diego. Of the meeting house, residence, recreational facilities, and laboratories, only the last was built.

Form and Design

Pennsylvania. We went out together on a rainy day. He said, "How nice, a beautiful building. I didn't know a building that went up in the air could be nice. How many square feet do you have in this building?" I said, "One hundred and nine thousand square feet." He said, "That's about what we need."

That was the beginning of the program of areas. But there was something else he said which became the Key to the entire space environment. Namely that Medical Research does not belong entirely to medicine or the physical sciences. It belongs to Population. He meant that anyone with a mind in the humanities, in science, or in art could contribute to the mental environment of research leading to discoveries in science. Without the restriction of a dictatorial program it became a rewarding experience to participate in the projection of an evolving program of spaces without precedence. This is only possible because the director is a man of unique sense of environment as an inspiring thing, and he could sense the existence will and its realization in form which the spaces I provided had.

The simple beginning requirement of the laboratories and their services expanded to cloistered gardens and Studies over arcades and to spaces for meeting and relaxation interwoven with unnamed spaces for the glory of the fuller environment.

The laboratories may be characterized as the architecture of air cleanliness and area adjustability. The architecture of the oak table and the rug is that of the Studies.

The Medical Research Building at the University of Pennsylvania[5] is conceived in recognition of the realizations that science laboratories are studios and that the air to breathe should be away from the air to throw away.

The normal plan of laboratories which places the work areas off one side of a public corridor and the other side provided with the stairs, elevators, animal quarters, ducts and other services. This corridor is the vehicle of the exhaust of dangerous air and also the supply

5. Alfred Newton Richards Medical Research and Biology buildings (1957–65), Philadelphia.

of the air you breathe, all next to each other. The only distinction between one man's spaces of work from the other is the difference of the numbers on the doors.

I designed three studio towers for the University where a man may work in his bailiwick and each studio has its own escape *stairway sub tower* and *exhaust sub tower* for isotope air, germ-infected air and noxious gas.

A central building to which the three major towers cluster takes the place of the area for services which are on the other side of the normal corridor plan. This central building has nostrils for intake of fresh air away from *exhaust sub towers* of vitiated air.

This design, an outcome of the consideration of the unique use of its spaces and how they are served, characterizes what it is for.

One day I visited the site during the erection of the prefabricated frame of the building. The crane's 200-foot boom picked up 25-ton members and swung them into place like matchsticks moved by the hand. I resented the garishly painted crane, this monster which humiliated my building to be out of scale. I watched the crane go through its many movements all the time calculating how many more days this "thing" was to dominate the site and building before a flattering photograph of the building could be made.

Now I am glad of this experience because it made me aware of the meaning of the crane in design, for it is merely the extension of the arm like a hammer. Now I began to think of members 100 tons in weight lifted by bigger cranes. The great members would be only the parts of a composite column with joints like sculpture in gold and porcelain and harboring rooms on various levels paved in marble.

These would be the stations of the great span and the entire enclosure would be sheathed with glass held in glass mullions with strands of stainless steel interwoven like threads assisting the glass and the mullions against the forces of wind.

Now the crane was a friend and the stimulus in the realization of a new form.

The institutions of cities can be made greater by the power of their architectural spaces. The meeting house in the village green has given way to the city hall which is no more the meeting place. But I sense an existence will for the arcaded city place where the fountains play, where again boy meets girl, where the city could entertain and put up our distinguished visitors, where the many societies which uphold our democratic ideals can meet in clusters of auditoria in the city place.

The motor car has completely upset the form of the city. I feel that the time has come to make the distinction between the Viaduct architecture of the car and the architecture of man's activities. The tendencies of designers to combine the two architectures in a simple design has confused the direction of planning and technology. The Viaduct architecture enters the city from outlying areas. At this point it must become more carefully made and even at great expense more strategically placed with respect to the center.

The Viaduct architecture includes the street which in the center of the city wants to be a building, a building with rooms below for city piping services to avoid interruption to traffic when services need repair.

The Viaduct architecture would encompass an entirely new concept of street movement which distinguished the stop and go staccato movement of the bus from the "go" movement of the car. The area framing expressways are like rivers. These rivers need harbors. The interim streets are like canals which need docks. The harbors are the gigantic gateways expressing the *architecture of stopping*. The terminals of the Viaduct architecture, they are garages in the core, hotels and department stores around the periphery and shopping centers on the street floor.

This strategic positioning around the city center would present a logical image of protection against the destruction of the city by the motor car. In a sense the problem of the car and city is war, and the planning for the new growth of cities is not a complacent act, but an act of emergency.

The distinction between the two architectures, the architecture of the Viaduct and the architecture of the acts of man's activities, could bring about a logic of growth and a sound positioning of enterprise.

An architect from India gave an excellent talk at the University about the fine new work of Le Corbusier and about his own work[6]. It impressed me, however, that these beautiful works he showed were still out of context and had no position. After his lecture I was asked to remark. Somehow I was moved to go to the blackboard where I drew in the center of the board a towering water tower, wide on top and narrow below. Like the rays of a star, I drew aqueducts radiating from the tower. This implied the coming of the trees and fertile land and a beginning of living. The buildings not yet there which would cluster around the aqueduct would have meaningful position and character.

The city would have form.

From all I have said I do not mean to imply a system of thought and work leading to realization from Form to Design.

Designs could just as well lead to realizations in Form.

This interplay is the constant excitement of Architecture.

6. This was probably Balkrishna Doshi, who visited Philadelphia in the fall of 1960. He was instrumental in securing for Kahn the commission for the Indian Institute of Management (1962–74) in Ahmedabad, assisted him on the project, and participated in overseeing its final stages of construction, which included some portions of his own design.

5 The New Art of Urban Design: Are We Equipped? (1960)

• •

Kahn offered the following speech to a "New Forces in Architecture" conference sponsored by the Architectural League of New York and *Architectural Forum* magazine. The other speakers were public housing advocate Catherine Bauer, Dean José Luis Sert of the Harvard Graduate School of Design, and Ernest van den Haag, professor of jurisprudence and public policy at Fordham University.

Kahn's interest in city form ("immeasurable" form as discussed in the previous essay) arose during World War II and continued throughout his career. Although he had briefly referred to "viaduct" architecture (freeways entering from the suburbs) with its "gateways" (city-edge parking garages), "rivers" (major streets), "canals" (minor streets), and "docks" (downtown parking areas) in "Form and Design," his first comprehensive statement about it was "Toward a Plan for Midtown Philadelphia," *Perspecta*, 2 (August 1953), of which this speech was a succinct précis. "Architecture is also the street," he had contended in that earlier essay, "because the street is design for movement." His nautical references are perhaps manifestations of his lifelong interest in water as an aid to architectural design.

• •

From the "Louis I. Kahn, Architectural League" folder, Box LIK 61, Kahn Collection.

I want to tell you about a Polish architect who came to visit me in the office and asked questions.[1] The question was: He tells of dreams he has of spaces—wonderful spaces that have no beginning and have no end, are made of seamless material and when the joints are there they are eventful joints—all white and gold. He said, "When I try to put this dream on paper, the first line already makes it less. Why is it that it is less?"

"It's less because you deal with the immeasurable and the measurable. A line on paper is a measurable act; the immeasurable—the unmeasurable—is our aspirations, our dreams. And to try to reconcile both at the same time is difficult. It also explains why a man is always greater than his works—because it includes his aspirations which he cannot express. The expression must resort to measurable means; it must resort to nature of nature which deals with completely measurable things."

I think he took this as an answer, except that he said, "Yes, but I will not give up my aspirations. How can I meet more closely my aspirations with what I do?"

"Well, it's obvious, if you think. I think thinking or thought is feeling and order. Now this probably isn't a good enough word to use; let the order, the nature of nature, and let's say your thought—your feeling. An orderly thought is an unmeasurable thing because it contains a psychic quality. I advise you to give up thought, because as soon as you think, you have to make it less. It becomes less. And so I ask you to join a monastery and disown the order of the monastery, because already that's a kind of measurement."

And he said, "I object to this very strongly because I want to make things, and what you're telling me is to make nothing." True. I told him to make nothing. I said, "Well, of course that's intolerable."

Then one must think in terms of transcending beyond your own thought and your own feeling to, let's say, a religious state of mind— not a religion, but a religious state of mind. And a philosophic state

1. This architect is probably fictional—an oratorical device. Kahn changed the architect's nationality—or made him a student of architecture—from one speech to another.

of mind which could lead you to realizations. And realizations aren't really tangible things. But they are realizations in form and not in design. They are a recognition of a harmony of systems which distinguishes one thing from another. Form, I believe, is that which distinguishes one thing from another; and it is not tangible, but it leads to the active, tangible things in design.

I believe we design too quickly without realizing in form what characterizes one thing from another. And so the realm of spaces which is, let's say school, is not the realm of spaces which is, let's say city hall. But the buildings look alike quite. An Indian architect[2] spoke at the University of Pennsylvania the other day and showed many of the works, the fine, recent works of Corbusier. It is delightful to see a man of such wonderful resourcefulness as he. The architect also showed his own work, which was extremely interesting in his ability to, with frugal means, produce very good things. After the thing was over he asked me to comment on what I thought.

I went to the blackboard, which is standard equipment at the University, and I placed in the middle of the blackboard a water tower, which I tried to make as beautiful as possible, with a broad top and a narrow-waisted bottom from which I drew in starlike radiation aqueducts leading from this tower. I said, "This would be an appropriate beginning for a town in India."

Not building the buildings first, and not the hope of water, which I felt was more of a symbol—more of a beginning—more of a modern beginning for India than the drawing of (the architect's name) and the building and conceiving of architectural shapes—delightfully conceived, certainly—but out of context with what you might call a way of life which calls for water as a hope for the trees, and a hope for agriculture, and even a hope for the building itself. I think that beginning looks right to me in form, and it gives almost position to the buildings—a disposition for all things that make a city. It's a beginning—it's not a continuation—of something that is there, but something which gives direction and almost immediate participation by all.

2. Balkrishna Doshi. See selection 4, note 6 (page 74).

I believe that modern cities need a distinction between the aqueduct, not the viaduct, architecture and the architecture of the living or the art of the activities of man, because the buildings we build are really indicative of what the activities of man need in the way of space. But the architecture of the viaduct, of the street, the expressway, and the garage which is part of it, is not expressed at all. It is generally homogenized into the building of what I call "Picasso and the Spoon," or whatever you want to call a building which belongs to a man; and the color of that piece of tin is given equal position in many ways to that of spaces which we work in, study in.

I think this is a great mistake. I believe both architectures must be separated from each other, because they are *not* the same architecture. One is a tough, kickable architecture, and the other is delicate—could be gossamer, in our present technology, could be completely remarkable. And if we knew the distinction, I think it would become even more remarkable, because we would not place that building out of context, but would place it in relation to the tough architecture of the viaduct.

And these viaduct architectures in the outlying areas coming into the city must be more respectable. They've got to come in and doff their hats and be better materials. They must also integrate other services with those viaducts and not be just the same old stilts and the crude construction only gathering newspapers and dust below. And the terminal points of this architecture, which could be the garage if you want to call it that, but I'd call it the gateway—those gateways could be marvelous structures. I think architects would all be jealous to do such structures, structures which would give you the sense of entrance into certain areas and give direction to the growth of those areas. At the present time garages are nothing but real estate ventures—helter-skelter decisions, not part of the design of the street. And they should be part of the architecture of the street, of movement, and that architecture of stopping, which in itself can be a marvelous architecture. If there is distinguished enough buried under the streets and put into lower basements of buildings and placed, let's say, at three stories of the building before it begins, I believe that is the great fault where we do not really study the forms sufficiently—that which, in any case, the distinction between our way of life now and the way of life before.

We constantly think in terms of squares which once reviewed troops as being necessary in cities, because squares are nice. They are. But they have to have a meaning in context with a way of life. And these streets now, these expressways, are really rivers; they need harbors. And our smallest streets are canals; they need docks. They cannot just be anywhere; they have to have a definite relationship to the logic of movement. I believe streets should be zones—not lots, but streets for their movement, and the lots would take their logical position. I agree with the second speaker in saying that there should be not such a strict zoning distinction. This is causing much trouble, because if the center point of cities—in such a place like New York could have many centers—protected by the architectural stopping, I believe those centers could become cathedrals in themselves—great concentrations of buildings which have a logic with the place of stopping. Those would not be interfered with cross-movement at all; they would be the stopping places, places to go to and not go through. And it would be equipped immediately with those conveniences which would make it possible to circulate as you would in any kind of pedestrian way.

But it never occurs to anybody, because the strong logic—the big logic—isn't there; because they try to kick the car out of the city. And I believe you can't deny the man who is simply satisfied with the fairy tales of yesterday—of being able to fly like a bird and swim like a fish and run like a deer. We do better than they do now, and only recently you were awed by the flying carpet. Today it's just something you're not too excited about. We definitely need the new fairy tale; there's no question about that. And that represents really our aspirations. We can't deny these aspirations, but we can't give them position in the making of things unless we think in terms of form—that which distinguishes one thing from another—instead of design.

I want to suggest just a little bit about institutions. If you take our institutions, you think in terms of City Hall. City Hall today, in

Philadelphia, for instance, is a quarry—it's a great quarry. The mayor doesn't want to be there; it's a place where you pay taxes; you pay inspection fees, licenses; you go to court. But nothing in the way of participation. There is no so-called City Place, a place where great men could be invited into the chateau of the city. A place where fountains play; a place where boy meets girl. Such places are given to you by commercial means? No. They should be really that which the mayor inherits and has key to as he inherits office; something which one can feel ownership to himself as a man. The sense of patriotism of the city can be given by giving great city places to the city instead of one stream of commercial enterprise all fighting for a kind of place in the—in the—not in the sun; I couldn't think of where it is—but just fighting for a place, I would say.

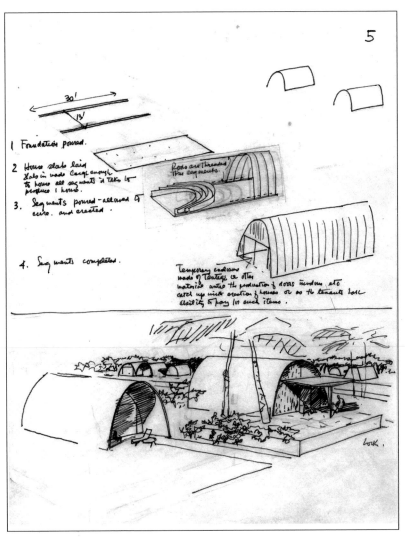

Jewish Agency for Palestine Emergency Housing (1949, unbuilt), Israel.

81

Richards Medical Research Building (1959–65), Philadelphia, Pennsylvania, under construction.

Richards Medical Research Building (1959–65), Philadelphia, Pennsylvania.

United States Consulate
and Residence
(1959–62, unbuilt),
Luanda, Angola,
exterior wall system.

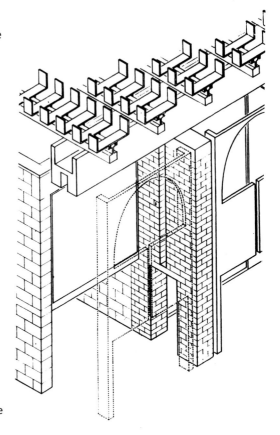

United States Consulate
and Residence
(1959–62, unbuilt),
Luanda, Angola.

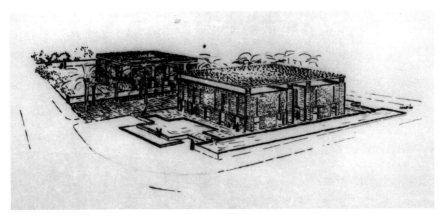

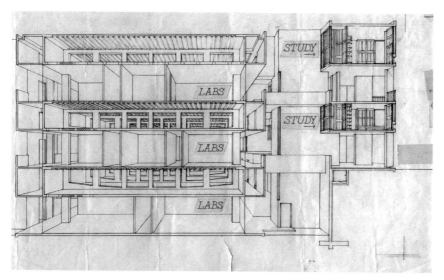

Salk Institute for Biological Studies (1959–65), La Jolla, California, section.

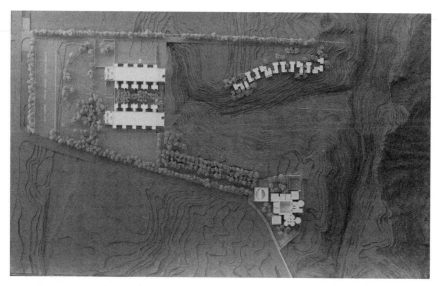

Salk Institute for Biological Studies (1959–65), La Jolla, California, site model of laboratories (left), unbuilt residences (upper right), and unbuilt meeting house (lower right).

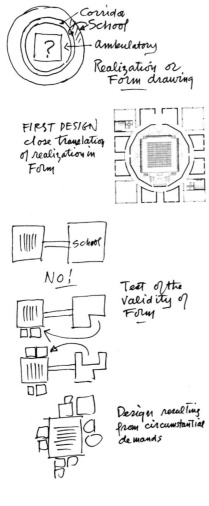

Corrida
School
ambulatory

Realization or
Form drawing

FIRST DESIGN
close translation
of realization in
Form

School

NO!

Test of the
validity of
Form

Design resulting
from circumstantial
demands

First Unitarian Church and School (1959–69), Rochester, New York. From top to bottom: form-drawing, first plan, manipulation of program elements.

First Unitarian Church (right) and School (left) (1959–69), Rochester, New York.

First Unitarian Church (1959–69), Rochester, New York, alcove seating.

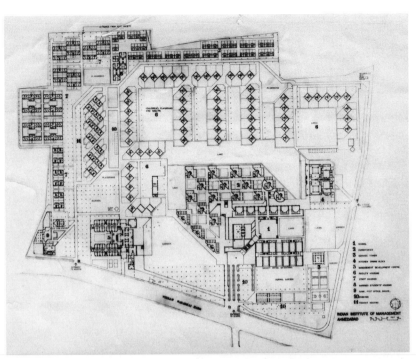

Indian Institute of Management (1962–74), Ahmedabad, India.

Indian Institute of
Management
(1962–74),
Ahmedabad, India,
wall fenestration
system.

Eleanor Donnelley Erdman Hall (1960–65), Bryn Mawr, Pennsylvania.

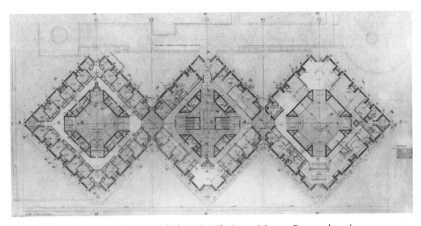

Eleanor Donnelley Erdman Hall (1960–65), Bryn Mawr, Pennsylvania.

Fine Arts Center (1959–73), Fort Wayne, Indiana.

Sher-e-Bangla Nagar (1962–83), Dhaka, Bangladesh, East Hostels (upper left), National Assembly Building (center), and West Hostels (lower right).

Sher-e-Bangla Nagar (1962–83), Dhaka, Bangladesh, construction for pouring and pointing concrete.

Phillips Exeter Academy Library atrium (1965–72), Exeter, New Hampshire, view from second floor to ceiling.

Phillips Exeter Academy Library atrium (1965–72), Exeter, New Hampshire, view into stacks.

St. Andrew's Priory (1961–67, unbuilt), Valyermo, California, model.

Discussion in Kahn's Office (1961)

6

The editor of *Perspecta*, Yale University's magazine of architecture, asked Kahn about three recent or ongoing projects, the first two never constructed: the United States Consulate and Residence (1959–62) in Luanda, Angola, the M. Morton Goldenberg residence (1959) in Rydal, Pennsylvania; and the First Unitarian Church and School (1959–69) in Rochester, New York.

Kahn spoke of wrapping the consulate in "ruins." Literally he meant fenestrated walls that would stand a few feet outside of the building's actual walls and were intended to minimize sun glare and deflect wind, a device he used in subsequent commissions for especially hot climates. Figuratively, ruins were what remained of "beginnings," reminders (for those caring to look) of the origins of those Platonic-like "forms"—traces of "basic principles"—that had characterized architecture from its inception.

Two things should be noted about Kahn's comments on the Rochester church, as well as its ten-year gestation and construction: what Kahn called a "form drawing—as opposed to a design," in which he tried to depict the essence of Unitarianism in order to understand how to conceive a particular structure for a specific Unitarian congregation, and the patience and care with which he worked, reworked, and then worked more on the actual design, a process not atypical of Kahn's *modus operandi*.

From *Perspecta* 7 (1961): 9–28. Reprinted with permission of the Dean of the School of Architecture, Yale University.

AMERICAN CONSULATE, LUANDA, PORTUGUESE ANGOLA

K AHN: One of the things which impressed me very much during my stay in Luanda was the marked glare in the atmosphere . . . when you were on the interior of any building, looking at a window was unbearable because of the glare. The dark walls framing the brilliant light outside made you very uncomfortable. The tendency was to look away from the window. Another thing that impressed me was the importance of breeze . . . the importance of breeze in carrying away the warm air that accumulated around the building. And I thought wouldn't it be good if one could express . . . find an architectural expression for the problems of glare without adding devices to a window . . . but rather by developing a warm architecture . . . which somehow tells the story of the problems of glare. Some of the buildings used place work, grillework . . . wood or masonry grillework in front of windows. This was unsatisfactory because of what it did . . . because the wall itself was dark against the light; it gave you just a multiple pattern of glare . . . little pin points . . . little diamond-points of glare against the dark ribs of the grillework. And that tended to be unsatisfactory. I noticed that buildings which were very close to windows were very pleasant to look at from the windows. I also noticed that when people worked in the sun—and many of them did—the native population people—when they worked, they usually faced the wall and not the open country or the open street. Indoors, they would turn their chair toward the wall and do whatever they were doing by getting the light indirectly from the wall to their work. That gave me the thought of a wall a small distance in front of every window as a kind of indigenous architectural sense. Now, placing a wall in front of a window would cut the view and that is not pleasant. One doesn't feel like having the view cut away, so I thought of placing openings in the wall, the wall then becomes part of the window. When that wall got the light—even the direct sunlight—it would modify the glare. So therefore I thought of the beauty of ruins . . . the absence of frames . . . of things which nothing lives behind . . . and so I thought of wrapping ruins around buildings; you might say encasing a building in a ruin so that you look through the wall which had its apertures by accident. But, in this case you'd want to formalize these openings and I felt this would be an answer to the glare problem. I wanted to incorporate this into the architecture instead of it being a device placed next to a window to correct the window desires . . . I don't want to say window desires . . . window desires is not the way to put it. I should say: desire for light, but still an active fighting of the glare. Another thing that impressed me: I saw some buildings that were conscious of the heat generated by roofs. They had large areas in the roof . . . large separations between the ceiling and the roof . . . small openings which were visible from the outside in which the breeze could come in to ventilate the areas in the ceiling and roof planes. And I thought how wonderful it would be if one could separate the sun problems from the rain problems. And it came to mind to have a sunroof purely for the sun and another roof purely for the rain. I placed them six feet away from each other so that one could maintain the rain roof . . . which was the important roof to maintain because the sun roof could take care of itself . . . it being a loose roof, one in which the rain can go through. It can never become a problem, you see, except for minor repairs. The sun roof naturally wanted to be made as light as possible . . . because it should be in a way a gossamer . . . something which is just there as an interceptor . . . and I thought of the insulation . . . that the actual sun roof might become the insulation so I would eliminate insulation on the rain roof entirely . . . have no air space except for what you get from the separation between the two roofs, the rain roof and the sun roof. Now there were other thoughts which came to my mind, outside of plan, outside of any aesthetic notions I may have had to begin with about how I build the building. I felt the building should have a restful, a reposeful character, and not be particularly aggravated in contour. I wanted very much—as has always been my desire—to demonstrate to the man on the street a way of life . . . so when he sees a building as he passes it he feels as though . . . "Yes, this building represents or presents a civic story to me of my relation to this building. I expect a dignified building for a dignified activity of man." But those were feelings about a sense of appropriateness which may have come from learning and from other things but are not really deeply fundamental. They are aesthetic considerations and aesthetics are, of course, the laws of art. You learn them by seeing a lot and by being told a lot and by sensing a lot, but the other things come out of the very characteristics of the air, and of light ... very simple everlasting presences that should constantly talk to you in architecture. You cannot forget that light of a certain character has to do with that which distinguishes the architecture of one region from that of another. Even if you took the demands of a company for their identification in one country or another, you couldn't build a prototype as a kind of business principle, rather than as a building principle. You would have to give not so much a building but a vision, an image. But the image must change from one region to another because the requirements of an area are different in one place or another. The integrity of a building could be one stamp of identity with a company, the excellence of performance could be one ... certainly their sign could be ... but when you take the very same building, a prototype, an actual duplication, and place it anywhere regardless of the area ... this would be a ridiculous building. I also realized that natural ventilation was an important thing to consider in these buildings because of the state of mechanical ability; the repair of air-conditioning systems or plumbing systems was something that would take a long time to develop in this country ... you can't just import devices without regard to their future performance. But even if you were to have good mechanical maintenance for air conditioning and the other modern devices which control your environment, the protection against the sun and glare and the channeling of wind is still important so as not to impose too much load on the air conditioning. So a non-air-conditioned building can look just the same really as an air-conditioned building except that the windows would change. In Luanda you can just have slats—you don't need any glass at all. You just allow the breeze to come through and you control it with your louvers. But, when you have an air-conditioned building, you've got to have glazing—you've got to contain it ... you don't want to condition the whole atmosphere. So I felt I was not doing the wrong thing by making the building look like a non-air-conditioned building except for the glazing.

EDITOR: Is it or isn't it air conditioned?

KAHN: This is an air-conditioned building. Only, you must figure that it could at times be one in which the air conditioning would not be functioning. There will be some louvers and operating windows in there anyhow so you can get some ventilation in case the thing goes bad.

The glare walls are designed to present a non-bearing wall. You feel the openings are done with the idea of giving you a sympathetic place in which to view your . . . whatever you want to see. I feel, off hand, that they're now a little too large, that they can be made smaller. It's only that I still haven't developed a kind of sense in lieu of experience to tell me whether they're large or small. I haven't developed this because they must be tried . . . probably anyone could have greater caution . . . I think they can actually be smaller than those indicated. I feel the openings should be smaller because you can have a side view anyway . . . you always have a side view. You can look out and see everything you want. But here you have a controlled view and it can actually be smaller than I have indicated. I feel this is a good approach to architecture . . . a true approach to architecture . . . in that you're constantly aware of the natural forces and trying to restate and to reestablish a way of life in architecture. So a building really aspires to something, and it answers very much a way of life. But, this aspiration has to be constantly renewed and reborn and what is presented by the art of building or the art of painting or sculpture is in light of new techniques. The new techniques will help you . . . it brings before you new measurable means of doing that which your aspiration calls for and that's how you view technique: as a measurable means of expressing closer and closer the desire and the existence will of aspirations.

From the main thoroughfares I developed an entrance court which is really a parking space for the chancellery and the house . . . the residence. I used trees to divide areas of parking and to shade the parking, too . . . right in the street itself. This much of the street would be paved with limestone . . . a material prevalent in Angola. This answers many of the problems which are unsolved in some of these consular buildings . . . I'm not saying it very well . . . let me just say it in different words . . . I'm conscious of this thing for a moment. The government board of architectural review liked the scheme very much because they saw a sense of privacy in the parking . . . in that the paving is different from the usual run of paving . . . which seemed like an ordinary consideration, but they didn't think it was ordinary because it gave a kind of gate . . . a court entrance to these two buildings. The chancellery is surrounded by a play of pool areas which empty one into the other; the upper pool empties into this lower pool and the lower pool empties into a pool at a still lower level . . . and that keeps the water running into this pool . . . which is very essential to water use in these areas. And practically the entire landscaping ideal on the chancellery side is the pool and the various terraces sitting in the environment, a rather stark environment. On the other side you get an environment of green . . . though it's not indicated on the plot plan, this will be a green area, a treed area . . . whereas this will be (the chancellery area) rather an untreed area with the court itself giving shade and direction to the parking and entrance. The residence is treated in the same way as far as the recognition of glare and the recognition of the sun roof. The four courts on the interior of the residence give interior light and afford a positioning of the columns which hold the sun roof. This shows, of course, a lower story . . . and you notice that it has a continuous walkway under the building. I feel that in bringing the rain roof and the sun roof away from each other I was telling the man on the street his way of life. I was explaining the atmospheric conditions of wind, the conditions of light, the conditions of sun and glare to him. If I used a device—a clever kind of design device—would only seem like a design to him—something pretty.

I didn't want anything pretty; I wanted to have a clear statement of a way of life. And those two devices I feel very proud of as being strong architectural statements from which other men can make infinitely better statements. These are really crude statements . . . they're actually done with almost the feeling that they should be primitively stated first rather than in high degree of taste. The purpose was to state it in a rather primitive, unknowing, unsophisticated way. And I think that in the arrangement of spaces required, the sense of entrance, and the sense of reception, the plan has again a sense of the appropriateness of such devices . . . or the space feeling that one should have considering the type of building it is. One should have a feeling of entrance and reception not by the way of sign but by its very character and this every architect who is conscious of spaces does one way or the other. And, I think this plan does indicate that. Notice also that the piers that hold the main girders for the sun roof are completely independent of the rain roof. The rain roof is never pierced. The sun roof rises quite independently out of the architecture, so that at no point do you pierce the rain roof. That accounts for these piers . . . these four sets of piers. The girders go across and the joists—concrete pre-stressed joists—hold the tiled—the clay-tiled leaves which form the sun tree on the sun roof which covers the entire building all together. You're completely conscious of this because when you enter the building . . . here, for instance . . . this is all open through there . . . the rain roof only follows this little portion here . . . is only this and there and this is all open, so . . . when you come into the building here you sense the entire leaf-like structure above . . . they'd be open enough so that the light can come through.

EDITOR: Why is the opening in the pier greater in the lower story than in the upper?

KAHN: There's a lintel that allows me to have a smaller opening above . . . it can distribute the load that way. I wanted it open under there because I want to pass through everything and I pass through this beam in order to get a continuous promenade under the building. I then put the building off the ground . . . it is current practice in these areas to raise all important rooms above grade. Also it gives you a feeling of greater protection . . . in a way the chancellery building of this government function is, in a sense, a fort . . . it's a protective building . . . and the extra floor gives it a kind of extra sense of protection.

EDITOR: The physiological reaction to sitting in darkness and looking to light is a problem like the adjustment of the diaphragm of a camera . . . I was wondering why then this interval—the double window—will ease the adjustment the eye must make. You either know or are hoping that when you do finally—after looking through the void of shade—see the bright area, it will be toned down enough so that your iris can adjust instantaneously without having a painful physiological reaction.

KAHN: Listen to what I think. I say it more this way: When you see this wall in front of you light framed in a window surrounded in darkness is what causes the glare. That's glare, a glare condition.

EDITOR: It provides a shade of gray between the black and the white.

KAHN: Grilles or anything like that—which are prevalent in front of a window like that—give little pin points of light which are very

glaring. You needn't see it, you can just draw it.

When these members get smaller and smaller, it's all right again . . . you don't feel it as much. Then you get a great modification of the glare.

EDITOR: Well this would presumably be easy enough to make a model of . . .

KAHN: Yes, we have made a model of it . . . you can see the difference. You put a large bulb—a 500 watt bulb—in front of you and you can see plenty of glare right close to it. And as soon as you move that thing (the model of the light wall) in front of the bulb it's completely different. You saw the difference right away.

EDITOR: This shape begins to recall . . . almost an eye . . .

KAHN: It does in a way yes. Of course, I use it as a device to get some grace into a box-like building. The requirements being so little—I mean the building is so small—the desire to breathe something into it was there too. You have this privilege, this device, you see. You can go overboard very, very easily—you can make something frivo-lous in a second. I don't know that's even good—I just feel it's good—somebody said it looks African, which was awful. That reminds me—Yamasaki, who said that he was doing a building in Iran says he likes the idea.[1] I've used this device recently very, very often. These are beautiful windows. I think it's well to play not so much on the com-pleteness of the design . . . after all . . . everybody's problem is differ-ent and this is only how I designed something. It's one of the reasons why I also think that the completeness of the drawings is not terribly important; I believe it is more important to just simply state some-thing fragmentarily in order not to say: I like the design, I don't like the design. This way it becomes easily a part of the architectural mind without the minor likes and dislikes . . . one can judge it another way . . . and then from this many people can do better. I think that . . . that design is a very personal thing. But I feel that these other things are not really personal . . . it's just simply a sense of architecture, you see, which you feel you want to install within the framework of this, your work.

GOLDBERG[2] HOUSE, RYDAL, PENNSYLVANIA

EDITOR: The obvious question is: why couldn't this wall be contin-ued and then you frame from here to there? (That is, have solid cor-ners.)

KAHN: Because that really is the way it works and there is a desire to respect the fact that a building can end up . . . that the ends of a building are different from a prescribed thing like this.

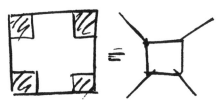

1. Minoru Yamasaki; Iranian building unidentified.
2. Goldenberg is incorrectly spelled.

You start with this but sometimes the interior wants to move out and break the walls out.

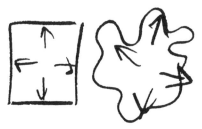

And you hold it in because of the preconceived shape that you have chosen. And that discovery . . . that the diagonal can be something to which you can frame . . . that it can be a kind of circumstan-

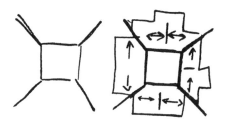

tial ending . . . which this is because if I had more money, I probably would have come up with a little bit more. It's purely circumstantial. I felt this was rather a discovery in the desires of interiors—interior spaces . . . a house is a building which is extremely sensitive to internal need. In this satisfaction there was an *existence will* of some kind . . . but there was an *existence will* for this house not to be disciplined within a geometric shape.

EDITOR: You've wound up with a much bigger periphery than, say, a square . . . you could obviously juggle these parts and wind up with a full square . . . it can be done. But the point to me is this: That in this particular configuration you have a circulation ring to which each room relates—all except the living room—by way of the passage through the functions . . . as a sort of buffer zone . . . the major rooms then take their needed configurations independently of each other. If you had filled in the corners or made it a regular volume it would not

Discussion in Kahn's Office

have been, it seems to me, nearly as clear a relationship as when you shove these things out.

KAHN: In an ordinary square you always have the problem of these ends which are hard to reach. You must penetrate this (the "functional" areas) to come to the spaces—the final spaces being what they will be. You penetrate this to come to this—and so this—these become servant areas and these areas served. The servant areas also serve as insulation ... they insulate you from room to room.

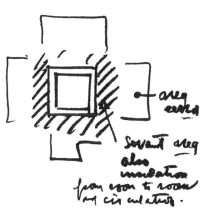

EDITOR: Also from room to circulation.

KAHN: From room to room and from room to circulation.

EDITOR: Aren't the inner servant spaces always sky-lighted and the others lit from the outside?

KAHN: Yes, I'll draw it for you.

EDITOR: The artist copying his own drawing out of the *Architect's Yearbook* for *Perspecta*.

KAHN: What could be better? Do you want a tree?

EDITOR: How about the light now?

KAHN: All spaces need natural light. I can write that in if you like.

EDITOR: For a house—or period?

KAHN: I would say all spaces need natural light ... all spaces worthy of being called a space need natural light. Artificial light is only a single little moment in light . . . and natural light is the full of the moon and it just makes a difference.

EDITOR: So doesn't this imply a tautology . . . in saying that you define a space as something which does have natural light.

KAHN: Yes, I can't define a space really as a space unless I have natural light. And that because the moods which are created by the time of day and seasons of the year are constantly helping you in evoking that which a space can be if it has natural light and can't be if it doesn't. And artificial light—be it in a gallery, be it even in an auditorium—loses one a great deal. I would like to—sometime—build a theater which has natural light . . . which you later blot out when the show is on. But why must the rehearsal be in a dingy place? Is the rehearsal a play? No—the play is the play and the people see it, not the rehearsal. During the rehearsal the theater should be as pleasant as possible with a different kind of atmosphere. I'm not so sure that a theater should be always artificially lit unless you rehearse somewhere else. With the absence of the people you probably are producing something which is completely artificial, you see, in the sense that you make the same space but with natural light present. I think natural light should be in spaces that you may call spaces. And interestingly enough I think that the way a space is made is almost made with the consciousness of possibilities of light because when you have a column you see, you are saying a column is there because light is possible. A wall does not say it's possible . . . but when you have a column or a vault or an arch, you're saying that light is possible. So therefore the means of making a space already implies that light is coming in . . . and the very choice that you make of the element of structure should be also the choice of the character of light that you may want . . . and that I think is truly an architectural demand.

EDITOR: If it's so dark you can't see the room it can't be a space. Like the inside of a refrigerator with the light off.

KAHN: Is not a space . . .

EDITOR: When you open the door and the light goes on it is a space . . . if it's natural light.

KAHN: If it's natural light . . . Some of the darkrooms which are used in laboratories . . . they always tell you . . . the doctor will always tell you "Well, there's one place where we don't need a view out . . . I don't mean a darkroom . . . I mean to say a coldroom where they have experiments. But you usually find that it is the man in charge of a project who says that while some student who is working for him is suffering . . . who has to do without light. He can't tell whether there's a bird outside, or if it's snowing or raining. When I got to talking to some of the underlings I soon found that they were very unhappy without a window so they could look out at something.

UNITARIAN CHURCH, ROCHESTER, NEW YORK

EDITOR: When you were in New Haven you touched on the various stages you'd gone through . . .

KAHN: Let's put these four plans down. The idea which I sketched on the board before the congregation was my first reaction to what may be a direction in the building of a Unitarian Church. Having heard the minister give a sense of the Unitarian aspirations, it occurred to me that the sanctuary is merely the center of questions and that the school—which was constantly emphasized—was that which raises the question . . . and I felt that that which raised the question and that which was the sense of the question—the spirit of the question—were inseparable. And so, when I spoke, before the congregation . . . they had a blackboard on the platform . . . I drew this diagram:

From Drawing,
NOT A DESIGN

A square, the sanctuary, and a circle around the square which was the containment of an ambulatory. The ambulatory I felt necessary because the Unitarian Church is made up of people who have had previous beliefs—they still have beliefs but they're simply beliefs of a different kind . . . they were Catholics and they were Jews and they were Protestants. I don't know much about religious ways except that I feel religion. So I drew the ambulatory to respect the fact that what is being said or what is felt in a sanctuary was not necessarily something you have to participate in. And so you could walk and feel free to walk away from what is being said. And then I placed a corridor next to it—around it—which served the school which was really the walls of the entire area . . . so the school became the walls which surrounded the question. The first plan was almost a literal translation of the form drawing as I would call it: form drawing—that which represented, which presented inseparable parts of what you may call a Unitarian center or Unitarian place. Although I did not know the specific requirements—I knew them in general. I felt that a direct, almost primitive statement was the way to begin . . . rather than a statement that already had many expressions of experience . . . which may modify so strictly translated a form as in this diagram. It was modified somewhat: The exterior became a square, the interior corridors were round and the sanctuary was still square. The four corners become larger rooms—they were immediately questioned because four larger rooms had to have four purposes. They couldn't have equal purposes very well because they were positioned entirely too—where the positions were too important. I tried to argue that they could be classrooms like any other classrooms—there are large classrooms and small classrooms. But this was a congregation which didn't have endless resources and money and they questioned everything that I put down. In dealing with the committees which were formed from various activity interests: the committee for the nursery, committee on nursing, committee on entertainment, committee on religious activities, etc., I developed their sense of program as I developed drawings. At one point they insisted that the sanctuary must be separated from the school—that was a terrible blow to me. All this form that I thought was really inherent to what you might call an inexperienced ritual—or rather a ritual which is not established, but a ritual which is rather inspired—could not then state its shape and dimension to follow the ritual. Therefore I thought: The closeness of all parts was a better expression than that which already separated us from the two—in which you can say a school is a different thing than a sanctuary. And so I felt that it was something more than just a primitive statement of this, the beginning statement you might say which can make a Unitarian Church. Dividing may be just doing lip service to the many other activities of man, and imitating how others have made their churches which have a different kind of sense of ritual than this one has. And so at one point I had to simply show the auditorium as a separate thing—but I did this only in diagram, not in actual plan. I never could be forced to make a plan which satisfied this. I resisted making any kind of plan. I wouldn't have done it. But I did at one point draw what it would look like roughly on a piece of paper, a sanctuary in one instance connected with the school square, the school area.

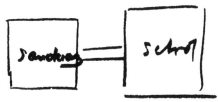

I asked questions about the sanctuary: What do you do after services are over? They say they have a coffee hour; they discuss the things that were talked about in the auditorium. They felt that it would be very good to have a kitchen close to the sanctuary. So I took a piece out of the school block and put it next to the sanctuary. And then they felt another room was necessary next to the kitchen to serve the kitchen. So I placed that and took another piece off of the school. And so it was with other rooms that were necessary, placing them around the sanctuary.

Discussion in Kahn's Office

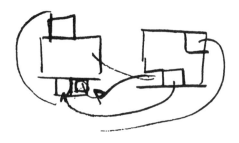

And pretty soon they all began to realize that we were back where I had started. It had to be that way because of the very nature of the activities, and I sensed right from the beginning that these things had to be close. I realized they didn't know what school really was; that a school was an adult room as well as a schoolroom for children. They wanted a kitchen, they wanted a sewing room . . . they didn't want a Chapel—somebody said it would be nice to have a chapel—any one of these rooms could become a chapel . . . such an indefiniteness as to what would be the actual space requirements of a ritual which is not established. With an unestablished ritual I felt that the most resourceful expression was not making distinctions, not making strong distinctions except distinctions of function—because it's a noisy thing on the exterior and a quiet thing on the inside. This also proved to be economically good because the interior required little heating and it's proving to be a very economical building. Now in the development of the various plans: The first plan is a literal expression of the form drawing. A form drawing—as opposed to a design. But because of the demands of the various committees and the drive for the naming of every room, the accounting for the need of every room, the first plan fell apart because the corners could not be justified; that is, the balance of rooms on the four corners . . . The various grades . . . school grades: kindergarten, junior classes and senior classes . . . wanted to be grouped together. And so all plans that follow give in to the design demands of the various committees and, of course, the limit of financing which disallow extra rooms prevented the development of a clear geometric form on the exterior of the building. At first there was a feeling of losing a great deal by this . . . and a formalization of

Discussion in Kahn's Office

these rooms on the exterior ... which is expressed by this drawing in that rooms were kept as much as possible the same size so we could develop a structural system with some inherent unity in the system.

EDITOR: At this [third design] stage it was still a series of calls ...

KAHN: Yes, and they still had little things over them, but it was losing itself there.

EDITOR: Well, they're all different sizes ...

KAHN: Some of them are ...

EDITOR: Should the cell be say—from here to here?

KAHN: No, from here to here.

EDITOR: Then they'd all be odd-sized ...

KAHN: It's just another development, a plan—which has not yet lost all these other earmarks—from the more formalistic stage which preceded it ...

KAHN: And the [fourth stage] is this ... and there the smaller rooms were getting larger ... there were just constant changes, that's all I can tell you. I don't know what else I can tell you. At this point I felt this is the big change here: Before the window's flat, here the windows punched out of the walls. We felt the starkness of light again, learning also to be conscious of glare every time ... whether it's the glare in Rochester or glare in Luanda, it still was one realization ... if you looked at a Renaissance building with a ... or rather a building in which a window has been highly accentuated architecturally—with its ... well like this, for instance:

You have a window that's made this way . . . this pediment and a window of this nature . . . this is not a very good detail at all . . . this is not a good drawing . . . you know what I mean: a window that's made in this form—windows framed into the opening . . .

This was very good because it allowed the light that came in on the sides to help again to modify the glare. When you saw light on the side of a wall, it helped you to look and so I felt that it would be well to have a framing of the window and to have blinders on the side of the window to give you a softness so that when

you're not looking starkly out . . . when you're in the room off at an angle you can choose to see the light directly or not, depending on the reveal of the window itself. I felt a need to reveal. And this is the beginning of a realization that the reveals are necessary. And this came about also because there was a desire to have some window seats—there's a great feeling that a window seat should be present because there is no telling how the room will be used . . . it adds a friendliness, a hate of comfort[3] and kind of getting away from someone and being alone even in a room where many are present . . . a room which is—its purpose is not settled—but is constantly full of human relationships and nothing starkly in the way of purpose . . . one that has a flexible purpose. I felt this window seat had a lot of meaning and it struck me as a demand of several people in the committee . . . this window seat had a lot of meaning and it became greater and greater in my mind as meaning associated with windows. And that's what this is. There's a true beginning of it in this plan. And it became really well expressed—I would say—in this plan when the windows—instead of being so very prevalent as in this plan—became much more carefully considered [in the fourth planning stage]. And

---

3. Kahn was probably thinking of the window seat not as a place of relaxation but of stimulation akin to the ambulatory in his original form drawing.

the windows were in a place where really you need them you see . . . and that's what finally resulted . . . this is the final plan . . . not quite the final plan, but pretty much the final plan . . . and these represent on the elevation . . . you'll see it here much better:

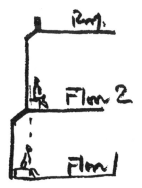

For instance, there's a window seat here on the first floor and there is another one on the second floor, but it is not the same configuration as the one on the first floor as the wall recedes inwards . . . In other words it steps in there and forms a window seat which is against the wall rather than in an alcove. In the lower the light in this case is gotten from the side at this joint and above it's gotten at this joint.

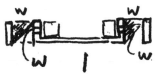

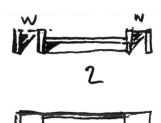

It's a play really of wall and variety in the getting of various conditions around the windows which caused one to make these changes. And in some instances this window seat turns into a thing which you don't need at all above and that would not be expressed here. At this [fourth] stage, the window seats were equal on two floors—were the same, I mean to say, on the two floors. And . . . what I did was to consider that you back up you might say, a façade to the line of the floor seat. And you back it up to it as though you were just wheeling something up to the façade. But in this case I reconsidered this idea of wheeling to it because these walls can be so much aid in the construction of this space because you get much more . . . you wouldn't need a beam if you actually used these walls in bearing. That was the way I arrived at this whole business . . . by backing it up to this . . . which later became an integral part of stage four. A very important development in stage five is this: That above the library, coffeeroom, is a chapel for the school—the school for the students, the pupils. The getting of light below was a problem . . . though one could get light to shape this room above it was difficult to get light to shape this room below. So I devised four walls for light in the four corners. The light came in above and went down to define this space below. This space being an oblong . . . only two sides in light was not sufficient to express the oblong . . . and therefore I felt that getting the light from above and down a well into the corners of the space gave expression to the form, to the shape, of the room chosen.

EDITOR: When you use light this way, you're using it to define the limits of the room.

KAHN: Yes, I do. I find the limit of the room you actually give . . . I was concerned about the light in this particular room—the others were minor rooms and they get their light from, let's say, from one side—which probably is quite sufficient for the size of the room.

EDITOR: I'm still not clear, sir, about the stepping in of the wall . . .

KAHN: The slab goes to here and this turns, the slab turns down to support this. And this turns down this way and the window seat is here. It avoids the development of a continuous roof line . . . it takes

the boxed in windows which reach all the way up to the corners of the rooms—and frees them as elements.

Actually one of the elevations is drawn incorrectly, the roofline is behind the window. Yes . . . you see . . . that should be out because that should really be freestanding. The idea is to develop really quite frankly a silhouette.

EDITOR: But the end result is that the stepped wall begins to look like a buttress . . .

KAHN: No, I don't think so . . . this is just a seat.

EDITOR: No, I mean the inner part—the stepped part does.

KAHN: Yes, well it might—of course, it might . . . This is really, you might say, a way of playing with the walls to give you a variety of impressions on the interior. It may look like a buttress, yes. That may be its criticism, if you like.

EDITOR: I wasn't implying anything one way or the other . . .

KAHN: No . . . it makes it look like one. It's a way of controlling what you want below and above.

EDITOR: Colin Wilson[4] said that when he was down here you were working on a new way of spanning the center part . . . he said something about three-legged tables . . .

KAHN: You get your light from the four corners . . . four columns here and this is a concrete wall here. And off this concrete wall is cantilevered the roof. And this wall also holds these slabs which intersect—the beams are out—I've taken the beams away . . . but you get the light. I think we have the sections through it . . .

Also, there is an isometric . . .

This is a terribly, terribly difficult drawing . . . you've got to see the inside looking out . . .

. . . Now this, interestingly enough . . . this, acoustically is good (referring to the roof of central area). The turning of the slab upward . . . and these are good for reverberations . . . that you would get in the music. One of the corrections which the acoustical engineers have made is that they'd like us to make this slightly longer . . . this slightly down so that you've got more of a unity in the space and so that you don't get separation of the two . . .

These spaces and those spaces . . . in form . . . it's a very interesting truth . . .

4. Colin Wilson, a prolific English writer of self-improvement books.

EDITOR: The angularity on the outside which will then be picked up with the horns.

KAHN: . . . there were many more developments than this, by the way, because I had, at one point, four umbrellas with a column here, there, and there and there, an umbrella here, an umbrella there and there and an umbrella here. That was very nice—in fact, the one that represents this thing here with the four domes over it was really . . . I gave up the idea because I hated the idea of the columns on the side . . . and I had to admit also that the columns on the side were encumbering. However, the umbrella scheme with the column inside and the things going off the umbrella was really a truer expression of that construction than the other . . . of being supported on beams at this point. I thought this was still necessary . . . up until the very end . . . until recently I found they were not necessary. A sense of structure . . . that's something I still have to learn a lot about—I have it but I don't. I have other things too that interfere with each other. I have the usual artful fainting spells, you know.

I derived the lighting of the big room—actually, it's the same problem—from the small . . . but I couldn't really use the same construction that I did everywhere else . . . it became too important . . . in the hierarchy of spaces it became too important . . . this plan is strangely reminiscent of something which is derivative. You know, it's funny. This plan looks very much as the older Saarinen did it[5].

It looks somewhat like it and it came with very little consideration of this . . . it came by backing a façade to it, various ways which were brought to it and then the rightness of it . . . as you felt the rightness of it is what established it.

It's very Gothic, isn't it? Does that bother you? I like it myself.

5. Kahn may be referring to Eliel Saarinen's Tabernacle Church of Christ (1940), Columbus, Ohio

7

The Nature of Nature (1961)

According to Kahn, the architect's responsibility is to make the nature of things evident by analyzing what they truly are and expressing them as such. Even a parking garage should look like what it is, not like something wrapped in "a nice little candy bar" of design in an effort to upgrade its image. Every aspect of the city needs redefinition, greater architectural clarity, so that its residents may understand their "way of living." Otherwise, civic life deteriorates into the alienation represented by "just I"—a reference to the philosopher Martin Buber's immensely influential book *I and Thou*—as opposed to what Kahn calls the "in-common-ness" of humankind represented by "thou."

These comments were made at an American Institute of Architects–sponsored "Education for Urban Design" seminar held at Cranbrook Academy of Art, Bloomfield Hills, Michigan. They were published in 1961 in the *Journal of Architectural Education*.

Built into us is a reverence for the elements, for water, for light, for air—a deep reverence for the animal world and the green world. But, like everything which is deeply rooted in feeling and a part of our psychic existence, it does not come forward easily. There are times when we feel strongly, but the simple matter of doing daily chores and solving daily problems keeps us away from the feelings about such simple, wonderful, motivating things.

From the *Journal of Architectural Education* 16 (Autumn 1961): 95–97. Reprinted with permission.

Design is a circumstantial act. It is a battle with the nature of man, with the nature of nature, with the laws of nature, with the rules of man, and with principles. One must see all this to put it into being. Design is a material thing. It makes dimensions. It makes sizes. Form is a realization of the difference between one thing and another, a realization of what characterizes it. Form is not design, not a shape, not a dimension. It is not a material thing.

In other words, form is really *what* and design is *how*.

Find the form and from it many designs can come—many notions and many personal acts. Design is a personal act, it is how you see it. But the principles, the unique characteristics, are something which do not belong to you at all. They belong to the activity of man of which you happen to be a part and which you must discover. In planning, the central business district or housing areas are nothing but question marks. What are they, really? Where is the beginning? What is the nature of the place for living, or of the place where business is conducted?

We must look back into the nature of man and the laws of nature. We will find very good answers there. We will find selfishness, hate, love, sincerity—all these things. We will find what is called "good and bad" and we must account for it. Don't say you don't want any "bad." You will have it, whether you want it or not. It is in the nature of man.

There are wonderful things in the nature of man which can be brought out, if you think of design in a fundamental way. Empathy, for instance, is a realization of in-common-ness—that which is true of all men. In-common-ness is not just common place. It is a kind of transcendency, commonness in transcendence. It is where you and I become "thou," instead of just I.

This is not accomplished by a committee or by many people. It is the work of a single person right from the start and supported with unquestioning enthusiasm because it is so true to existence itself.

In city planning, connection is very important to me. Not passage, not going from place to place, but simply places, areas which are treated as events in the plan and which give a feeling of connecting one thing to another, a feeling of belonging to everything in the city. A square can do this. Well-placed squares provide a sense of connection between one part of town and another.

This does not mean that a passage does not provide connection. But it is often confused by planners. Going from place to place you need established reference points from which you can sense the city in a certain way, in a certain aspect, a certain point of view. It makes you more loyal to the city. You can be a participant in the city only if there are logical and very strong statements in regard to movement and institutions of which you are conscious.

The architect should give spaces to an institution which evoke new meaning for it. Our institutions need spaces which will evoke a greater sense of dignity, a greater sense of loyalty to the institution and its relationships. For institutions are establishments of responsible civic living. The architect should think of new institutions as reflecting the things which are deeply ingrained in the nature of man and which, when expressed more fully, can make a city a city. And one can put new life into existing institutions by giving them other spaces, by creating new connections and by redefining everything: buildings, streets, lighting, traffic lights, gateways, entrances—everything the city needs to make the passerby understand the way of living in a city.

To put garages under buildings and to sort of hide them, or to wrap a nice little candy bar around them, or a nice grille, may appear as though something has been done. But, actually nothing has been done. It only confuses everybody as to the way of living in a city.

To prevent things from being done in an ugly manner, or in a manner which tends to deteriorate the original motives, our principles must be so true and real that they cannot be easily destroyed.

This applies to planning. It is finding the devices which obey the laws of nature and bringing them into consciousness. The architect must think of his responsibility—his responsibility to create something which is always true to the nature in man and to the Laws of nature, and which is conscious of water, of air, of light, of the animal world and the green world.

QUESTION: To what degree can we give such values as loyalty to a city which elicit from the people part of their innate fiber?

KAHN: It depends on the level of the important planner. If he is a doodler, a designer, a red, green, blue pencil man, I am afraid, nothing will happen. If he realizes the really wonderful natures of people and thinks of all men and what their motivations are, it can be done. I don't think the city will disappear someday. It won't, because it is a place which expresses the various aspects of man, the many points of view of man, how man is really varied. It starts with things that are indestructible, not patterns. Out present way of living puts us in close touch with distant points, it makes a fundamental beginning somehow different from what it was before. We must ask ourselves, "What is the first beginning, what is the first loyalty, around which you can expect the others to come? Today it is Levittown. It is the planned community, and it is nonsense, because back of it is nothing but profit.

QUESTION: One of the great problems in our cities today is the values people have and our children will have, and we are often told these are materialistic ones. I wonder if we can identify what, in terms of our environment, has contributed to this and what we might do to change these for our children?

KAHN: Your question should be the subject of a new conference. It is the only question that makes, to me, any sense. All the others are devices answerable to this question.

8 Law and Rule in Architecture (1961, 1962)

By the 1960s Kahn was much in demand as a speaker, both in academia and among art and professional organizations. His practice was growing rapidly as well. In 1962 alone, two especially demanding commissions—the Indian Institute of Management in Ahmedabad and Sher-e Bangla Nagar, the Bangladeshi capital complex in Dhaka—came into his office, which was already busy with several other major projects. In addition, he had been teaching full-time at the University of Pennsylvania School of Architecture since 1955.

Despite his many commitments, Kahn was always reluctant to turn down speaking invitations. Casual observers might have thought that Kahn was overextending himself, thus requiring shortcuts, like recycling speeches. But more discerning individuals could note that despite sharing a title, no two lectures were quite the same. What repetition actually revealed was Kahn's unrelenting intellectual curiosity, as the opening sentences of the following talks with the same title illustrate.

His confession that he "know[s] nothing about the subject" may be an example of false modesty, but it nevertheless indicates his "feeling of wonder" at the "harmony of systems in physical nature," which led him to contemplate not only its underlying order but also "the difference between one thing and another" within that order. For difference was a clue to essence—in social institutions as well as in nature—which meant to him those innate, defining characteristics that made one thing distinct from another. Each thing had its "begin-

Both texts from "LIK Lectures 1969 [*sic*]" folder, Box LIK 53, Kahn Collection.

123

ning," which, despite its evolution, still revealed itself in traces of how it came into being originally, what it is now, and what it might become. Or, as he often said, everything that is carries traces of how it was made. For Kahn there was always continuity, no matter how much things changed, a notion he distilled in his oft-quoted phrase, "What will be has always been."

Kahn's distinction between law and rule recalls his earlier distinction between form and design. Laws and forms are immutable, immaterial, and eternal; rules and designs are mutable, material, and temporary. If architectural designs are temporal interpretations of eternal forms, and architectural rules ad hoc codifications of immutable laws, then a successful building is simultaneously ancient and avant-garde, incorporating what "has always been" into "what will be."

The first version of this speech is from an open lecture at Princeton University in 1961; the second was delivered to the Royal Institute of British Architects, London, in 1962.

LAW AND RULE IN ARCHITECTURE I

I want to talk to you today about something that I've been giving some thought to only very recently. And therefore I can readily say that I know nothing about the subject. I just feel, however, the importance of it, and the few experiences I've had recently bear out how little a man really has to know if only his sense of wonder is always being talked to. I believe wonder is the motivator of knowledge. And knowledge is nothing until it comes to a kind of sense of order, a sense of the harmony of systems. And this harmony of systems can, to the scientist, give a sense of law. And it puts the artist in an enthusiastic state of wanting to express. Knowledge doesn't do that. A sense of order does. But in a way the artist and also the scientist who, after his feeling of the sense of order, somehow winks at wonder and says, "How am I doing, Wonder?" somehow feels that wonder is what one reveres, a well-source of all our desire to make things and to express things.

Recently I was asked to do a monastery in California.[1] I visited the monastery and I stayed there for a few days. I was asked by the monks to tell them what I thought about monasteries. Of course, it was my first real contact with monasteries. But I felt I had to know very little about the ritual, about the ways of a monk because essentially I was an architect. I could never really be a monk unless I were one. I had thought to be more of an architect at that point, not a monk, too. And when I heard that they had found water in this very high desert, I felt that they have that upon which a monastery can really exist. Without water and the laws that govern water, one couldn't begin to build, couldn't make a plan. I realized then that water is not necessarily in pipes. And I also realized that every planner should begin to think of his plan by saying to himself that water is not in pipes, or that regulations really are to be changed, that only laws cannot be changed, and that laws do not work in isolation but they work always in a great harmony. *We* isolate the laws; *we* make steam engines which nature can't make. We make them by making good rules so that this steam engine can be made.

Man makes rules. Nature is of law. Without a knowledge of the law, without a feeling for the law, nothing can be made. Nature is the maker of all things. The psyche desires things and challenges nature to make that which expresses the inexpressible, that which cannot be defined, that which has no measure, that which has no substance . . . love, hate, nobility. Still the psyche wants to express just that and cannot without an instrument. Law is the maker of instruments. Look at the violin. Beautiful, out of the law. How the upper and lower diaphragm of the violin lends itself to the stresses of the beam. And the column action of the dividing vertical undulating member dividing the two membranes are a series of columns. Even the little openings in the violin diaphragm are cut so that little of the continuity of the beam is lost. Without a knowledge of this law, a good rule cannot be made.

But rule is really spirits or you might say the psyche and law. And

<hr>

1. St. Andrew's Priory (1961–67), Valyermo, California, unbuilt.

since the psyche is indefinable, since it cannot be measured, cannot be felt, it is something which is changeable. I think anyone should approach rule as changeable, as something that can be changed, and approach law as something that cannot be changed.

When the Father asked me, "What would be your plan for the monastery?" I said, "The first thing I would do (and please excuse my infringing on your sense of what is important to you) but I would build a chapel where the water came from. And if you agree to do this, we can settle the fountain. And then I think we should build the architecture of water . . . the architecture of water being the cisterns and the reservoirs . . . not just casually but very consciously in the shapes and dimensions which assert themselves very clearly. And then build whatever modest or strong aqueducts that may lead from these water sources to logical places using the laws of gravity, and making good rules so that you don't spend a cent more than necessary. Good rules lead to wonderful economy. The law is free. This architecture of water and the thorough logic and economy of this architecture and because you know how to do it and you know the law, you get very proud and do things that can be seen very well. Those who know how to make a joint usually don't like to hide it. It's those who don't know how to make a joint who usually like to disguise it in one way or another. And from this order of water, you may place your chapel and the church and the cells and the workshops and the little community."

We know a lot about walls today that we didn't know before. We know many more laws or we know many more combinations of laws or harmony of laws. A wall long ago was thick, and it was expected to be one thing on the outside, something else inside. And it was wet here, supposed to be dry there, cold here, warm there, warm here, cool there. It had to be strong enough also to hold things. Today, you can make this wall one thing, make that another. And take this wall away and build yourself two walls, but so far away that you could

2. Probably a reference to the venturi tube (or meter) used to channel (or measure) the flow of air or liquids. Kahn reconfigured the venturi tube for channeling air (or liquids) between earth mounds to ventilate a village.

Law and Rule in Architecture

walk through. In the summer the two walls create a venturi.[2] In the plan, develop a very free view as to how these walls may relate to each other. In the winter, you can close this with a door and you have a space which can insulate you from the cold and the warmth. It's a kind of knowing of law, knowing the law of air, of temperature, and realizing this. Law is the nature of all things, and opens the mind to these realizations in form or in shape.

Then, knowing that they were an industrious group, I said, "Why don't you build your walls now out of adobe and store the adobe, and I shall build walls for you with great knuckles which can hold this adobe and these will span across for roofs and for floors—that which is very hard to make at all times. A floor is the hardest thing to make because it just must be straight, and all the laws try to make it this way, and you make a good rule and you make it deep enough so that it can stay this way. Whereas a ceiling which you don't have to walk on need not be straight, and if you curve it, you are acting in a good rule to counteract the law which wants to bend it in this direction. Nature wants to go this way, and you do this with a good rule and nature says "okay." If you want to know how relentless and completely nonconscious nature is, you get in front of a truck. . . . you're soft, it's hard, and you're a dead duck. You disobeyed the law. A man who drives a car resents the red light, but if he remembers his child crossing the street, he thinks it's a pretty good rule. The red light is easily obeyed by the man crossing the street, but the law in the man, the nature in the man is really following law very closely though it is a law and spirit both. He very readily obeys the red light.

Every building an architect does is for an institution. It's for the institution of learning, the institution of home, the institution of government. There are institutions growing every day or coming into being or want to come into being. It's hard to recognize the coming of an institution because it so gradually comes from other institutions. But many of them are completely distinct but never recognizable as such from the way architects express this urge. It has to be itself.

Consider factory buildings. An architect always considers a factory building as a great opportunity to do a very simple structure. And like a museum, it must be on a podium. And the vision of the stacks rising up like great towers—it somehow is a kind of a dream. It ends up by this kind of thing where you build a structure very simple—I won't go into the details—and the client who wants to have a cafeteria, which is a very humane and good thing to do in a carborundum factory. It is simply done this way and naturally there must be a painting . . . a Chagall . . . on one side and there are chairs by Herman Miller and partitions done possibly with new things. But this probably should be this. Differences tend to create their own species. There's nothing compatible or contributing to carborundum manufacture in this cafeteria and vice-versa. Therefore the cafeteria should be a little Pompeiian house outside the carborundum factory.

Now this is looking in terms of an institution, the institution of working, the institution of, let's say, a factory. In such a place where a variety of activities, all needed by man, occur. It isn't just a building cleverly divided for the various things it does. That which is different and that which is compatible as opposites must be found. And that is recognition of the law because the law will make this want to expand and throw this out. It won't grow naturally if you do not let it be what it is and let eating be what it is. The finding of these differences is knowing the meaning of form.

Form has no shape or dimension. Form is the recognition or the realization of the characteristics of one thing and another. Form also says it has no shape or dimension. It is merely a realization of its characteristics. When I say eight feet, I say design. I have designed in variation to this form. There's where design comes in. Design is dimensioning, design is finding the means for putting into being. You must remember that when I drew this circle, it did not exist. It was simply a statement or rather a realization and the difference between it and that. That is form.

And so this is form. Finding the differences, finding that one thing is not really the other, that creativeness in this realm of spaces compared to other realms which distinguish other institutions from each other, is the finding really of the distinguishing differences in the nature of the spaces and the inseparable parts which each form seems to indicate. A familiar example that I have used is the example of the spoon which in form is a kind of container and an arm. When you take the container away, you have a dagger. When you take the arm away, you have a cup. Together they are a spoon. If you make it out of silver or wood or paper, it's design. You're following the characteristics of the two inseparable parts, the parts which designate its form. Design is how you make it, how you put it into being.

I'm doing a dormitory for Bryn Mawr College.[3] The dining room and living room and what they call the showcase, which is a nice living room, music room and parlors, were in scale so different from the rooms, that I thought there was a difference between the construction of those rooms and the other, and thought of them as real differences in which I could really use a different construction entirely. If I were to make one of brick, I'd made the other of stone, let's say hypothetically. (I wasn't thinking of those two materials particularly.) But I found I was very wrong. Because I realized that if I had said to myself that it must also contain a penitentiary, then I would say "Yes, that is the difference." But the house is nothing without the dining room, without the living room. And I thought of it in terms of a chateau or a large house in which that which gives it a sense of hospitality, a sense that one belongs to this house, becomes inseparable . . . these parlors and the dining room. And therefore its construction must somehow be of the same fabric as you find so true of a chateau where large rooms and small rooms also exist.

But finding that there are really opposites and not differences was turning my design direction . . . with greater difficulty to accomplish, yes, but with a greater feeling that I was doing something and not just being smart. It is much easier to change the construction. I could do one thing one way, have a connecting wing, and have something else on the other side. I came to realize the differences, realize the opposites. These are opposite hands. They do different things, but they are very necessary to each other. Nothing can be created if you don't have opposites, a sense of playing against one of a similar kind of sub-

3. Eleanor Donnelley Erdman Hall (1960–65), Bryn Mawr College, Pennsylvania.

stance, but they're not the same because they don't occupy the same space. And of course they're largely still made out of the same fabric. It's difficult to do this, but look how wonderfully you can sense that it is an institution that you must serve. Because I think the first thing that an architect must do, and I really mean this, is to sense that every building you build is a world of its own, and that this world of its own serves an institution, something which has been instituted by man as being important to the way of life of man. It has nothing to do with life, understand. Life is one thing. It's a way of life and it has nothing to do with living except, of course, indirectly. But that's a personal matter. The way of life is an important feeling that one gets in sensing the meaning of institution. That's why the rules which bind the ways of the institution must constantly be in doubt. And one may even think of tradition as being a kind of very highly sensitized self-protection. So even that may be somewhat in question, but not as seriously because there is in that wonderful wealth of human wonder that which cannot be easily changed in the way of rule. But our work which is made up of repetitive mistakes, repetitive misinterpretations, can certainly stand a great review.

Think for a moment how we receive a program. The client asks for area. The architect must give space. The client asks for corridors. The architect must give galleries. The client asks for a lobby. The architect must give a place of entrance. He can't accept the stamp because right away it becomes an easy, lazy retreat to no-thinking. Now the demand of space (and all these are really spaces) is very great. As the architect goes from this to this, he's demanding a great deal. He remembers that space means a containment in which it is evident how it itself is made. No space is a space which does not show how it is made, indivisible in its own confines. You don't make a big span and then divide it off into little pieces. This span is its own thing. If you need something else, you make it.

Also, every space must have natural light, because it is impossible to read the configurations of a space or shape by having only one or two ways of lighting it. Natural light enters the space released by the choice of construction. I mean to say that every column is contrary to the wall—the wall does not want an opening, it resents an opening. When you make an opening, it cries. When you make it really well, it feels all right. But it must have a kind of sense of building the wall with the window being part of the building of the wall and not just a hole in the wall. With the advent of columns, you have a natural opening between the columns. And that is the beginning of light in architecture, and I believe it is also the beginning of architecture. And a vault and a dome are all light-giving elements of construction. The search for light, the light which makes it possible to read, the space which is framed by the construction, and the nuances of the time of the day and the season of the year, enter the space. It's constantly a world borrowing its light from another world.

But it is full of wonder, that which must be answerable in all buildings in the end. You may start with wonder, and you must go through the process of measurement which means you must abide by the law and find good rules to use the law, but in the end it must be full of wonder. And so it is with the space made with construction which is its servant in the making of this space—construction being that which gives character and light to the space. Its choice is a choice in the character of the space.

The architecture here is what does not appear on the program. Certainly the architecture of movement through the building, whatever it may look like, this architecture I would call the architecture of connection . . . that which connects the usable space. The institution is here in function, but it is institution truly as an inspiring space by reason of the entrance, the galleries of movement, and the harbors leading to the various spaces which the institution needs. This is the measure of the architect . . . the organization of the connecting spaces . . . that which gives the man walking through the building outside his specific niche where he works a feeling of the entire sense of the institution—not at his desk, not in his little room, but in the sense of the connection between all rooms and all functions of this institution.

And as you look up in your handbook and you find how many square feet per person is a lobby you say, "What is the heart of this institution?" Even if there are two people here it makes no difference.

Though it may be a hundred feet across, it may be the most appropriate, the most inspiring part of the life of this institution . . . those spaces which are public which do not belong to what the architects know as the twenty percent which goes to lobbies and corridors and toilets and walls! And what percent for architecture, please? And that must be somewhat more.

I'm doing a building for Dr. Jonas Salk in San Diego.[4] Though it was presented to me as a biological research center, of which there are many examples, I sensed from the start from a little remark that Dr. Salk made that it was not the same. He said, "I am more interested really in the nature of man. It's what really activates my sense of wonder more than does all this business of being able to make contraptions which can make microbes talk and what not. I want to invite Picasso, I want to invite other people, even you. I know you know nothing about biology, but I feel as though the fact that you have gone through life so far and have been so intensely interested in what you're doing is equal to the intensity of what the biologist feels about his work and the thorough importance of what he feels about his work. As a matter of fact, they all remark and say, 'You're crazy to think that anything is unmeasurable. Everything is measureable.' I think they're dead wrong." In that sense Salk rather believes that they're dead wrong, that sense of knowing in the wake of things which do submit to measurement, there are things which are unmeasureable. This sense may lead to more wonderful discoveries, more wonderful attitudes and realizations in even scientific subjects where there must be certainly no rule for expression because certainly a scientist expresses nothing. He simply discovers the ways of law. Realizing this, I separated differences from opposites. I would say the artist is really quite opposite but not different from the scientist. He couldn't be different, because he's man and the other is man.

When I talked to the scientists who were to occupy the laboratories of the institute and become members of the institute, they all

4. Salk Institute for Biological Studies (1959–65), La Jolla, California. See selection 4, note 4 (page 70).

Law and Rule in Architecture

seemed to be bothered by little noises. In their study which was isolated from the laboratories, they heard water baths which make the slightest noise. They heard water baths, refrigerators going, they heard the air-conditioning system. I didn't hear it, but they heard it. And I said, "Why are you so close to your laboratory where all these noises are if you hear them?" Oh, they couldn't possibly leave this place. "This is absolutely important that we must be close to our laboratory, naturally." Lunchtime came and out came a sandwich from the back pocket and after a few microbes were swept away, they ate their lunch! This is a very important project. Naturally, I realize that the trouble is that somebody probably in Oshkosh, Wisconsin, some little meek-looking fellow is probably inventing something that they're not quite finished with. And so there's a great impatience amongst the scientists, I find. And I realize also in speaking to some of them that they have a varying sense of what is clean and what is dirty. Some told you that they simply had to hose down their laboratories every so often in order to keep the microbe count down. Others said, "Hell, you can't do anything about it anyway. Some places get pretty cluttered up anyway." And so it went. I listened to all this, recorded it very carefully.

I realized that when I met some of them they were serious about this question of the air in laboratories. You cannot make it perfect. But one can assume that if you wanted to follow the laws and make good rules, you would make it the architecture of clean air. That meant that the air had to be thrown away, it had to be really filtered, and that the entire architecture be made so that all protruding instruments and equipment had to be either moved or recessed so that one could really take the entire room and clean it of all that which can spoil an experiment. And the studies were really not this clean architecture at all but the architecture of the oak table and the rug. And that's quite a different place. I decided that they should be placed not in the same envelope as that of the laboratories. I made that decision not from the way I was instructed, but from realizing that the institution was of a certain nature and that probably its most creative relationship could be that which is not now prevalent. I placed these studies over an arcade in a garden. And from this arcade, I entered the laboratories. If I had not that site which was generous, overlooking the Pacific Ocean and the canyons and toy pines . . . an incomparable, beautiful site . . . I still would have found a way in which the studies were not necessarily in the same space as the laboratories which demanded an entirely different architecture than the architecture of the study.

And even the dining room I did not feel had to be a large room where one said "Hi" even if he didn't like to, but rather a small room where one could be with a few. And they could actually act as seminar rooms, too, where they could discuss things because lunchtime is really a good time for that sort of thing. And most men avidly speak about their work. I haven't yet gone to a lunch where I haven't said something about a column or something which has to do with architecture. I check myself on it and I wonder sometimes if I'm completely sane. But nevertheless it's true. And the library, too, was rather different in this other house which I called the meeting place. There was also a little gymnasium, a place where the fellows could be, and a large entrance hall which I called nothing. It was just a place of entrance sixty feet by sixty feet. Because I know that if they have a banquet, they can hold it there. Why always build a banquet hall in which no banquet exists except just a lot of people whom you don't want to meet sometimes.

So this may be wrong. It may not be what really presents this institution properly. But all I do know and I feel well about is that I did not take the tenets of what is considered a good biological laboratory from the examples that exist. Because they are not cognizant of it's being really an institution. It's another building concocted in some way or other to suit the conditions all right, and it will work. But will it help in the sense of dedication to your work and devotion, which are the same.

I think architecture has this power and it's marvelous to think of the power of architecture when you, for the moment, reflect on the Pantheon which I consider a wonderful great building. It's great because when you think of the time before it was built, it was a kind of conviction, a belief on the part of a man who said that this, because of its shape, presents a statement in form of what may be a universal religious place. And the Oculus is also an expression of a world within a world. And just think that that was presented to a man who had the wherewithal to build it (the architects had never had it) and he agreed. It may have been twice as big on the sketch or on the presentation and boiled down to a more reasonable and buildable thing. But the belief in it and how that belief was so true to what rang true to the other man, was like the approval of the whole world, practically. The coming about of that which has no precedents—to be able to state this and to have others believe in it is wonderful. I believe that building today needs this kind of belief on the part of the architect. I think the belief can come from the recognition of the coming about of new institutions, and I believe also that once a thing has a beginning, if man receives this, then it forever is. It cannot ever have the strength of acceptance unless it has all the ingredients already of its perpetuation.

The first moment that painting was recognized as the undeniable need of man meant that painting will always exist. So it is with sculpture, and so it is with architecture, and so it is with writing and the play. I was appalled the other day when I was asked to speak before the ANTA group in New York.[5] The playwright who spoke said that his main interest in writing plays (when he was questioned about his main interest) was to fill the seats of an auditorium. I was glad that I spoke after him because I really expressed how I felt. Probably never was I more earnest about what I felt. I felt that if I were an architect building a theater, I would consider his influence the most detrimental. The reason for that is that I could never be an actor, nor could I be a director or a playwright, and I must never assume that I could be anything but an architect. But only in the presence of those who cannot do anything but write plays, even though they must starve, although not necessarily starve, can the real sense of the theater's undeniable perpetuating existence be conveyed to the architect. Only those who cannot do anything but direct, only those who must act and those who must write plays regardless, and not write so that you

5. American National Theater and Academy.

fill the seats—only through them can great theater be born. It will not be born through technical additions or ingenuity. It will be born out of the institution of play, of theater, recaptured in the mind of that one who must get it raw, must get it like a beginning. It must be a primitive beginning that he must feel again, because in that primitive beginning when theater began is the real strength of theater. If it got it off the ground, just think of how much strength was there to begin with. And if you sense this, if you sense how it must have felt to have realized suddenly that the play was something that you must see tomorrow again because it was shown for the first time before man, that feeling can make great theater, I believe.

And I believe that a playwright doesn't write just for any kind of house. He writes for a particular house just like Ibsen wrote for a room which was closed. Actors were inside, and he just opened this wall and said, "Look in." That's an Ibsen theater. And Shakespeare theater was different again. And then the theater-in-the-round. And to take an interesting play and put [it] on [in] the theater-in-the-round is tampering. I believe we should build this kind of a theater, that kind of a theater, and other kinds of theater so that man when he writes a play doesn't have to think of what terrible things a director will do with his play. These cannot be fooled with. You're talking about a man who cannot do anything but write a play and he writes so much better when he knows his conditions and when he knows his limits. And for the moment to think of limits is to think of really knowing your realm.

In the realm of your work, all the world really exists. All the emphasis is on your work. And it has a wall around it which is its limits. And to touch the limits is to know your field profoundly. If you go across the wall, you may be in business, where also architecture is or even painting is—everything, the entire world, but the emphasis is on something else.

The realizations in the limits of your field can be illustrated by saying that if this is architecture[6] (of course it isn't and I said that the

6. Kahn was probably referring to a blackboard drawing of several arrows aimed at a circle, illustrating different ways of perceiving a single phenomenon. See selection 10.

Law and Rule in Architecture

world looks on architecture from this point of view), we must think of Le Corbusier as being really around here and looking at it, for this is the same thing. It's still architecture. And because he sees it from here, he sees it from a different point of view. A different point of view isn't seeing two things but it's seeing one thing. He sees it from here and what comes out of it are images which are different from the images here. But we see these images, and from them see the point of view. From the unfamiliar we sense much more the walls of the limits of our field. We know that architecture is not sculpture, is not painting. One painter can paint the skies black in the daytime and can paint doorways smaller than people and dogs that can't run and birds that can't fly. Another is even more radical—with people flying in the air and cows upside down because he doesn't have to answer to gravity . . . like Chagall. A sculptor has to answer to gravity. He can make square wheels on a cannon to express the futility of war, but the architect must use round wheels. His rules are different. He is equally as cognizant of the law, but his rules are different. The walls of his limits are different.

LAW AND RULE IN ARCHITECTURE II

I chose a subject about which I can rightly say I know little. I am just beginning to understand the meaning of law and rule but I feel there is a great deal in it. The buildings I have done and the buildings which I sense I can do depend on being cognizant of the difference between one and the other. By law, I mean physical law; I do not mean legal law. I mean that law is unchangeable. The laws of nature are in a kind of harmony with each other and are not isolated from one another, whereas rule is made by man knowing law, and it is changeable. I feel very secure and full of delight in being able to think in terms of changing rule against law, whereas law I know I must respect.

I visited the site of a monastery[7] which I was asked to design very

7. St. Andrew's Priory (1961–67), Valyermo, California, unbuilt.

recently and I did not hesitate to tell the prior almost directly how to design buildings, because I was conscious of law and rule. I asked him whether he had found water on the site. This was a high desert near Los Angeles, California, a cold place in the winter and a very, very hot place in the summer. He said, yes, he had found water. I said, "Are you going to build a temple where you found water?" He said, "Yes, I think I will build a temple where I found water." I said, "You don't have to build a temple, just build a fountain. Something must be done to show your appreciation that water can be found where water is scarce." I told him that the plans usually assumed that water is in pipes, and of course, that is why plans look so ordinary, in my opinion, too. And I developed before him an aqueduct architecture in which the source of water fills the cisterns and these cisterns gave a system of water distribution, which I called the aqueduct system, using the natural places for the accumulation of this water and distributing it by gravity in the most economic way. I said, "When you have established this architecture, only then should you think in terms of placing your buildings, your chapel and your church and the place of meditation and rest," and also the village which they wanted to have.

There is, in other words, an architecture of water established; and then there was an architecture of the various functioning spaces which had to answer to the position most logical for water.

There is something poetic in following this law, and there was something very secure about establishing these rules which came from the law. I also showed him the way in which the thick walls of old construction should now be separated into an exterior wall in its own right and an interior wall in its own right. The separation became a space of its own; it became a kind of venturi to get the warm air away from the buildings in the summertime and it became also insulation in the wintertime by shutting doors at the ends of the venturi.[8]

I talked about Spanish architecture, which he at first was quite concerned about because he wanted some work in the Spanish way, but he soon realized that he did not want Spanish architecture at all

8. See selection 8, note 2 (page 126).

but something which is very true to nature, and something around which he himself could design and not always have the architect by his side to tell him whether it was aesthetically good or bad, one way or the other.

I said many other things, but I now have many more things to say to you, so I will continue some other time with that.

I wish to distinguish between design and form and I cannot help but start with a feeling of wonder and, as they say, wonder is the beginning of knowledge, and knowledge seems to be unsatisfied without a sense of order. Knowledge is almost worthless without a sense of order. The sense of order or the sense of harmony of systems in physical nature comes to realization in a form, and form has no shape or dimension. It is a realization of the difference between one thing and another, the inseparable parts of something. For the moment, in the glare of the lights, I can think of no exact example of that except what I have already given, and I mildly hate myself for doing it but there is a form of difference between spoon and a spoon, in that spoon is form made of inseparable parts of a container and an arm. If you take the container away you have a handle, and if you take the arm away you have a cup. Together they are spoon, and the way you design it is whether you make it out of steel, wood, paper, gold, silver or any other material. Therefore, what to do is form, it lies in form; how to do it is design. Often, we turn to design somewhat too quickly, because we have no information as to the form.

In the buildings I did for the University of Pennsylvania,[9] form enters in a realization that the air you breathe in a laboratory of this nature should never come in contact with the air you throw away. I will demonstrate how I designed this building, considering this as part of the form of the biological laboratory. Also, I considered the usual plan of a laboratory with a service set of rooms, a corridor, laboratories; the service part of the construction is built of columns equally spanned and containing the stairways, the animals rooms, the air-ducts, elevators—all noise-making—and also instrument dis-

9. Alfred Newton Richards Medical Research and Biology buildings (1957–65), Philadelphia.

charging areas. The corridor is an anonymous space which leads to personal areas of laboratories. The arrangement causes much political strife between professors young and old because soon, the older professor loses ground and loses space, into a kind of undistinguished position in the building.

What I did in the laboratory in considering a rule out of law was to place the service area in the middle of three spaces which became studios, not any space in a building but a special place in a building where a man feels secure in his own studio. The space would be 45 feet by 45 feet and would contain, if not his whole department, part of it. The simple space took care of all the requirements of elevators, noise-making equipment and animals, separating it definitely from the other. This could very well be the kind of space for a school where the laboratory required special considerations. Not only was the studio arranged in the way I have placed it on the sheet, but each studio had its own stairway and its own exhaust. All the exhaust air was taken in at four nostrils, and the fresh air came low into the nostrils and was distributed in the studios, and all the exhaust air was kept away and exhausted high above the entrance of the air. It happened that this laboratory was placed in a generous bit of ground and I was able to express it in this free way, but had I had a limited area, I would have given up the idea that the design must give separation between the air you breathe and the air you throw away. In this case, the air you throw away and the air you breathe are all in the corridor, separated by a thin layer of metal. In the other case, the separation is absolute. It is the kind of thing which says that an armadillo is not a giraffe.

The emergence of spaces characteristic of their use is evidenced as necessary in the high demand for new kinds of spaces today. Buildings that have different functions entirely are too much like each other. Though I only needed two stairways to satisfy the building codes, I have four, and I satisfied the need of this particular building, where escape from chemical experiment is important. In the Salk Laboratories in San Diego,[10] where I developed a keener idea of what

10. Salk Institute for Biological Studies (1959–65), La Jolla, California. See selection 4, note 4 (page 70.

Law and Rule in Architecture

a biological laboratory should be like, it started with Dr. Jonas Salk visiting my office, promising nothing, simply asking me to show him this building which he saw almost completed. He asked me how many square feet it contained. I said, "109,000," and he said, "That is what I need." That was the program, too. But he added something which was very wonderful. He said, "You know, I don't want to make a usual biological laboratory, which is rather a kind of engineering place where a man simply extends some of the findings of our great biologists. I want to invite people with minds, people like Picasso, because I feel the study of biology, living things, is essentially an immeasurable thing, and when the scientist is working closely to his scientific approach, somehow he should realize that that is not necessarily the answer to the problem." This inspired me to think in terms of a new institution. It was important. Institutions remain for ever and were somehow born with man. It made me also think that an architect's first duty is to think in terms of the institution that our minds create.

If you think in terms of a school building, it began possibly with a man under a tree who did not know he was a teacher, talking to a few who did not know they were students, and you realize that the institution of schools came from such beginnings and that the usual program comes from the school board, which talks about the height of fences to keep people out, and lobbies in terms of so many square feet per person, and corridors that are measured in terms of lockers or return air ducts, and rooms which must be all light because you usually have 25 to 30 pupils in them; and the basement can well hold the boiler because you only use it for an hour. Then you begin to realize something must be done about such a program, and this wonderful event under a tree looks pretty sick.

So I believe the architect somehow must hark back to the time of the beginning. The beginning is a wonderful time because nothing could take hold unless that beginning, when it does take hold, is true, thoroughly and deeply, to the nature of man; and that, although it may have a very primitive beginning and a very modest one, is bound to continue if it is something that is close to the desire and subsequently to the needs of man. So the beginning is true to man; school is true to man; government is true to man; home is true to man. All these institutions are true to man, and the architect's search for indications of how the institution can be amplified or how a new institution can come out of an old one is probably one of the most delightful mental experiences that he can have.

Dr. Salk's statements, his feelings—he did not think in terms of architecture at all—were just feelings that he wanted that could be the beginning of a new attitude, a new point of view of what is an attitude. He did not call it an institution, he said "a biological laboratory" should have this or that—more than is usually required.

Immediately, I thought of in what way I could express such an institution. I visited the scientists; they were all, to a man, very busy. They had their studios very close to the laboratories.

In fact, they were chiseled out of the laboratory space, which was already too small. They sat in this miserable corner, insisting that that was the place they had to be, and they heard all the noise of the water and the clocks and the air-conditioning equipment and the refrigerator. All the noises that I did not hear, they heard—because they were nervous.

Also, when I had time for lunch, they took sandwiches out of their coat pockets and brushed aside some of the microbes and ate their ham sandwiches, claiming that they had no time to have lunch and take time out. Actually, I was sure what they were thinking about—whether somebody in London was doing the same thing that they were doing, and it was only a question of time who would be first!

I thought this over and said that if I were to get a program of what seemed to be the dictation in this direction, I would come up with a quiet room in each laboratory, probably. I decided that the study was really not the same thing as a laboratory because in the process of development of things I have done before, I realized that even with the laboratories I built in the University of Pennsylvania, there was not a clear statement of law and rule, because a laboratory must essentially be a kind of stainless steel place, a clean-air architecture, where the air must be thrown away because you are dealing with microbes that are in the air, you are infecting animals with diseases to experiment on them, and there are noxious gases. To try to filter or try to recirculate the air is nonsense. It costs money, but it is nonsense not to spend it. So I divided the architecture of the laboratory, which is really a study on its own, from the study, which is truly the architecture of the unmeasurable. I placed the studies close to the laboratories but away from them in an arcade facing a garden which, though it was San Diego and a desert area, grows beautifully when a little water is added. In this way, I was trying to express the difference between that which is measurable and that which is unmeasurable, although the unmeasurable is always present. And someone will quite rightly say that the scientist is really essentially an unmeasurable animal: and he is. But from this wonder and sense of order and realization, his realization is a different realization from that of the architect because the architect realizes to express, whereas the scientist realizes to find the laws of nature. So we go off on different paths though they are both essentially unmeasurable things.

The meeting-house I separated also from the laboratory space. I placed the laboratory in one area, the meeting-house in another, the housing in still another. The laboratories entered by a garden and each laboratory is an autonomous space, not answerable to any corridors, which savor of strife, incompatibility, and other things. There is a dining room and the Greek Library and the gymnasium and the meeting-hall and a religious place—a place which has no other meaning but is just a good place to go to.

All these activities are tied to a place to which I gave no name, because I felt the dining room should not be made as one baronial hall but rather there should be seminar rooms, where one scientist could meet another in a small room and smaller groups could gather together; also, they serve as seminar rooms at the same time.

The library also had one large stack for books but there were small rooms both for seminar and meeting. Then when there was a larger gathering, the space could serve; at present, it is nothing but a circulation space, 70 feet by 70 feet—a space waiting to be used. In other words, the space induced a project. It was a kind of space where it was good to meet in a way compatible or in character with the individuals that are here. If you ever met these people, you would know that each one lovingly hates the other: I felt that this was not wrong because it should flow with this feeling rather than try to contrast with it. Incidentally, the fact that I separated the studies, as places to sleep rather than work, from the laboratories, was immediately taken as being right by the scientists who originally thought they could not get away from them.

This is an architect making a program, thinking in terms of spaces where it is good to meet, where it is good to work, and serving them a certain way and not developing a building which has a variety of service needs all put in one.

In a carborundum building I am doing,[11] by virtue of carborundum material, I first thought, like every other architect, that the dining room should be placed in a very good position near a lot of light and away from most of the other dusty operations of carborundum which is probably the most unbelievably obnoxious work in the world; I could fit it out with a marble floor and furniture and that was all you needed to make it a dining room. But I soon learnt from the biologists that there was something in differences and opposites. This was a difference and not an opposite. It was not like your two hands, each working together, the one helping the other; because dining does not help carborundum and carborundum does not help dining. So I thought of a carborundum building which had great dust chambers above the ceiling and a building which you may say is a little penthouse where you dine as the kind of thing which must enter our buildings, not buildings necessarily on podiums; but because of the very nature of this building, a rule was made which somehow tells every man that there is a way of life even in a carborundum factory. The separation was good. The separation gives division between the measurable and the unmeasurable and the unmeasurable and the measurable.

If you put them together, there is a taking for granted of the facil-

11. The Carborundum Company Warehouses and Offices (1961) in Chicago; Mountain View, California; and Niagara Falls, New York. Kahn's 1961–62 plans for a fourth facility in Atlanta, Georgia, were not realized.

Law and Rule in Architecture

ities which you have. Someone could make a very clever plan by simply combining them, but I believe that separation, as a primitive beginning of what I believe is a new institution (and Dr. Salk thinks that too), is a better way than one which is always somewhat sophisticated in design. Though I know if I were in a position where the site and the acreage covered by the buildings was very little, if I was forced into a very small site, I believe the separation would still be very apparent. The point of separating these buildings could be achieved by separation of a single building in which the air is thrown away, and here, where they can use the natural air of San Diego, it would be difficult to design, but it can be done, if the separation is apparent. Even the architecture in very large span can cause difficulty because the large span is necessary to the success of the experiment, which must have no inhibiting architectural structures. It must be clear but always be completely resourceful even in a very large space.

Going back to the architect's duty, I feel that the client starts with areas and you must give him spaces; the client starts with a budget and you give him economy. He says "lobby," you say "place of entrance."

Here, as an architect, you can take this literally; you feel like a druggist with a prescription. Architecture deals with spaces; it is the thoughtful and meaningful making of spaces, and those spaces should be of a nature where the structure of those spaces is apparent in the space itself. Never do you build a big structure and put little spaces in it; a big structure is worthy of a big space, and a small structure takes its place in the hierarchy of spaces in its own way, and also, a space may have its own structure and must have its own light. The structure is really the beginning of light. The vault is a light-making structure. The dome, the beam, the column—the choice of the structure, is only a choice in light, of making a space light, not artificially but naturally, because the nuances of the seasons, the time of day, come into play with light. Even a space that must be dark must have enough light in it to see how dark it is. *This* (Areas–Spaces) is space-making; *this* (budget–economy) is book-keeping. To go from one to the other is the act of architecture. The galleries, the place of entrance, all form what may be termed the architecture of connection. This architecture must also have its light; corridors without light remain corridors. Galleries emerge as a kind of nobility of space, an arcade where the hierarchy is expressed in the areas of service, the functioning areas and the areas which lead to the functioning areas.

I think an institution which is highly restricted by arbitrary budgets, usually brought about by getting across from the inadequate examples, tends to whittle down the inspiration that a space itself can give to a person working, living, or studying in it. I think you will find that the memory of space, where the architecture of connection has given nobility in space, is what you really remember about a place, and not so much the rooms in which you studied or worked.

The architecture of connection has its own position in the arrangement of spaces of function and it must be thought out with equal reverence as for any functioning space; it brings about the possibility of double walls, flanking, possibly, the connecting architecture, because they both have to be served equally—that of the gallery and that of the functioning space—so you get a doubling of walls where the services go. Thick walls at one time induced the making of niches but now they can be separated, as I tried to indicate in the monastery building.

The law says this, really: to find good rules which tend to bring about that which the nature of man demands; and the rules should come easily into mind too, because you satisfy that intangible part of man, in his spirit of love, nobility and sincerity—all those indefinable, unmeasurable aspects of man which, in the end, a building must evoke.

In a dormitory building I am doing [for] a college in Pennsylvania, which is a girls' college,[12] I developed a system which, at first, looked like this. The connectors of the three units were little buildings in the architecture of connection, which disturbed me because I could not make them very well, and when I made them, one looked into the other. There was something unlawful about it. It worked very well. It

12. Eleanor Donnelley Erdman Hall (1960–65), Bryn Mawr College, Pennsylvania.

Law and Rule in Architecture

never occurred to me that I could take the square and turn it this way, so that it made its own connection. It took me a year to find that out. Of course, the other feature was the development of three interior spaces all having rooms around them and the center room getting its light from above. . . . You will see the analogy between the Scottish castles and this. The wall is thick, but it is made of thin members, within which are the rooms of the girls; the recreation space, the entrance space are very different. There is a little sitting place and a dining room with a kitchen, and some other smaller dining areas.

I have a book of castles and I try to pretend that I did not look at this book but everybody reminds me of it and I have to admit that I looked very thoroughly at this book. It was so inspiring to see these thick walls and the gift that is given to the interior of the space. Once you have satisfied the law which says that the wall must be thick, the rules and the unmeasurable enter and you see that it must be thick. But I know where I can do one thing or another where I have certain things, and the central area is given to you in a most wonderful way.

This building interests me greatly because it does not throw away tradition, but you learn, from the problems of one tradition or the complete adherence to law and rule, that the same thing must be true today. Certainly, in buildings of a walled-in town, the walls were made by the order of the day; there was no tomfoolery about whether you liked it one way or the other. You knew that large openings invited trouble, and that was something which was part of the law of shooting arrows, and you made a good, tidy rule, which made the discipline possible and the design possible. That discipline made castles look somewhat alike, though circumstantially, there were design problems with regard to the materials available which made them different from each other. Design is a circumstantial act. Design is something to do with how much money you have, where you are building, who your client is, whether a tree is there, whether a rock is there. All those are design problems but form says, "before you design, know more," and the design is guided by this sense of forms, which looks for characteristics.

Dealing with planning problems of a city, I am becoming increasingly conscious of the architecture of water, the architecture of air, the architecture of light, the architecture of movement, the architecture of sound; from which came notions—because they are not yet developed ideas, about viaduct architecture, which tends to give a new sense of form to cities. And I also realized that water for the cleaning of streets, the serving of fountains and air-conditioning systems, does not have to be drinking water, so redistribution of the system of aqueducts and reservoirs might well be thought about, instead of relying on a few high-powered places, which causes one to use the filtered water very wastefully. So there is an order of water, and there is an architecture of water, and maybe, when the water is close in certain areas and you think in terms of the water supply as being in architecture, more fountains will come to the city, because it will be quite obvious that you can use the first water for such purposes.

The architecture of light: I have found in San Diego that glare is a contrast of light and dark. I found this out when I was in Africa, when the people were hardly contrasted against the light, and the people who live there all the time do their work by having the sun bake their backs, and they work from light that comes off a wall. In this way, they work without glare. In San Diego, I devised the idea of placing a wall in front of every window. The wall is free of the opening in front of the window, not too far away, but it is necessary for the wall to be in the light. The light on the wall instead of the darkness modified the glare, and making an opening in the wall made it possible to see through the wall. Therefore, if you see the meeting place, you see something that looks more like the rules of Kenilworth.[13] You see no glass; you see only the walls that are modified with the wind and the glare; so there is an architecture of wind and of light and there is an architecture of water. In the San Diego project, the rainwater, scarce as it is, is gathered in a cistern and then sent up to a higher point where it is distributed by gravity, and these pools are linear and shaded by trees so that

13. Kahn may be referring to Kenilworth Castle (12th century and after) in Warwickshire, England.

evaporation does not too quickly occur. This is a kind of design out of respect for and understanding of the nature of Nature.

There is a little development I wanted to mention in Israel which I am likely to do, in a town of 50,000 people.[14] The usual plan was submitted, of a road with two roads coming off, and the town center became larger and larger to make a town of 50,000. The plan I proposed was a series of mounds which contained water, and they had next to them a venturi, the venturi being produced by the courts of houses and a place for the air to go in, with a large area between; even the mounds were used to develop some mild hillside houses where the site was favorable. It began with the gathering of rainwater, which happens at certain points at certain times of the year, which goes to the reservoirs and the town was formed in this way rather than by the not too deeply thought out development, which would look more like the ordinary way of approaching it. But with the consciousness of the light, given by the closeness of the buildings to each other, and the spacing of the courts, in such shapes as to cause a venturi, there was an architecture of the air, there was an architecture of the water and of the light, from which perhaps the architecture begins.

There is another thing which comes to my mind, which is the importance of recognizing the growing instruments of building, which still do not appear in the specifications and in the plans in the minds of the architects. You never think of a crane as an instrument in your specification. I had an interesting experience when I was doing the Medical Research building, of a crane which kept being there; with its 200-foot boom, the 26-ton elements—the beams—which I used looked like matchsticks. I resented the presence of this crane. I could never take a good photograph because the crane was always in it. Then it suddenly occurred to me that this crane was really quite remarkable, and I realized that a column was not a column and I said, "Why doesn't the crane lift more tons?" I was not satisfied with 26 tons. I said, "A building could be built with columns quite at random, with spans

14. He was overly optimistic. His 1949 plans for the Jewish Agency for Palestine Emergency Housing in Israel were, by 1962, thirteen years old. The project was never built.

across the stations." After a while, you can get very big in your mind. I began to neglect the buildings and make them very significant events, which they were in the conception of building; I even thought that the façade in this case was something completely different from that of the interior spaces, framed by these large mounds. I thought, "Why must you build with prefabricated units? Why can you not build façades with buildings inside?" Merely by thinking, I found a crane is a positive thing, not something you resent because it does not hold the charm of an axe or hammer or saw. If man became more resourceful, he could design with the crane in mind.

I even thought that glass and stainless steel mullions are too well served with these strong members. Why not make the mullions out of glass? It all came from sitting for twenty more minutes at the site.

A little note on sculpture, painting and architecture. I think they are in realms of their own and an architect is not a painter and he is not a sculptor. Perhaps those who have read all I have written will recognize these words. A painter can make doorways smaller than people; a sculptor can make square wheels on a carriage to express the futility of war. The architect has to make doors bigger than people and has to use round wheels. His wheels are quite different from those of the painter. There is infinitely more latitude in being closer to the pictures of wonder that come before the painter, and though he may be very close to realizations in order, he winks at wonder and says, "How am I doing?" The architect is the same but he does not have the same prerogatives. He has a harder time. He has so many things to do, in the way of the timing of the program, the sketches, belief and decision, budgets, committees, contracts and building; but I think we architects know that we would not trade our profession with anyone.

Lecture at International Design Conference, Aspen, Colorado (1962)

•••

Kahn posits a pool of knowledge to which all humanity has access. The pool's contents are finite but the "wonder" of life lies in the realization that they will never be entirely known or understood. Yet everyone has an insatiable desire to learn, which yields "a sense of order" about the universe. Art is the need all humans share to investigate that order. Architectural art involves manipulating "rules" in order to implement the eternal "laws" of "form," which collectively constitute universal "order." Because a building is an interpretation of order, the architect may be obliged to eliminate what the client thinks necessary and/or include what the client thinks unnecessary. Kahn's discussion of the carborundum factory is especially pertinent here.

This lecture was given to an International Design Conference held at Aspen, Colorado. Its text—lightly corrected and amended here—differs slightly from the version printed in *Arts and Architecture* (May 1964), titled "A Statement by Louis I. Kahn."

Life to me is existence with a psyche; and death is existence without the psyche; but both are existence. I think of the psyche as being a kind of prevalence—not a single soul in each of us—but rather a prevalence from which each one of us always borrows a part.

•••
From "Aspen Conference—June 1962" folder, Box LIK 59, Kahn Collection.

This applies to every living thing, be it a flower, be it a microbe, or be it a man or an animal. Every living thing. And I feel that this psyche is made of immeasurable aura, and that physical nature is made of that which lends itself to the measurement. I think that the psyche prevails over the entire universe. It demands an instrument of expression which it cannot hope to have in some other area of the universe. I am sure that this very psyche hammers at the door of the sun and says, "Give me an instrument here upon which I can express love, hate, nobility"—all the qualities which are, in my opinion, completely immeasurable.

The instrument is made by nature—physical nature, a harmony of systems in which the laws do not act in an isolated way, but act in a kind of interplay which we know as order. Man isolates the law and makes every good use of it. But it must not be assumed that the law, when gotten by the tail this way, is very happy except when it is in relation to other laws where its real life actually exists.

When I hear a scientist speak in categorical terms of what he has discovered, I feel that as he grows older, he will change his categorical term into something which is not quite so sure. He discovers that the law is in a degree unchangeable, whereas rule is changeable; you check it off and say, "one down, and so many to go." It isn't quite as simple as that in my mind. Now we are made out of what nature makes of the demand of the psyche for an instrument to play the wonderful song which will never actually be finished. We must take potluck from nature, because nature has no consciousness whatsoever. Nature is not conscious of the sunset; nature is not conscious that the sunset is beautiful. As a matter of fact, if a painter were to faithfully duplicate the sunset, the sunset would laugh at him and say, "I'll make a better one tomorrow." But if man paints a sunset as a reaction and his product says to the young man, "I'll have a good time tonight," and to the older man, "I haven't got long to live," then nature is very jealous, because it cannot do this. Nature is unconscious, but the psyche is conscious, demands life, and gives life. Nature makes the instruments which make life possible. It will not make the instrument unless the desire for life is there.

International Design Conference, Aspen

Wonder in us is—you might say—a record of the way we were made. It is a well, which is completely full of all the things you will ever learn; because nature, in its making of things, records every step of its making. It is, one may call it, a seed. But it's understood much more if you realize that in wonder lies the source of all that we'll ever learn or feel. Knowledge which is derived from wonder is unhappy unless it relates itself to other knowledge. And this relation of knowledge to knowledge is what you might call a sense of order; a sense of the position of this knowledge in relation to other things around. When we get a sense of order—not just knowledge or information— then we are very happy. We wink at wonder and say, "How am I doing, wonder?" Because wonder is activated by this knowledge and better still, by this sense of order. And wonder becomes more reachable, more full of that of which we were made.

From wonder we can also derive the position of that which is intangible; because you cannot measure love; you cannot measure hate; you cannot measure nobility; they're completely unmeasurable things. We may, though, come to points where we know the nature of man sufficiently to know there is a commonness in all of man, because man is man all over. I don't believe that if you can think of a soul belonging to one man, it is different from another soul. I think all souls are alike, because they are first of all, unmeasurable; and secondly, they are gathered from all of earth. But what is different is the instrument. Nature, being an unconscious thing, cannot make the same instrument again, as we do in factories. Nature cannot, because the moment, at another moment in time, is a different thing entirely to nature. Nature is the interplay of these laws; any one time is not the same as any other. It's a kind of readjustment of equilibrium. When you come about, when you are born, you are not the same person as any other—you are a singularity, as an instrument, but not as a soul.

Nature is the instrument maker. Nothing can be made without nature. In fact, you might say that nature is the workshop of God. With a sense of order, and with the greatest moment in feeling—the feeling of religion in general, combined with the highest moment in thought, which is philosophy—you get the area of realization; you realize something. This realization is very true somehow, but still you cannot describe it. This is a great moment for the scientist as well as the artist. The artist feels with expression; the scientist does not feel with expression. The scientist (through his realization) goes excitingly to find again the real definition or position of the law in order. And he works without his feelings at that moment, but through experience, and from realization, which is just full of feeling. At that moment he must be completely objective. And men who speak objectively, speak truly as scientists—not necessarily as creative men but as scientists. Scientists who are interested in the law and finding the relationship of one law to another, find that the nature of man is already in a different kind of working than science. When a man works in biology, he is nervously concerned only with the laws, the physical laws of nature because his concern is so much with that which is undefinable; that which motivated the making of life altogether. And so, he must surrender the excitement of this for the moment in order to discover better means, tools, to evaluate if not measure the commonness of man biologically, psychologically and any other way. So you see, the scientist, I believe, is concerned with measures and with the nature of nature.

The artist is concerned with expression, but he starts with the same sense of realization as the scientist does. And there it might be well to say that the difference between a creative man and an artist is that a creative man is one who brings about the new image. He sees a new point of view. From this new point of view he sees different things. And through this point of view, which others are not in possession of, he sees and makes images which are different. The artist is one who senses from this image. He senses the meaning of a new point of view. I can draw a circle on the blackboard, to show what I mean about that. If I can be so arbitrary, I will say what I have drawn is the realm of architecture. Of course, it isn't. We know this is not the realm of architecture, but it has limits, we know that. We know that an architect is not a sculptor, and he's not a painter. Because a painter can paint people upside down. A painter can make people fly in the area, he can paint doorways smaller than people. A sculptor can convey the futility of war by making a piece of sculpture of a cannon with square wheels. But an architect must use round wheels, and he must make doors bigger than people. He is not the same man; his realm is different. I make this circle of what I call the realm of architecture. If we see architecture from this point of view today, the creative man sees it differently. From the same realm, the same architecture, the same eternal qualities which make architecture architecture. And he makes an image, and this image is seen by men today. This image reflects another point of view. Men immediately see that the realm of architecture has grown to be more rich; the walls, the limits are more understood. The creative man makes this image; the artist works towards the beauty of this point of view.

Now this brings us to what is realization. Realization is really realization in form, not in design. Realization has no shape or dimension. It is simply a coming to a deep, revealing understanding in which the sense of order and the sense of dream, of religion, becomes the transference of I into thou. A man does not live a philosophy—he lives what he lives; but he lives philosophy as though it didn't belong to him, because he can't live the philosophy that he senses. From this sense of order and sense of dream come realization. Realization in form. Now form, in my opinion, has no shape or dimension; form is merely a realization of the difference between one thing and another—that which has its own characteristic. A circle is not a triangle, though tautologically it may be the same thing. It isn't the same thing in form. It has characteristics for rather inseparable parts. If you take one thing away, the form is destroyed. Each part must be accountable to the other. This is realization in form. When the scientist realizes this, he can work for years and years and years on this realization, making many designs, many experiments, many extensions of this realization.

Dr. Jonas Salk calls men who work towards extension in this light "biological engineers." But the biologist he visualizes he would like to have in his institute is one who recognizes the immeasurable as well as the measurable. To think that men can really put down a statement saying, "We now know what hope is when we can measure it." I believe this is not so. I believe the unmeasurable will always remain unmeasurable. I believe also that if you continue to think this way, even the unmeasurable will become much closer to you, because you recognize that you'll never get it by the tail. You'll know it much more that way than you will by assuming that you'll ever know it.

In the same way, I believe that you'll never really measure nature, unless we extend for years and years our wonder source, the well, which tells the whole story of how we were made. Now design is the exercise or the putting into being of that which you realize is form. I will give a familiar example, because I can't think for the moment of another: If you think in terms of a spoon, you think in terms of a container and an arm. If you take the container away you have a dagger. If you take the arm away, you have a cup. Together they are a spoon. But spoon is not a spoon; spoon is form. A spoon is made out of silver, out of wood, or paper—when it becomes a spoon, that's design. The realization, spoon. Form. Spoon is not design. This can be extended to buildings as well as it can to everything we make. Take the example, for instance, of that which can come together and that which can be separated. I had a problem for a carborundum factory.[1] If you know what a carborundum factory is, it's a pretty terrible place to work because the dust is very bad. The whole architecture should be shaped to take care of a human working in such an atmosphere. Therefore, it's a completely hooded kind of architecture in which the dust is gathered before it ever reaches the room. That's what the building should look like, although I don't know of any carborundum factory that looks that way. If I were given the assignment, I would do it that way: If you consider, from the present standpoint of architectural thinking, the placement of a cafeteria in this plant, there are many architects who would assume that you merely have to assign a certain corner of this temple for carborundum making. And this is definitely wrong, because a cafeteria does not contribute to carborundum and carborundum doesn't contribute to the cafeteria. It should be outside of this building; maybe a little Pompeian house,

1. See selection 8, note 11 (page 144).

next to the modern factory would be more appropriate than to try and integrate both. Because form-wise they do not come together; they mean nothing to each other. The realization of this separation, and the realization which does come together, is unexplored in our architecture.

This brings me to law and rule, which is my present concern—not that my architecture changes radically, because at present it isn't changing at all. Law cannot be changed. Law is there. You may not understand it fully, but it's there. Always there. Rule always should be considered as on trial. Rule is just made from realizations of feeling and the law. And when more is known of the law at certain times, then the rule must automatically change. Think of the wonderful discoveries of science today, and think of how much our architecture is at a standstill. I believe our architecture looks like Renaissance buildings, simply in new materials. I do not think it looks like modern buildings to me. It's all because the rules have really not been changed.

When we think of our cities for a moment, we can review again the new knowledge we have, the new sense of order we have, in relation to water, to light, to air, to movement. Just think of law and rule in this sense. If I get in front of a truck—the truck is hard; I'm soft—I'm a dead duck. I disobeyed the law. The rule is the red light and the green light. When I am driving a car, I resent the red light, the rule. I like to drive right through it. But I think of my own child, and I obey the rule.

The law is relentless; it has no feeling; but the rule has. Think of cities that have reservoirs miles away from where the water is used. Why do we have to use drinking water for air-conditioning plants, and drinking water to feed fountains that don't need filtered water? And why must we clean streets with filtered water? Why can't we have an architecture of water that goes through the town easily, recognized in deference to the very precious water? The order of movement today is based on an extension of the horse and buggy. You feel as though the manure has just been swept away. There has been no thought given to the motor car whatsoever. The same streets serve the motor car as served the horse, which was a pedestrian. The hitching post is really the garage, but the garage is a piece of real estate which should be part of the design of the street, it should be the extension of the street. The garage, therefore, is really a roundup street, and must be made part of the design of the street. The streets must be completely redone in the center of town. Why must you rip up a street and put in a new line every time you have to repair or improve services for comfort and control of environment? We dig them up every time as though they were the Appian Way. Why isn't there a building in which a room is dedicated for piping only? The dead center of the city, where those mistakes are most unprofitable, should be completely redone. In the center of town the streets should become buildings. This should be interplayed with a sense of movement which does not tax local streets for non-local traffic. There should be a system of viaducts which encase an area which can reclaim the local streets for their own use, and it should be made so this viaduct has a ground floor of shops and usable area. A model which I did for the Graham Foundation recently, and which I presented to Mr. Entenza, showed the scheme.[2] This is finding new rules out of realizations of law.

In the Salk project again, I am developing walls around buildings to take care of the glare.[3] I do not think that venetian blinds and curtains and all kinds of window devices are architectural. They are department store stuff and don't belong to architecture. The architect must find an architecture out of the glare, out of the wind, from which these shapes and dimensions are derived. And these glare walls are based on a very simple principle, which I got out of observation when I was in Africa, where the glare is very startling. There the peo-

2. In February 1961 Kahn received a $7,500 grant from the Graham Foundation for Advanced Studies in the Fine Arts (Chicago), John D. Entenza, Director, to study traffic movement in central Philadelphia with an eye toward applying "viaduct" architecture to other cities.
3. For the unbuilt Meeting House portion of the Salk Institute for Biological Studies (1959–65) in La Jolla, California, Kahn proposed fenestrated walls that would act as sun and wind screens and stand a few feet outside of the building's actual walls, an idea he developed in his unbuilt design for the United States Consulate and Residence (1959–62), Luanda, Angola.

ple worked with their backs against the sun, and they got the light off walls near where they worked. Their buildings are close together, and their windows look into walls. They modify the glare, by looking at something that is in light. These walls I'm developing for the Salk Center in San Diego are in recognition of this discovery of the law of light, from which I have made a rule for myself in the design of the building.

Recently I was asked to design a town in Israel.[4] Unfortunately I could not go to convey my ideas. But I thought of the desert being reshaped in mounds, which would contain reservoirs. And these mounds would be so placed against the winds that they would help in creating venturi which now are just flowing freely, not being controlled.[5] And that a village be built around a venturi principle of air so that the air would be guided through small avenues and large receivers. The shape of the streets will follow the need which the buildings have there. This would not be applicable in Germany. Some of the buildings which are built in Israel today, follow the rules set down by German architects—good rules for Germany, but not good rules for Israel. This indigenous architecture is, I think, the great excitement of architecture.

In a dormitory I'm doing for Bryn Mawr College,[6] I had a feeling that the dining room, living room, reception rooms and entrance were different, in every respect, from the sleeping quarters. And I kept the sleeping quarters apart from these rooms, believing that I was expressing that one was different from another. But I discovered my mistake. I realized that a person sleeping in a room felt well about his house if he knew the dining room was downstairs. The same way with the entrance to the building. The sense of hospitality, or reception, of getting together must be part of the fabric of the house itself. I changed, much to my delight, the whole conception, and I made these spaces part of the fabric of the other spaces. To me, this is realization in form.

4. The unbuilt Jewish Agency for Palestine Emergency Relief Housing (1949).
5. See selection 8, note 2 (page 126).
6. Eleanor Donnelley Erdman Hall (1960–65).

Now if I had just looked at it as design, as I did before, I would have been led to something which may look well, but which had no power to convey one very wonderful thing about architecture. Because architecture really is a world within a world. When you build a piece of architecture, you build a kind of location for an activity of man which is, let's say, different from another activity of man, even though it may be in the same general realm of activity.

One of the most wonderful buildings in the world which conveys its ideas is the Pantheon. The Pantheon is really a world within a world. The client, Hadrian, and the architect, whom I don't know the name of, saw the demand of this pantheonic requirement of no religion, no set ritual, only inspired ritual. He saw the round building, and a very large building. I imagine that he probably thought the building should be at least 300 feet in diameter; he changed his mind because there were no craftsman who would make such a building, and it was out of the stream of economy. Economy meaning here that there's no man around to do it. I don't mean money—I don't mean budget—I mean economy. And so the Pantheon is now a hundred and some feet in diameter. The dome, the first real dome made, was conceived with a window to the sky. Not because of ethereal reasons, but because it's the least distracting, the one that is most transcending. And there is a demand that form say nothing specific, no direction; that's what form says to you, feeling and philosophy. It says no direction to this . . . no oblong . . . a square not satisfying here . . . too far and away at the corners. The round building is something which is irrefutable as an expression of a world within a world.

Now architecture—if you think of it in terms of school—also probably began with a man under a tree who didn't know he was a teacher, talking to a few who didn't know they were pupils. They listened to this man, and thought it was wonderful that he existed, and that they would like to have their children and their children's children listen to such a man. Of course, that was the nature of man made impossible. School then became a room, and then an institution. Read a program today from the institutions called schools, and what do you get? You get a program that sounds like this: There should be a nine-foot fence around the school; there should be corridors, probably nine feet wide because statistically this is supposed to be enough. These, being corridors, are possibly the best place to have the air-conditioning return system and lockers.

In this environment you go to your classrooms, which, by reason of the fact that all classrooms have thirty pupils in them, are all alike. You have perfect air conditioning, ventilation and light—this is always given. And the cafeteria can be in the basement, because actually you don't spend much time there. This is the kind of a program you get from the school board.

Now I think the first act of the architect is to change this; to change the program for what is good for the institution, for the continuation of the institution of learning. Man has established that for which he feels an inner need to know, to relate knowledge to himself. And that school is as much a part of him as though it actually grew with him. That's really what an institution is. It's an extension of man and his needs. And this must be made greater and greater by the architect. He must refuse the program, he must change the client's program—which reads in the form of areas—into spaces. He must change corridors into galleries; he must change lobbies into places of entrance; he must change budgets into economy. Architectural space is a space within which you read how the space is made; within the space, the columns, the beams, and the stones are in the space itself. A great span must have nothing in it, but that which is captured by the span. And the decision of the structure of the span is also a decision in light. A column next to a column is an expression of opening and light. A vault is a choice in character of light. You shouldn't open one room to the other to find out how the space is made. Within the space itself is the structure of that space. That makes architecture different from building. Just building. All building is not architecture.

10 Lecture at Yale University (1963)

●●●

Kahn began this lecture by discussing his Fort Wayne, Indiana, Fine Arts Center (1961–73), originally conceived as an integrated complex including a philharmonic hall, small theater for drama and ballet, fine arts building, historical museum, and related service facilities, which he reconfigured several times as he rethought the plans. (Only the Performing Arts Center, 1970–73, was built.) During budget discussions with the client, he reported, Kahn discovered two realities with which architects deal: belief and means, which are apt to work at cross-purposes. "Belief" is the sensing of the "psychological entity of something," whereas "means" is the wherewithal to express the belief.

What a building really is, he contends, is an expression of the inexpressible. It accommodates a human activity, such as creating art (a fundamental impulse of humankind), but how one creates art can never be satisfactorily explained. The logic of his argument is that if a tangible building (the "means") is called upon to house an intangible or inexpressible "belief" (the psychology of creating art), then a successful work of architecture will be both functionally appropriate and spiritually enriching.

I'm scared stiff of people who look at things from the money angle. I had to meet some of them the other day at Fort Wayne in connection with an art center I'm doing there—a small Lincoln Center. The

●●

Revised transcript from *Perspecta* 9/10 (1965): 304–05. Reprinted with permission.

project is to locate the separate organizations. It contains a full-fledged philharmonic orchestra (that's really remarkable for a population of 180,000), a civic theater and, distinguished from it, a theater in the round, an art school, school of music, school of dance, dormitory, an art museum, and a historical exhibit. All this is to be in one bundle on one piece of land, and I had to say what it would cost. This is a very ticklish situation for me because I wanted them to want the project first, and then to talk about cost.

I was armed with just one fact: that the square foot areas which they required (which, of course, had nothing to do with cubage) were equal to what areas I developed in the design. This was nothing short of a miracle: Most architects, not excluding me, exceed their square foot areas and have various reasons for justifying it. In this case, however, all the member organizations had written their programs individually, and they had a reasonable cushion in there for contingent areas. Such realism to begin with made it possible for me, in the composing, to equal the required area. And I was armed then with accepted area, though not the cost. Except, yes, I had the costs: I knew they exceeded very much the costs that this committee had in mind.

I presented the plans to them in as inviting a way as I possibly could, described the new philharmonic especially so that they could never refuse its existence, and did the same with the other buildings. Then, when they asked me how much it would cost, I said, "Well, gentlemen, I must first introduce the fact that the area which you have asked me to have is the same as the area on my plans." They said, "Well, all right, but how much does it cost?" I said, "Well, it will cost twenty million dollars."

They had in mind something like two and a half million dollars as the initial expenditure, but the way the buildings became interdependent made it seem quite impossible to begin meaningful choice with such a low amount. I waited for a reaction. I felt the quiet shock the new figure caused and one man did venture to say, "Well, Mr. Kahn, we only expected to spend two and a half million dollars. What can we get for two and a half million?" I said, "Nothing. If you had asked me six months ago what you could get for two and a half million, I'd have said you'd have gotten two and a half million dollars worth; but as you see it presented now, there is an entity present: The philharmonic is dependent upon the art school, the art school on the civic theater, the civic theater on the ballet, and so forth." And it is so: The plan is so made that you feel one building is dependent on the other. I said, "After all, what was the purpose of coming here? Was it to make a convenient arrangement, or was it to make something with an extra quality? I've found the extra quality," I said, "which makes the coming together more than what they are when the buildings are separated from each other. Therefore, for two and a half million dollars you would probably get the hind leg of a donkey and a tail, but you wouldn't get the donkey."

After a little bit of a wait one man asked me, "Well, suppose we simply said to you we want an art school built; it's part of other buildings which we're going to build, but now we want to build only the art school. Could you have done it without an elaborate program including all the buildings?" I said, "Yes, I could have done that, but you would have a mosquito and not a donkey." Well, they had a donkey in their minds—half a donkey, not even half a donkey—and a mosquito (a whole thing which they didn't want, of course), and that was it. Finally, one said (because they did like the entity, and they realized that there was something about the entity which was not the same as having each organization represented in its own way), "Well, I can see, Mr. Kahn, I can see spending ten million dollars, but I can't see spending twenty million." Of course, at that point I realized that I was having an easier time than I had anticipated.

"Well, I will try everything possible to pare down expenses and pare down costs, but you realize that you have to give up something in order to do this; and, for the moment I can't promise anything because I, myself, think that this entity is now hard to destroy."

For if you sense something which is a coming of a now-accepted thing in man's way of life, which is expressed in a realm of spaces or in a form which is different from any other form, once that happens you cannot take parts away because every part is answerable to the other. Form is of that nature. Form is that which deals with inseparable parts. If you take one thing away, you don't have the whole thing, and nothing is ever really fully answerable to that which man wants to accept as part of his way of life unless all its parts are together.

I was really happy to have realized why I was so ready to give up the whole commission if they wouldn't build it all; or rather to feel that all could be built even if it had to be done in steps (as it was done in many wonderful enterprises of man, where the belief was so strong and it was understood so clearly that if you took one part away you didn't have—and everybody understood that you did not have—the entire thing). And I said, "At this moment, I realize something I've never realized before: that there are actually two realities that an architect deals with: He deals with the reality of belief and the reality of means." For example, I now read Goethe (which I had a very hard time reading before), and I find there is wonder in it. He calls his autobiography truth and poetry. This is a wonderful realization of life and the course of living. Though he reported what happened to him, he always avoided confining it to the circumstantial, or what happened, but reflected on its meaning, which transcended his own life. And this I think was marvelous. When you read it, you feel the objectivity and you feel the restraint that he gives you in regard to that which you may get too sentimental about, because he knows it only affects him and shouldn't be imposed on you. If you're reading it, you shouldn't listen to him; you should listen to that which belongs to eternity.

That was wonderful, I thought, and that is really art. It isn't you that you're making. It isn't just a question of believing something yourself, because the reality you believe isn't your belief, it's the belief of everyone: You are simply the radar of this belief. You are the custodian of a belief that comes to you because, as an architect, you are in possession of those powers that sense the psychological entity of something. You're making something that belongs to all of us, otherwise you are really producing very little or almost nothing—if not really nothing. Of course that tells you that almost everybody fails, and it's quite true.

But I don't think that Mozart was a failure, do you? And don't you think Mozart makes a society? Did society make Mozart? No. It's the man, the man only, not a committee, not a mob—nothing makes anything but a man, a single, single, man. This is so true again of Goethe. (I'm only reading Goethe now because I have a great reverence for a person who loved Goethe, and because I love this person I had to read it.) Before this I struggled to read *Faust* page by page. I met Faust for the first time and discovered a wonderful thing: that Gretchen was more soul than body, that Faust was a balance between body and soul, and that Mephistopholes was really all body, the body of man. He had no soul. Two people can't have the same sense of soul. The singularity is a soul and a body, though I believe that soul is a prevalence and that soul is the same in all, no different in anyone. The only difference is the instrument, our body, through which we express desire, love, hate, integrity, all the unmeasurable qualities of soul. Isn't it really true that only a singularity discovers the essence of the nature of man, and, in turn, an institute of man, not several people? So don't think that by research you'll discover anything—let's say, by collaborating with somebody. Either you will be able to reach only the kind of understanding in which you are the custodian of something which you discovered as being true, or you will never discover it. I met a person the other day who had never had an education, and that person, without question, has a remarkable mind—one that needs but a single, tiny fragment of knowledge in order to piece together the most fantastic sense of order. And why should that be so very, very peculiar? After all, the Greeks didn't have the knowledge that we have now, and look what marvelous things they did, only because the mind was highly respected. Somehow or other, because of frugality, because you haven't got so many things to choose from, you begin to think of how gloriously you can express, with the little you have, the nature of man's strivings to express his will to live.

I really felt very religiously attached to this idea of belief because I realized that many things are done with only the reality of the means employed, with no belief behind it. The whole reality isn't there without the reality of belief. When men do large redevelopment projects, there's no belief behind them. The means are available, even the design devices that make them look beautiful, but there's nothing that you feel is somehow a light which shines on the emergence of a new institution of man, which makes him feel a refreshed will to live. This comes from meaning being answerable to a belief. Such a feeling must be in back of it, not just to make something which is pleasant instead of something which is dull: That is no great achievement. Everything that an architect does is first of all answerable to an institution of man before it becomes a building. You don't know what the building is, really, unless you have a belief behind the building, a belief in its identity in the way of life of man. Every architect's first act is that of either revitalizing a prevailing belief or finding a new belief which is just in the air somehow. Why must we assume that there cannot be other things so marvelous as the emergence of the first monastery, for which there was no precedence whatsoever? It was just simply that some man realized that a certain realm of spaces represents a deep desire on the part of man to express the inexpressible in a certain activity of man called a monastery. It's really nothing short of remarkable that a time comes in the history of man when something is established which everybody supports as though it were always eternally so.

And at this point it would be well to speak about the difference between the eternal and the universal. That which is universal is really just what deals with the physical. But that which is eternal is a kind of completely new essence that nonconscious nature does not understand or know about, whereas man is the conscious desire that exists in nature. And I believe that because of this dichotomy, nature will change because of the presence of man, because man is of dream, and what nature gives him as instrument is not enough. He wants much more.

Architecture is what nature cannot make. Nature cannot make anything that man makes. Man takes nature—the means of making a thing—and isolates its laws. Nature does not do this because nature works in harmony of laws, which we call order. It never works in isolation. But man works with this isolation, so whatever he makes is really quite minor, you might say, compared to what is really wanting to be expressed by the desire and the spirit of man. Man is always greater than his works. He could never, with his instrumentation, bring out that which is completely full.

And another thing I feel very strongly: that if a belief always carries with it a great deal of sophistication, I'm afraid it's the limited interpretation of it: one does not know so much about the belief as to make it always fully aware and beautiful. One has to sort of sense it must exist first, and at best it must be called at later times archaic—something which didn't quite express itself in all its beauty, but had such power of existence that others did not change its spirit but worked toward its emergence in beauty. And I believe that beauty somehow sits in that light of being something we work toward. It's a selectivity. It's something which has to do with a completeness of the harmony of a presence.

Lecture at Yale University

11

Lecture at a Conference on "Medicine in the Year 2000" (1964)

In this lecture at the Sixth Annual Conference on Graduate Medical Education, held at the University of Pennsylvania, Kahn used two of his designs to illustrate the virtually inevitable cross-purposes of the client and architect (especially an architect as determined as he was to infuse his buildings with meaning about the nature of humanity and its institutions) but also the wonderful results that come out of those rare instances of philosophical agreement between the two parties. He also stressed the importance of thinking through the essential nature of every aspect of a building, even an elevator, in order to determine both its best placement in relation to every other element of the whole and its potential for accommodating change, insofar as that can be anticipated.

I will not speak with any formal knowledge of either the present and certainly speculations that must be considered speculations in the future. I think we cannot anticipate circumstances; that what we think we can build, I think we can build today.

If one knows the order, knows the ordered content of something, one knows a lot more than what can be found out by experimenta-

From "Report of Proceedings" folder, Box LIK 54, Kahn Collection.

tion in design. I am interested in the form realizations which to me mean the undimensioned and unshaped, yet unshaped, but which defines itself as characteristics that are different from other characteristics.

When I think of a hospital, it cannot be a hospital unless it begins not to look like any other building, and until that happens I think the hospital has yet not been given its characteristic shape out of the order, the realization of hospital as distinguished from any other building.

Our present buildings—and I am including the hospital among others—and research buildings of a biological nature, tend to be yet not properly realized buildings because there are too many functions included in the one envelope. I believe that if a function is so particular, it must be separated so that it can develop its characteristics, or be expressed in its characteristics, rather, and develop in its adaptability, mobility, and change that must take place; and if it is inhibited by certain restrictions which are placed on it by other characteristics, then I believe that part of the activity begins to fail.

You can see buildings which are made to suit the garages on the lower stories of the building and the spacing of columns, of support, for such a use is so different from the spacing that is required, let's say above, which would require possibly a modest distance, while in a garage you need large distance. Therefore the garage, because of its characteristics, must separate itself from the building so that the building is not inhibited—that is to say other parts of the building are not inhibited by the demands of parts with a different function.

The functions of buildings cannot be considered purely physical. As a matter of fact, I believe it is only the balance of the psychological and the physical that will produce what may be called a workable architecture or in which architecture serves all other activities of man.

I believe also that a building must be answerable to an institution of man. What is instituted by men is that which has the approval of man, and this approval, or rather this sense of institutionalizing or making of the institution of man, comes from our inner inspirations.

170   "Medicine in the Year 2000"

The inspiration to learn, the inspiration to live, the inspiration to express, the inspiration to question, are all the source—motivations of our institutions.

I believe that the institution of learning actually stems way back from the nature of nature. Nature, physical nature, records in what it makes how it was made. Within us is the complete story of how we were made, and from this sense, which is the sense of wonder, comes a quest to know, to learn, and the entire quest, I think, will add up to only one thing: how we were made. I think our entire quest for knowledge is only that: how we were made.

From this grows a man under a tree who doesn't know he is a teacher, and talks to a few who don't know they are students, and from that comes a sense of wanting to learn. And then the first enclosure is made because it is more comfortable to meet such a man, and it is a place also to meet, and from it grows classrooms and other complexities; and then also grows the whole system of poor directors and good directors and bad programs and good programs, and directors which have absolutely no bearing on the original inspiration.

So when we start to do let's say a building for medicine or a school, in my opinion we must begin from a very most primitive beginning; never to take the examples of what has been done. I think it is the worst start a man building a building can take. He must begin by saying: What is a hospital? Why is a hospital different from an apartment building? Why is a hospital different from a research center? Why is a biological laboratory different from a physical laboratory? If he doesn't begin this way, I think it all homogenizes into some kind of almost useless thing right from the start.

When I started the biological laboratories for Salk, I thought I had something pretty hot there.[1] I had a very clear distinction I made in the areas that serve the main areas. I made a system of construction.

1. Salk Institute for Biological Studies (1959–65), La Jolla, California. In the laboratories, nine-foot-high Vierendeel trusses spanning sixty feet were placed on top of each laboratory floor to contain mechanical equipment. Kahn knew these more costly "buildings within buildings" were a better solution, though less visually exciting, than his original proposals. See selection 4, note 4 (page 70).

Here is a floor, here is another floor, and here you work. I will draw a man working at the bench. Here they were spaced very closely, ten feet apart so that one can get at this source any appliance, any service, any power, air, any control.

But you had to crawl through the space in order to adjust the piping, and though this distance and this truss system actually supported the building, you had much integration there, it proved to be of less value than a building in which the room you work in and the room with pipes are equal in size so that a man can work here as well as work there.

That cost a lot of money, but when you say, "Should this be built over the other?" there is just no question. In other words, the discovery of this characteristic, this form characteristic, is worth all the money it cost.

Now, the control of such an area, especially in biological research, is a mess. Not only did I say from this came the realization that there must be rooms within rooms; why impose the ordinary partition system or the general services or specific services? If I need a cold room which had to be controlled at a certain temperature, why must I have the walls also take in the hermetically sealed characteristic that such a cold room needs? Therefore, I build a room within a room and that will have its ceiling and must also have its floor, because its floor is different from the general floor. Its ceiling again is different from the ceiling of this room. Therefore, an ordinary building can be a space and all the specific characteristics should be considered buildings within buildings.

If these sense themselves as being the characteristics which, let's say, a biological laboratory needs, then it fits very much the characteristic of man who cannot, once having reached a level of comprehension, move back to a lower one. So, therefore, the directive that a client must give an architect should be one which says: Define for me. I give you the things I need, what controls I want.

We cannot project ourselves so many years back. There can be the smallest unpredictable invention that can happen tomorrow that can make any speculation today ridiculous. I cannot design for the future,

"Medicine in the Year 2000"

it is impossible, but what one can do is distinguish the inevitable from the circumstantial, and the inevitable is somewhat a sense of order, a sense of what is characteristic of one thing or another, and that will have tremendous lasting qualities.

This space where you make up air, where you make up special compressors or anything you place here, which is a laboratory of machinery, you might say—the floor is a laboratory of machinery—it is so necessary and so far superior to any hung ceiling with all the dust you raise every time you make a change, especially in biological work, and you distinguish very distinctly that that room is just as changeable as this is, only in a completely different way.

Now, this building can last a very long time. I say this building can be just as good one hundred years from now and the building we build now, without considering the nature of a building and how it distinguished itself in form from another building, has a very short life. If I said ten years I say it would die of old age. That is the difference.

This was not the only problem. This was only a small part of it. This building looked much dumber than the building I originally conceived. The building before was much more exciting. It would make every architectural magazine. This one may have some difficulty—but this is true and the other is false.

It has nothing to do with eye appeal. It has to do with the emergence, I think, of a new image which, if you take the problems today, is the kind of thing one should see today; and the emergence of a new image is not at all a scary thing to the creative man. He is not afraid of it. He knows it is true, as the original paintings of Picasso, which certainly were condemned in many circles but now hang in everybody's bathroom, were true. He knew it was true. It was true to art because he knew that art was the making of a life and the life that nature cannot make. He knew it; it was in his bones. Whatever he did, he wasn't afraid of anyone in expressing it.

The creative man, as contrasted with the artist, is the man who can, by his realizations and the realizations within the prerogatives of the realm he is dealing with, can see and create and express the new image, and the artist is the one who works in the light of this image and perfects it, believes in it, and makes it beautiful.

I think what we should see right now are very archaic looking buildings, buildings that will be considered archaic in the future, the beginning of a new realization or a new expression of a realization which is not familiar. The buildings all look alike. Office buildings look like apartment buildings. City halls look like office buildings, which they are not. Schools look like—well, sometimes like mortuaries, and the other way around.

There is really no sense which says, "School, yes." School—it is the place of God, certainly. It is the place where the students have their own classrooms. Why not? All of these are characteristic. Why must a student always be in the light of the teacher? Why can't the teacher teach himself? This is so much a factor and in the characteristic of school must be present no corridors but galleries; no lobbies but places of entrance; no budgets but accounts. This is economical and the other is not, even though it costs twice as much, and the other is a budgetary solution and is worthless.

In addition to the physical characteristics, here is where a man works. This building must be made characteristically to comply with the demands of the success of his experiment, and that means an awful lot of duplication here of power—two if necessary, or even a third one to guarantee the two, so that an experiment is not destroyed by a negligence of some kind.

People need light and I place as much emphasis on light as I do there. To place something near the light is only a momentary advantage. I can build a room here and build a file and borrow the light from here. I shouldn't think I have to get near the light, necessarily, if I need light. It is the idea, again, of not accepting a general consideration for what cannot take care, in the ultimate, of your problem.

If you take it another way, if you could build, if you had the fanciest room here and one that is required here, you can still pay the greatest servitude to complete aseptic conditions if you just build your house here and forget all about this. You can teach where it is very, very important how you build material. In other words, whatever "Madison Avenue" approach you may have to it, the important thing is the realization that one is one characteristic and one is another.

To go on, I would just like to have one of these pictures I brought with me spread before you here. This is a plot plan of the biological laboratories of Salk. Here are the laboratories, but here is a meeting center. I did not mix the meeting center with the laboratories, because the characteristic of the laboratory is so completely different. Also, the studies were outside the laboratories and they are associated with a garden, because one is the architecture of the success of the experiment, it is the architecture of stainless steel and controlled air, and this is the architecture of the oak table and the rug. The studies don't need pipes, don't need compressed air, and I placed them outside but very close to the laboratory buildings.

How expensive it is to put a little office or a seminar room in a place which is loaded with pipes and capabilities in other directions! They are placed outside but connected, and they are built in a completely different architecture than these buildings because the architecture of the man is completely different.

Here is the meeting center which is the place again requiring no piping, the place where you eat, which is developed as little seminar rooms rather than go into a baronial room where you meet everybody you don't want to meet. Lunchtime is almost a natural time when you discuss your problem, and you like to discuss it with certain people, not with anybody. And so I have arranged a series of small rooms where problems can be discussed. I have the large room, too, and I will tell you about it and how it works.

Also, there is a gymnasium because I think physical well-being is absolutely essential to any plan, no matter where it is—that presence, the presence of the bath, the presence of the exercise room, should be everywhere—everywhere where it is logical, where men work and need it.

In the same way, here also the library is a seminar room. There is also a residence there, as a point of invitation, but in the center of all this, in a square about seventy feet by seventy feet, is a room unnamed, entirely unnamed. It is a place of entrance but which becomes a banquet hall and becomes a exhibition hall when the time arises. It is ready for the general thing but it is always in characteristic as a kind of seminar environment.

Here is a little village which is just for the convenience of those who want to stay near their experiments, who want to live, let's say, for a short period of time on the project. It therefore has three characteristics, two of the most important: That is, this is a center, you might say, of the unmeasurable, and this is the center of the measurable. The laboratory I just sketched on the board is the way this is constructed, and these are constructed partly in wood, partly in concrete, partly in marble and tile. They are very different and they are associated with the garden. There are no such things as thinking areas. They are everywhere. They are predictable. To call them such is just a small minute kind of consideration.

How did I arrive at this plan? I arrived at it by Dr. Salk having visited the University of Pennsylvania Laboratories and he said he liked them, but he said, "You know, I have one idea which you may be surprised at. I would like to invite Picasso as a resident in my biological studies."[2] He realized that a biological study, without the realization of the smallest living thing that belongs to man, has in a way a soul, it has an existent will, it has something which says, "I want to be a microbe" or "I want to be a tree" or "I want to be little."

He believes that great symphony which you call man totally, with a feeling of self, probably brought about as Mr. Mitchell suggested, who sketched a beautiful picture of, we hope, a kind of more organized, and in that way I think possibly better, use of time of cities. The city, as was brought out in a little book I read just recently, uses the past. You know it—it is by Mueller.[3] It is a swell thing, really, because it just simply touches on the person of the man. It gives no answer to anything.

He just makes you conscious of things, and one thing he said that

2. The Alfred Newton Richards Medical Research and Biology buildings (1957–65), University of Pennsylvania, Philadelphia.
3. Mitchell and Mueller could not be identified.

"Medicine in the Year 2000"

I think was very good was that he thought the city would never die. He said the city is the place where man realized his self-consciousness. When you see the villages of India and Pakistan as I have seen them, they are absolutely nothing but pure servitude to your job. You eat all right, and you do your job, but men come from those places into the city, where they don't eat and where they sleep on the street, and you couldn't get them to go back to their villages because they feel something, even though death in a way, but there is where they feel a touch of independence.

You can't deny that force and you can't deny the force because it began, because I think that everything that begins in man does not die. It is revived somewhere. Once an institution is established, I believe that establishment is there forever, because the acceptance of the confirmation of it is truth and it is just barely managed throughout the ages, and yet to lose its visual inspiration, and that must be brought back.

I had no other program than just that: "I want to invite Picasso here," and of course he included many others in that—a pure physicist, a pure chemist, the man who is a philosopher—because he realizes that in living things, no matter how small, there is this will to exist which can have an influence, a psychosomatic influence on your discoveries; and just to say that this man leans to some other expression of man than the scientist does, and to make him aware that, let's say, his findings are not necessarily the truth—they may border on the truth or may lead to other findings, but there is a great gap left unsought.

Fundamentally, every living thing is unmeasurable, and just the presence of these people who deal with unmeasurable things, as the artist does, because art really is the language of the soul and it is completely unmeasurable, and knowing that men tend toward this and devote their life to it and are willing to die for it, is enough to put the proper humility in a scientist who would take him out of the class of being merely, as he would call it, a biological engineer.

In this, I realized that the place of meeting, which is a place where you let your hair down, where you are not concerned with measurement, you are concerned with the mystery of existence all together and the great dichotomy that exists between physical nature, which by the way can exist if all living things were gone, including trees and shrubs and everything. The wind would still blow, the sun would still shine, the snow would still fall if all of these things went, so physical nature is separated from the nature of man or the nature of all living things as being that which had its spiritual beginnings where nature, in my opinion, is the workshop of God, is the tools with which everything is made—everything, including ourselves. But it is the tool of making; it is the materialistic thing.

Realizing this is the realization of the separation between the place of meeting and the place, I would say, of measurement, if we are brought in tension with each other, that they have more meaning in their physical relationships. They can be across the court, but just so they are made differently. In other words, you are really expressing a dichotomy, and it caused me to make the change.

Of course, the location, which is three points on a canyon structure, had much to do with my choosing the distance between them, but that is only the drama of architecture and one must be excused for this, especially in the good walking distance, the good walking environment of San Diego or La Jolla.

The other example that I wish to bring before you is an example of just architectural thinking along the lines of establishing or expressing the emergence of new institutions. If we think in terms of creation of new institutions or new expressions of old institutions, a revitalization of the realization of its parts, I believe the directive that the man gives to the architect would result in infinitely better things. The architect needs the inspiration, he needs a man who trusts him, someone who says, "I don't want to give you a program." I received no program from Salk, and he had a program, also. He had also a budgetary amount of $3 million. It now costs $25 million, and this isn't yet built, because the faith in this thing grew out of the realization that if you built anything else, you would not express what was the original intention; and if the original intention has meaning—and certainly it can't have meaning alone when you have nothing in your pocket—

the meaning must be translated into dollars, and that was translated into dollars.

No funds are loose funds, they are all difficult to get, but belief can be transmitted if you do not have a closed eye to belief. Building is being done by the university constantly without any belief whatsoever. It is just a budgetary amount, and a lot probably in the wrong place, just so it is a building. I don't think so. Well, I could go on and on.

The other is the assignment I had for the new capital for Pakistan.[4] It is the second capital, which is the legislative capital, and the executive capital is in West Pakistan. I received a program which was in acres. They said, "Supreme Court, ten acres. Meeting room, five acres. Hostels, eight acres."

I had no other program, and that was a wonderful program because then I knew that I had to think of what a hostel is, and the hostel they had in mind was a hotel and I changed it to studies in their gardens on a lake—quite a transformation—because I realize that when the legislators come from various parts of the country, even though they are politicians, something happens to them in the assembly that causes them to take transcendent views—and this is so different from a hotel. There is very little transcendent in a hotel.

I also realized, by just observing their religious habits, that the assembly room itself had to have a mosque interwoven into it. I knew how dangerous this was but as soon as I realized that some building had to be there or something interwoven, a mosque, some relation to the assembly, I felt I knew the entire program. The complexity meant nothing to me. I knew that the assembly is a transcendent place, even though there is much shenanigan going on, and that the mosque was very much related to this transcendence.

I proposed this idea to the director. He answered me by picking up the telephone and talking for half an hour and finally turned to me and said, "I think you have something there." I let on as though it was my usual way of handling the problem. Actually, I was terribly excit-

4. Sher-e-Bangla Nagar (1962–83), the capital complex in Dhaka, Bangladesh, known as East Pakistan before 1971.

ed inwardly, because I had discovered how to put things together immediately. The relationship became clear to me at that moment, and I also realized that the acts of the assembly are really the making or the establishment of the institutions of man, so that part of the program which had to do with other buildings other than the assembly also took their place, because I realized that they should not be mixed with each other but, rather, be expressed as being not counter but related one to the other, not necessarily together.

The picture I have here, then, is the assembly building. Here are the hostels on the lake. All this darker area is the lake. This is also lake here. The garden intervenes between the citadel of the assembly and the citadel of the institution, in back of which are the housing areas which belong to the staff and other workers of the government.

This is a diagram which was done hurriedly in clay and photographed merely to indicate what I must constantly keep in mind, and from which I developed the building. The development has gone very far now and it looks very different from this in detail, but essentially I have not changed the position of this building in relation to the other buildings.

This will show you the influence of my approach to the problem. In this assembly building is a little triangular area here which is the mosque. I started out with four minarets to prove that I knew a mosque was a mosque, but I had no intention to show the minarets finally, because it was quite clear that minarets weren't any more the same thing in the Moslem countries as they were a long time ago, because now they wire them for sound.

One little story in connection with this. When I told them the idea of the mosque and the assembly—well, before the mosque I was warned that the chief justice of the Supreme Court does not like the idea of being near the assembly. He expressed it quite clearly when he said, "I don't want to be near those rogues."

I said, "Is this your decision or is it also the decision of the chief justice that will follow you?" And he had to admit it was his own personal decision, and then I started to tell him what I had in mind, and

I made a quick sketch, not this one for I had no notions of this yet, of an assembly building with a mosque attached to it, sitting on the lake and the hostels wrapped around it—that much I did have in my mind—and he took the pencil out of my hand and put the Supreme Court where I would have put it, and that was in back of the assembly, and he said, "The mosque is sufficient insulation for me."

I needed it very much, you see, in the composition of the whole. Otherwise, what I would call a dream, a symbolism, although I don't really believe it was that, I couldn't work after I had realized. I couldn't have changed it and it holds as of today and we are putting piles in the ground.

I just want to end by saying that it is a search for the character of the program, which seems then to indicate a new institution of man, and to find in what way it differs from other institutions of man. It is the development of characteristic spaces which are different from other spaces. Those who serve and those that are being served are different from each other. We shouldn't just throw around places of closets and utilities in not the exact specific locations, not let them float around, and not allow the budget to ruin the possibility of a lasting building.

A building is not like a piece of transportation that by its use you can say wears down. A building is one which is very different. It is really a part of the landscape. It becomes a part of the city, of the treasury of spaces of the city. There are very few buildings of significance, old buildings, that you want to tear down because they have a psychological effect on you. It tells you continuation of history, and as Mr. Mueller has said very beautifully, "Every act is an act in the past." It is not an act in the future. It is not even an act in today, because the idea of today is entirely spurious, because as you act already it is yesterday, and from this sense we get also the sense of what man is. We don't get it from the future, we get it from the present, what he calls the spurious present.

You really get a sense of it only by a sense of action which is inevitable and that which is circumstantial.

DISCUSSION

QUESTION: I wonder in what way a hospital differs from, say, a research laboratory. What would you say is the essential character of the hospital?

KAHN: In the hospital you have the places where the patient is and where facilities for change of patients are. Today, hospitals are completely cognizant of this but uses are stacked upon uses in the central core area, let us say. It is made to be almost cramped into a certain physical area and some of these facilities are in their very nature only good if they are expandable, and others may not have to be expanded. In almost all cases, I think, expansion is wanted.

The number of beds should be considered an independent problem from the services area. I can't sketch a new hospital in front of you. I think there must be—instead of trying to make a single place of all the facilities, I have a feeling that pavilions for special work, which can expand and have a feeling of expansion about them, and not to frustrate their expansion by being tied to other things, may be a good thing psychologically, and also for the giving of funds for such an expansion.

You may have emergencies in one place and not in others, and so I believe these pavilions should not be tied so much floor to floor, but be in areas expanded in their own way, and that the area for the treatment of the patient be its own entity, because the nature is really quite different one from the other, though I know you need some duplicating services.

It is a place also where every patient has no desire to stay for any particular length of time, and also where the kinds of services that the patient requires cannot equally be given by one nurse or another. I believe that systems such as Mr. Mitchell has talked about will certainly come about in the hospital construction to equalize services and the personality angle, though terribly important, I think the interest in building the hospital isn't there, whereas in a biological laboratory it is really a study. It is not the same as a hospital. Even the

"Medicine in the Year 2000"

laboratory areas are essentially studies, although their studies differ from studies which we call studies.

I am sorry I can't answer it any better than that, except just to note that unless they are drastically different after much thought has been given to it, certainly more than I have just now, then you can be suspicious that you have not solved your problem. It should be such a glaring difference that the question would be unnecessary.

QUESTION: Mr. Kahn, what about the elevator in the hospital today? Do you feel, as Mr. Mitchell seemed to say, that we should walk these short distances?

KAHN: I don't think Mr. Mitchell said we should walk in all cases. I think he means walking which is very much a part of our nature. You do walk sometimes, you are forced into it; you realize the need. It is so different from the need of an elevator, which is a project thing. An elevator is a project thing. Walking is not a project; it is a delight, you see. So therefore the elevator is, again, characteristically completely different and we must work on it with greater professionalism, so the elevator of a hospital isn't just so much bigger but we should know it so differently from any other thing that even emergency treatment could be given in the elevator.

You see, the elevator is wrong because the elevator company has found out that the elevator has to be just big enough to take a bed, and the doctors don't think any more about it, either, and the doctors transmit the same kind of dumb information to the architect, who is overwhelmed by all kinds of problems.

The doctors don't think at all, I can tell you that, when they give you a problem, not at all; and the architect thinks, well, of glory in the realm of architecture, and the elevator company wants to sell elevators. It is all wrong.

QUESTION: Mr. Kahn, I can't stand not knowing what is going to happen at La Jolla. There is a discrepancy between $3 million and $25 million. Who compromised? Did you, or what?

KAHN: There was no compromise at all. It was the wrong figure, that's all, originally.

QUESTION: You mean someone found $25 million.

KAHN: No. The laboratories alone were to be $3 million. The program called for laboratories and meeting place. The laboratories would have cost somewhat less, in fact considerably less, if my first scheme were built. I think we could have built them for in the neighborhood around let's say $6 million. But this costs twice as much and still this is right, and recognized as such by the scientists and by the donators because this was more in the nature of a biological laboratory.

It is being built. In other words, the laboratories, which cost about $12–$15 million, the laboratories alone, you see, are almost completed, so there was no compromise here at all. It was a case where the client, you see, actually demanded a better building. He came to a realization and charged the architect to change his plans, which was very painful. I was told all along, "You are doing an inferior building. You are going from a superior building to an inferior building," but I really believed in what Dr. Salk and his advisors thought could be a better building.

QUESTION: Is much thought given by you, Mr. Kahn, to the changing times with regard to information handling and information processing as a coming thing in hospital design?

KAHN: I personally am not acquainted with it, I don't even know if the right kind of minds that know the problem very intimately, what is to be related, are working on it. I can only challenge the means that are available today, including machines, to give related answers. Once challenged, the architect will find completely new shapes and means to produce the hospital, but he cannot know what the doctor knows. It takes him all his life to know what he is supposed to know, and then doesn't, so, therefore, I believe he needs the order sense to be brought to him, which is translatable into building materials and spaces and their services.

12

Conversation with Karl Linn (1965)

• •

Karl Linn, a University of Pennsylvania professor of landscape architecture who spent his later career in Berkeley, California, deleted his comments from the recording of his conversation with Kahn, making this difficult text even more impenetrable. But attentive reading reveals Kahn's unflagging optimism about the capacity of national institutions either to reinvent themselves or to adapt to the 1960s' widespread demands for social and political reform. Clear also is Kahn's uncompromising commitment to individuality and to dismantling social constraints that encouraged programmed responses to life. For him this meant creating spaces flexible or neutral enough to accommodate spontaneous activity rather than discourage it. Hence his remarks on the absence of courtyards in a proposed school of fine arts building.

Well, I'll tell you, my own paths have not crossed yours, but they have run parallel to mine. One is always primarily serving an institution, and an institution comes from inspiration. And these inspirations are the inspiration to live, the inspiration to learn. These are not surface things, because even when we consider the inspiration to learn, it might be that all we want to learn is how we are made. If we knew how we were made, we would know all the laws of the Universe, because everything that Nature makes must make it by the laws

• •

From "Linn, Karl" folder, Box LIK 58, Kahn Collection.

of the Universe, not by a few simple things, not by the isolation of a few laws of Nature, but by every single thing, be it the smallest thing or the largest thing. And when you think that we are the custodians really of all the laws of the Universe, we really know everything. Only some of us don't have sonar radar about this knowledge. I have always felt that knowing things must be distrusted and that no one has ever written the book, which is what we need, about what we know. This book lies outside of us, and it has not been written by anybody, but the book still is there; theoretically, it is there. Idealistically, it is there, and when you take a thing out of the book, the book talks to you. It says all right, you can have it. But you must tell me everything, otherwise you can't have it. You must gently put it back into what you said before.

There is an inch of knowledge in all of us, but the inspiration to learn is really only a recapture of how we were made, because everything that Nature makes, it records in what it makes, how it was made. Now the inspirations of man, if you consider the inspiration to live, and this "inspiration to live" is a revolt against that approximation of Nature which makes us live for only a short time. It is the most numbing revolt we have, this dichotomy between Nature, physical nature: physical nature and our unconscious nature that is the workshop of God, you might say. The maker of all things only approximates living things, what they really want: but they accept it, first of all, it's so very necessary. And much of our indecision, the lost effects of the instrument itself, is unfortunate.

I myself see the juvenile delinquency problem as you do. I see it as stemming from a gross dissatisfaction, and a high sense of inspiration. The inspirations of man are stronger in a violent person than in a complacent person. Naturally, the mode of expression must, in that case, be in keeping with social mores. The violence that I read of in the paper, of a gang-up of two or three people to, as they say, "clean somebody," results in the death of a young boy, who is completely unaware of what is going to happen to him. This must be compared to the whole course of war.

But I fear for my own point of view, the ever-reviving consciousness about things that are true—the great excitement of change, you know. When I find a better answer to something or a better expression of something, nothing stands in my way except to express that very thing. I feel always in terms of what way I can serve the Institution of Man. None of the thoughts that serve the Institutions of Man are complete; it is almost a marvel that they even exist. And every era can be measured by the creation of the new institutions of that era. In the institutions lie the germs of new institutions. The ones that exist are taken for granted in a very mediocre way. Almost every generation has something in it which demands a restatement of every institution. Only by restating institutions can one really revise the program that an architect gets in his plan. This is his first duty—aside from the details of treating space. They add to the creative stimulation that architecture could give, being a world within a world. If the place, the institution is a place, then architecture is the place of the institution. If I were to say anything about you, I would say that I see in my feeling out of the sense of the inspirations of man that which is the nature of the institutions. Because our inspiration to learn is actually expressed in all the institutions of learning. When I read recently "is the university good enough for students?" I see the real truth—not is the student good enough for the university. This means that the program at the university must change, in the same way that our streets must change and our land must change.

We speak about the places where we can give of ourselves by reexpressing, you might say, the spirit of knighthood. Not in the historic sense of knighthood. A lot of that was more bigoted than knighthood. But a spirit of knighthood and often the exercise of the spirit gives far, far less to the spirit itself.

I can give you one example which you have spoken of with some elaboration. When I was recently in India, I was told by the minister of education that they have a hundred applicants to study chemistry at the University of Calcutta. You may imagine that this is a lot of students because there is such a small proportion of students who even think of education in India, that this hundred students is nothing but phenomenal. The minister there was faced with the fact that he had only ten benches to offer to a hundred applicants for chemistry. He gave them a very stiff exam in the English language, and he emphasized the stiffness of the exam to make sure that he had the right people. I reminded him after he had spoken and had felt the powers of his righteousness that I had told him I didn't remember anything that the ten best students did in our class. Those that did express themselves, and those that were always late, and sometimes were marked because they were late, are the only ones I know now, and value. So there's no indication that the examination method is of any value in the emergence of significant physicists. Not at all. So I said to him, "Well, of course, maybe you have to use your examination and do pick the ten best," but I said, "Wouldn't it be a good idea, because of the privilege of the ten, that you demand that those ten teach nine others? And that the privilege, and I consider it a privilege, of a bench and the teaching of the nine others, means he doesn't have to take the final exam." After about ten minutes, he said, "You know, it would work."

So I said, "Now since you're so receptive, I'll give you another idea! Suppose you had also, as a privilege of being taught, which is marvelous to have in your possession, suppose the students were obliged to go to a village to teach everyone in the village to write his name? Do you realize how curious the villager would be to see how his name was written? And you know, they would all learn to read the newspaper almost immediately."

We need a kind of will to *live* the education, because you want to live the inspiration to express. Not to express as much as to learn. But the will to express is art, and art is never functional, but always describes something undefinable, and still belongs to poverty which is the greatest inspiration that we own, even greater than the inspiration to live. To express means to express that which physical nature is unable to do. This is the great distinction between nature and man. The will to live is the will to trust. To express hate, love, integrity, nobility, are all that are demanded by man. Although nature gave man a terrific violin on which to play things, it's still completely inadequate. The nature of our institutions is the building point in the greater fight to emerge as humans who are greater than nature made us.

Conversation with Karl Linn

So I can see that what you're trying to do is completely parallel in this sense—that you do not accept the programming—you see, programming and motivation is the difference. You see motivation can lead to a program. The program can merely motivate less. Most programs have no motivation behind them. They are simply extensions of things that have already been done. And the things they're written from were written from things that had already been done. All the way down the line. And there is nothing that states it so creatively as the first monk, when he made the first monastery, which is nothing but remarkable. The individuation of spaces gave such a sense of environment for dedication. This is remarkable, the most remarkable. To me the coming of your first neighborhood commons is equally remarkable, and has equally remarkable connotations.

The faith in and inception of institutions is complete perpetuation, because nothing will be accepted by man except that which is true to man. That is why the first institution is the inspiration for all others to come. We need new first institutions, but we don't have them, and the atmosphere is full of a desire for them. It takes a person to see it. And then he must surrender his right to having seen it, because it belongs so much to man. Only the way he expresses it, does it belong to him. I have the greatest reverence for those who can point to an institution. To me it's like pointing to living, not life. Life is the broad existence. But living is patterning, designing, it's creating, it's all these things using life as a medium of creation. Living is different; living is a personal thing. That which can give living possibility is the sense of an institution of man.

I'm not listening so closely to what you're saying about the way you're doing it, as I am about the importance of having it exist to do it. This to me is the most important point in what you said. Unless we can allow these ideas to almost spontaneously come out, what you create is only a sense of an institution of man. Then your institution is wrongly conceived. If it is a way of doing it, I would say it is not enough. In *what* to do is the secret, not in *how* to do it. And the what to do is there, in the evidence you've gathered, Karl. I don't know of anything that could be more important in conjunction with a physical problem. Even the physical problems I think have to be answerable one to the other. Physical problems are incomplete unless they take into account the nature of the problems. New words must be found too. Instead of landmarks, social marks, people-marks, man-marks, life-marks, which is even better. Still they're bad words, because they sound too biological. But the word can serve the doing, and then the word can be found. Man doesn't have the word before the new institution has been made, and you have to have the name—to raise funds.

This is the most exciting part of my work today, this sense of the new institution. I sense it in every building I do today. I sense institution first; am I serving an inspiration? Is a dormitory part of an inspiration? I did a dormitory at Bryn Mawr,[1] and tried to make it a house, and it wasn't a house. What can you do? I put fireplaces in there to place a man in the house—this is a dormitory for women! How do you make the woman feel that she has a sense of hospitality?—it isn't just sitting in the house. Do it by working with a remarkable woman client, like Mrs. McBridge.[2] Terrific person. If you took a position that some one else was responsible for what went wrong, her whole point of view changes.

I found the same thing with Mrs. Kennedy.[3] In Mrs. Kennedy, I found a beautiful kindness. I noticed that when I made apologies for something I did, she always reminded me what a struggle it was to do anything. I realized right away that I had to talk straight from the shoulder to her. Things are not what you want them to be—she understands that. Never apologize about anything. Bare, naked. That's how she likes you. She doesn't like you with your clothes on. That's what's remarkable about Mrs. Kennedy. She's the complete existentialist. She even told me that her children don't seem to her as they did before—now usually a woman doesn't admit this. She'd say,

1. Eleanor Donnelley Erdman Hall (1960–65), Bryn Mawr College, Pennsylvania.
2. Misprint for Katharine Elizabeth McBride, then-president of Bryn Mawr.
3. Jacqueline Kennedy, widow of President John F. Kennedy, invited Kahn to serve on the Arts and Architecture Committee for the Kennedy Presidential Library (1977–79) in Boston, I. M. Pei and Partners, architects.

"Now I must hug my children, they must be protected now that Jack isn't around." No, she saw them differently. She saw things differently, and not unkindly, the associations with her husband were so strong. She didn't say, don't tell me about eternal life, and she's Catholic. She would trust when she had the inspirations.

Of course you'd want those who have had some experience, and often those would be people who would know the least. However, it is the case that experience is good to be confronted with, but offhand I can't think of anybody who has experience I could trust. I know many experts who are worthless, because they are too expert. If I think of younger architects who are talented, who have enough experience, then I would invite them simply because their minds are not cluttered with the usual ways of doing things. Then too these people must also be respected, but usually, if they don't have experience, they're not respected. You cannot extract things from people who are not given to inspiration, especially if they are adults. You will certainly only get it by the work of a few people. The work of a few people which will give a certain instrumentation because it is right. It will be used—I think that an artist changes life first, and in this way he serves best. If it were for someone else, he would never serve. The image is always implied.

I don't like people who say cities are for people. There must always be a city. As soon as you say they are for people, then I wonder what part is for cockroaches. It can't be stated this way; it must be stated so that people are always implied. Then the work always becomes great. People are not always sought out in too intimate detail. You must include all people. You just must be yourself. The belief in it is your best service, working towards it, expressing it. The more you can get this expression of inspiration out to express, the more art it is; the more you want to exist, the more you must adhere to the laws of nature—otherwise, expression will destroy itself. It must be strong in itself, not an affectation with momentary satisfactions. So I would like to—this would be a great help to me—talk to you about more specific things, like the kind of environment and what it means. If you say that this doesn't answer one major thing, and you make people see the profundity of this; I like it. But, when I say all architects must build the institution of man, I then say what the institution of man is. This avoids generalities and confusions. Take the example of a school, then develop a theory of coming to a new institution.

I talked to the dean[4] the other day, when he was talking about a school of fine arts to be built on a corner, a most ridiculous place to build it. And then with a pool to boot. I cannot understand any man, any city planner, who builds a building in the wrong place because someone told him to, and then is going to accept a completely insufficient statement as to what a school is. I said, "Tell me this: Do you have one thing, a courtyard, where you can make any damn thing you want?" He said, "No." "So, do you have a school of architecture, crying out to be a school of architecture, which has yet to be built, to be the simplest thing in the world, where you can have places to make noise and places where noise is not permitted?" Simple notions like this. You know the test of a man's work. It isn't sufficient to say, Well, does it appeal? Does it have service spaces, etc.?

The Naguchi[5] playground in New York is something else that I want to talk to you about. I would not exclude from your mind anything that is seemingly out of context—this playground in New York, *you* could have done. You could have inserted just those things they're talking about now. I know you could have done it. I'm not even sure that you can't enter the project now. But it's pretty nearly completed. I would like you to enter it at any rate. . . . It must be entered with a sense of service, so that your belief is felt. If for instance you sense the nature of children who look at everything as if they were going to destroy it—those forces in them—that intimateness—the spontaneity of participation, where it exists, if you sense this, you also sense

4. G. Holmes Perkins, dean of the Graduate School of Fine Arts, University of Pennsylvania, hired Kahn as professor of architecture in 1955 and was later the first curator of the Louis I. Kahn Collection. Kahn may have been hard on Perkins because he was not asked to design the School of Fine Arts, although at that moment he was preparing a campus expansion (1964–66, unbuilt) for the nearby Philadelphia College of Art.
5. Kahn collaborated uneasily with sculptor Isamu Noguchi (here consistently misspelled) on the unbuilt Levy Memorial Playground (1961–66) in New York City.

Conversation with Karl Linn

that a thing is *made* to be incomplete for play. This sense of incompleteness has to be affirmed. I'll have to speak to Naguchi; there are many things that need tremendously harsh criticism. I just hope that what is there can somehow be pushed into position without seemingly changing it. It must be done this way, and I think your sensitivities will be needed. You've got to help destroy what we did. I think that would be a very good thing.

Did you know Lady Allen of Hurtwood?[6] She's very much akin to what you are doing. Very much. I like the emphasis of Lady Allen of Hurtwood, and I think you'd get along. She's very much associated with children and that sort of thing, and she thinks very much as you do. Really a very wonderful woman.

Lady Allen of Hurtwood is sort of object minded, and in that sense, isn't the same as you. But in a way, she would be very much inspired by you. And to know her, would be inspiring to you. To know Lady Allen, would be to have a contact in England, which would be marvelous. Your work should not stop anywhere.

In you lies a tremendous amount of experience, and out of difficulty comes real experience. My daughter, who lives in New York now, has this terrible time getting started. She plays flute and many others play—and it's hard to distinguish because so many play better. She only plays well. So at one point, she was thinking of going to Chicago. I told her not to. I told her to go where the going was really hard. What you get from this is much more, though the opportunity is less.

Momentarily. You'll come on better in the long run. To think of a thing in two ways, you must not only think of it as confined, to where you might use material which was only thrown away. You see after all that's not the only type of material. It must be considered something which is good too. In this way, the broader attitude, of the institution of quality, cannot be had by treating it as a local affair. It must be something which is cross-sectional too. You must make it applicable in Russia too. If you can't do that, then it's too confined. It becomes not a matter of adjusting to conditions only. A school must be applicable

6. Lady Allen of Hurtwood, born Marjory Gill, was an English landscape architect.

there as well as here. It must be important in that sense. Now in that sense, you see I'm just bringing it up to this point, from the standpoint of the landscape architect. But I feel this is something I would have to find a broader use for. You can design things well, I know this. When I saw this brickwork, and the wood done on a lathe, I loved that. Today, can I assign a wall to a painter? I can't. Because I haven't learned, you see, one of these things to the point where I could really do it myself. After all, I'm not a youngster. I haven't found it. I haven't found a co-trust which doesn't cause me to be in any way resentful of this thing.

But I think you can also bring in so much in this Institution of Man. My mind always runs this way. I always assume the people are there.

I learned much from my first teacher. He said, "Don't show all you know in one problem. You have to have this restraint."

But you must express an institution that is growing, an institution of learning. You should think of chemistry as the same as architecture, or of architecture as the same as chemistry. You can't think of this thing belonging to that way, and of that thing belonging to this way. It must somehow always be the same. From which we will learn great things. Like I learned to revive study from the laboratory. But the kind of man who does this has to think—we have one room here of 400° temperature, and another of 400° below zero temperature, and where is there a room for study, for the pencil? Or a fireplace room? Which is really a different kind of space? We must build something that satisfies this, and satisfies the other. We must express dichotomous things. We must express them because the dichotomous things inspire.

Unity to me as a word doesn't mean unity. Unity could mean fight. What's the use in expressing it then?

I think your work can—should inspire a real sense of a program for urbanism. I want to call it urbanism for want of a better word. Something else. Urbanism immediately makes all minds as heavy as lead. You don't think any more because it's all finished. Urbanism needs to be redefined. That's one of the most important things that you can do, Karl, I really think so. And your mind can do it, I know. The images you can work very well. Now to revise the vocabulary of urban life—urban life is becoming the exchange point where a boy understands himself in relation to other boys. And this is very important. A boy makes a choice in the city. He merely serves a term in the country. It's quite a different thing. And because of this, what does it mean? Where are the places, where are the nodules that one recognizes? Even in the Paris streets, where you can take a pee. It's important. You know where it is, when you go walking, and you have confidence when you go walking. Otherwise you have to walk close to hotels. These things are important. Karl, you have a sense of people, which is a way in which you can derive a new program. Whether they're white, Negro, or yellow, it makes absolutely no difference. I would not worry that one type or combination is more right than the others. That problem, you might say, is in the department of circumstance. These things change. Circumstance.

Not thinking correctly but positively instead. Thinking *there* is actually a new way of expressing a new institution, instead of how to correct a present one. The creation of a new institution naturally buries those things which were problems in the old. One must never try to anticipate circumstance. In the making of something, the circumstances can never be anticipated. Even some of the plans, which say that this can happen, must all somehow be reserved. What must be created is something that is infallible. Something in a sense of the institution where these things can happen. This is expressed architecturally, in space, whether you cover the rooms or not. It must be also created in such a way that it is anonymous enough to be similar enough for any man to be comfortable in. So, therefore, when you say, "What is a school of architecture?" I always envision a place where somehow you have walls you can defile. I always felt it should be a place where nobody is inhibited by anybody else. Nothing precious. But a variety of light, and low and high spaces. Nothing to tell you where something *should* be. Or where music should be played. Simply an environment which in every sense is a kind of landscape. I saw it this way. I told this to the dean. It is the only thing that stopped him. Courtyard? Do you have a courtyard, an ingredient of the institution? This Princeton school—it's just like a beauty parlor, with desks. Rudolph's Building—a disgrace.[7] It doesn't even work in detail. This building—it could be for any other purpose. It's like, when you think of vandalism, you think of that building. It's like it's vandalized. Something has been taken away. Prissy things. A rugged face of a seaman that has been smoothed out. Makes a young boy look like a seaman. It's a ridiculous thing, taking time and forcing it. If you did that every time, something shallow would come out. Therefore, you can't force time; you can only allow it to do its part. No matter how you plan it, it'll go the other way. That which locks itself into position, and expresses in a most archaic way. Not the most sophisticated. The archaic way. You've got to do it, it's not more important to think about, but just do it. And out of this inspiration will come the building, and such that people will feel the institution, and will say that we are living in an era in which this acceleration that you speak about will bring about the most beautiful fullness of life.

You will be able to sense the coming of the new institutions; that's a key which should mean something, which should inspire. These institutions must be welcomed as not being corrections, which are ways of perpetuating old institutions. Therefore, of no value.

This must be put in your book. If I'd write about it, I'd write about it in this way. In order to explain what you are trying to do is very difficult. I can write how I see what you are doing, but I cannot write what you are doing.

I think the first thing I would do is have the university put on an exhibit. The work of the exhibition, which may take some time to be worked out, could be part of the classwork. To really make it a living thing. Discussions in the class can be written down and the material can always be had. You can say the essence of the second semester can be written in the third. I think that's the only way.

---

7. It is unclear to which building or buildings Kahn was referring. He may have been looking at photographs handed to him by Linn. Paul Rudolph did not design a building in Princeton, New Jersey but was responsible for the 1958–65 Yale University Art and Architecture Building in New Haven.

13 Lecture to the Boston Society of Architects (1966)

Again using his own projects as illustrations, Kahn explained in this lecture his attempts to put philosophical principles into built form. He referred to "elements"—architectural basics that one may alter only at the risk of violating the ancient verities upon which they are based. "Elements" include such simple things as doors, roofs, chimneys, and fireplaces, which, if misplaced or ill-considered, could compromise the integrity of entry, shelter, ventilation, and warmth both functionally and psychologically. According to Kahn, architecture itself is the most basic element: It is a spiritual enterprise trying to explain humanity to itself. No building *is* architecture; it is merely "an offering" to it. Architecture "can never be satisfied" because it is "completely insatiable," meaning that perfection will never be reached and "form" never realized, just as humanity will never fully understand itself. Nevertheless, it is humanity's destiny to try.

Kahn's projects reveal the seriousness—almost humility—with which he approached his work, his openness to advice, and his inclination to revise plans even when his clients were thoroughly satisfied with them. Kahn's explanations of his own buildings were sometimes even more illuminating than professional critical commentary.

This lecture was published in the Boston Society of Architects' *Journal,* 1 (1967), but the version reproduced here is from a revised text in the Kahn Collection (with some minor corrections).

From "Boston Society of Architects. Earl Flansburgh" folder, LIK Box 57, Kahn Collection.

would like to just introduce you to some thoughts that I've had recently. One being that everything that nature makes it records in what it makes how it was made. In the rock is the record of the making of the rock; in man is the record of the making of him. And in the making, the consciousness of man as contrasted with the nonconsciousness nature sets up in my mind a feeling of dichotomous existence of man and nature. So everything that man makes, nature cannot make. And everything that nature makes, man cannot make. The inspiration that is built in man is the inspiration to live, and the inspiration to learn the way we were made. Because all that man really wants to know, is how he was made. If he knew this, he would know all the laws of the universe.

So learning is a kind of inspiration. The inspiration to express is all of art. It has to do with the seekings of nature to express that which is fundamentally inexpressible. It is impossible to express love, hate, nobility, and integrity. Those qualities which are really, you might say, the *raison d'etre* of man's living. The reason for man's living is to express. And art is his medium. All of science is a servant of art. Science deals with what is; art deals with what is not. But rich in every way, science wants to be expressed, and inspired by the feelings, of nobility, feelings of integrity, and love. Every building that a man builds I believe is answerable to the institutions of man which he establishes through these inspirations. The inspiration to express is the establishment of all our places of learning. The inspiration to express is that which sets up man's urge to seek shapes and forms which are not in nature. Nature cannot build locomotives, nor build houses. So every building is answerable to an inspiration of man.

When a commission comes to an architect, he thinks of the institution it serves, and the environment of spaces which express one place of man, and another. It is almost the first duty of the architect, you might say, to take a program and to translate its area programs to spaces, so that the lobby becomes a place of entrance, the corridor becomes the gallery, and the budget becomes economy.

I met an architect in Mexico—Barragan, landscape architect.[1] His

1. Mexican architect and landscape architect Luis Barragan.

peers tell me that he is a land man, and I'll say nothing more about him. He likes wood and a few other things which are just sort of off-hand remarks. I've found that he is completely remarkable. A man who does not express himself in many works, but what he has done in the house I've visited can be seen every bit of what the man could do. His gardens which have nothing but a trickle of water, and still is so immense that all the landscaping in the world couldn't equal it. And we can't run to a place in his house which wouldn't let up until the ceiling reached thirty feet. And we sat down, because it was cold in Mexico, to some gin which he had (fine stuff). And we were sitting around just enjoying mere life, and he said to me, "What is tradition?" And I sure wasn't prepared for that one. But nevertheless I was determined (you know I'm a professor so I must answer all questions) and I said, "Yes, my mind goes to London somehow to the Globe Theater." And looking in through some opening when Shakespeare did *Much Ado About Nothing,* and people were on the stage in full *bragade* [*sic*] (it was a full house and Shakespeare was very popular). And the first actor who tried to make the first gesture fell into a heap of dust under his costume. The second actor, whose cue it was, had the same thing happen to him. The audience, reacting to the actors, also fell into a heap of dust and so did the men in the gallery.

I suddenly realized that everything that lives cannot live again. And any action which has happened cannot be re-acted. Forms simply are still. There was a first act of movement; somehow it disappears. But that which man has done, somehow, doesn't live. So that etching of Shakespeare, his image, lives! An old encrusted mirror which you cannot see your image in any more still lives, and you can anticipate and imagine the image of a beautiful person in it. Man's works belong to eternity. Not men as living things; they go but their works remain. And he felt that even the words that I've just said disappear again in the dust, so as it is now. But anticipation was life. If the sun wasn't what you anticipated, then the very razor edge that exists between the moments that have passed really doesn't exist because it's too difficult to calculate. And therefore, though I am not in favor of existentialism of any kind, all that I am really interested in is anticipation.

Now I met somebody in India who said he had a hot idea of how to teach world art. It's very systematic, and all of the artists would be able to communicate with each other on equal terms. I had just about a half a day's time before I left India. I was to have a meeting that night, and then the next morning I was to leave. And because this man was terribly sweet, a wonderful fellow from Berkeley, I couldn't imagine anything he said could be right. But nevertheless, if you had a measurable way of teaching art, I was that interested. But I was very equipped with my handy kind of words which I have studied very carefully for such cases. But he is such a terribly sweet man that I did not want to do this, and suddenly I realized that actually I didn't do with a good answer, the answer just came to me, and I told him what it was.

I felt there were three things that had to be taken care of in the teaching of the architect. One is professional, and that had to do with everything that is measurable—however a man can measure things it belongs to the profession. That which had to do with the strength of materials, that which had to do with the way you conduct yourself and the client, the office, statics, and science and technology. Also doing the right thing, you might say; make things stand out; the order of brickwork; the order of concrete must be understood; even the aesthetics that belong to it justifies the rules, let's say, of art. But that aspect, the second, was that of teaching a man. In teaching the man, one had to teach what was already in the realm of the unmeasurable, and there it was a question of teaching other arts and it was the distinction also between teaching and instructing. There the teacher entered because the job of the teacher is to teach another man, and that was a different realm entirely.

But there was a third realm which is even more important, and that was the spirit of architecture itself. The miracle that man can take upon himself the responsibility and love for the emergence of the making of a world within a world which architecture really is. And it is a very unmeasurable thing. And you begin to realize also, that a man does not do architecture, but he does a work of architecture as an offering to architecture. Architecture is a spirit that can never be satisfied, and it is completely insatiable. It transcends all

Lecture to the Boston Society of Architects

styles; there is no such thing as modern since everything belongs to architecture that exists in architecture and has its force. This is the spirit of architecture. Architecture doesn't know about styles. It knows nothing but simply its presence, and it's ready to receive an offering that is true. So man does not do architecture. He does a work of architecture which he offers to architecture. That is true with the sculptor, true with the painter, and even true with the scientist. I say even true with the scientist because I always consider him a servant of art. A servant of expression, because the *raison d'etre* for living is to express.

Now in this light, you take the Salk project.[2] Salk came to me and said, "I want a lecture building at the university." That was before it was occupied, because everybody hates it now (but for other reasons). He asked how many square feet it is, and I told him some ninety-one thousand square feet to be exact and he said, "That's just what we need because I need ten thousand square feet; I have ten scientists and they all tell me they need ten thousand square feet of space." But then he added something to the program when he said, "I want to invite Picasso here!" And that really made a big difference! And my mind went around, why I don't know, to some of those orbiting things. And the laboratory became very insignificant, and that was my commission, the laboratory as though it was a meeting house which was the center of the unmeasurable. And the science building was not described to discover the unmeasurable. And it was almost something dichotomous about asking Picasso to be there. And it was more usual to think that the man was so much obsessed by becoming a marking of a new institutional sense, something different from what he called the censure of biological engineering which most laboratories are—biological laboratories. It had to respect the fact that somebody else is doing something else and it is just as important to biology as it is to discover certain characteristics (which are endless anyway). So the sense of the institution is being made of three inseparable parts.

2. Salk Institute for Biological Studies (1959–65), La Jolla, California.

The meeting house, which was the center of the unmeasurable, and was the true address, from the human standpoint, of the laboratory. But it gave rise to the idea that the studies of the laboratory are also not the same thing as laboratory space because the laboratory space was so souped up with utilities that a poor little office surrounded by them would completely be swamped by it. And it seemed economically ridiculous to have so much equipment for a little office that contained nothing but a pencil and paper, and a filing cabinet. So the distinction is between the space which is usually the space of the oak table and the rug and pipe, and the place which has everything. One that could change the temperature in ten square feet away from another ten square feet [away] from some kind of ultimate temperature below and above. That sense of the difference between the demands of one space and another are essentially the differences between one institution and another, and the parts of it.

I've felt that there is really almost a [dichotomous] relationship between the study and the laboratory because they demanded different things. And I came to visit the laboratory people who were going to occupy these places, and they were so nervous about the smallest noise they reminded me that what they were mostly annoyed by when they were in their study (which by the way was only a smidgen of space) was that they were so afraid that some other scientist, somewhere not too far away who probably had no education at all would supersede him in some kind of experimental discovery. And so the nervousness of the situation was immense. But I realize also that they were all wrong about what they wanted. They wanted everything very close to them, and one person took out his lunch at exactly twelve o'clock, took out a ham sandwich, pushed the microbes aside, and ate his sandwich. And I felt it was a pretty good idea to have some place he could go to. And there was the idea of the meeting house. The meeting house was a place where one can really get away from it all. There isn't such a rush after all, you see, for the mind if it really is a mind at all, needn't worry about the other mind. Because fundamentally all are singularities; there isn't one alike.

Now in Pakistan,[3] I had a similar problem. I was given a program of about twenty-five pages, and that wasn't even a full program since the program was speaking about the assembly building. It said the requirements of the assembly building were something like this: THE ASSEMBLY BUILDING—TEN ACRES. That was the program! And a few other things which were really funny like, "hostels should have closets." Anyway, this is twenty-five pages of very meaty and serious requirements. The third day I was there a fellow with a good idea said why didn't you bring it all together into one unit. And the idea stemmed from this thought. That after all, an assembly building is a transcendent place. A place, no matter what kind of a rogue you are, when you go into an assembly somehow you may vote for the right thing. Now I thought that it had transcendent qualities, and so I observed that the Pakistanis do pray five times each day and very earnestly. So I thought of this preposterous idea of having a mosque attached to the assembly. I thought the mosque should be answerable to the assembly, and the assembly answerable to the mosque.

It was the next morning and I couldn't wait to tell Kafiluddin Ahmad, who was then in charge of the project.[4] He called, without much waiting, the president and several ministers in Hindu (didn't understand a word), and he came out to me and said, "Mr. Kahn I think you have an idea there."

In the program, there was some semblance of a prayer hall, which was three thousand square feet, and the instruction was also to have a closet for rugs. But I turned it into thirty thousand square feet, and the first translation of this was a mosque about the size of Hagaster Theater.[5] The point is to emphasize the idea. When I took this thought to the chief justice of the Supreme Court, he didn't want to

3. Sher-e-Bangla Nagar (1962–83), the capital complex in Dhaka, Bangladesh, formerly East Pakistan.
4. Kafiluddin Ahmad, deputy chief engineer of the Pakistan Department of Public Works. The president was Mohammed Ayub Khan.
5. Clarifying scale by speaking of something familiar to his audience, Kahn was probably referring to the Exeter Theater in Boston.

be anywhere near the assembly. He said, "I know why you've come; its no use, I'm going to make my office near the Provincial Supreme Court because they have the books there, the environment there, all the other judges are there, and I will feel much more happy." So I made a big sketch for the first time of the assembly. I showed the hostels on the lake overlooking the assembly, and the mosque which I attached to the assembly to make part of the entrance to the assembly. When he saw the mosque, he took the pencil out of my hand and placed the Supreme Court where I would have placed it. Then he placed the pencil opposite the entrance where the mosque is and said, "The mosque is insulation enough for me." The thought of the efficacy of trying for that quality which belongs to itself in whatever it may be, came from the nature of the way of life.

I think that if you were to judge the city as if it were an institution of man, and that the nature of connection is very vital in architecture. The sensitivity of the emergence of new institutions, even out of the old, seem to want to branch from it. The sensitivity to what may be willing to be an institution of man, and the spaces around which it could express itself are almost a first requirement. And all the other things like traffic and water supplies which have their own architecture, certainly you might say that the architecture of movement is one of its own. It's a kickable architecture compared to the gospel architecture of the institutions of man.

And so it is with the architecture of water which has a most romantic architecture. I am being asked to design a city in India.[6] The first thing I think of is just what is the architecture of water; which is a marvelous architecture. If only I could do that part of it I'd feel so happy compared to doing the buildings which I like to do where it is the framework which gives direction to the estates where things can happen. Such as the estates of working, the estates of living, the estates of government, that are really defined by certain surfaces. And

6. Kahn refers to his 1961–66 plans for Ghandinagar, the new capital city for the State of Gujarat, which was eventually designed by Indian architects.

how you express these surfaces architecturally is how they have their architecture of woman, the architecture of light, the architecture of movement, and the architecture of water. All of this has its distinct architecture and are expressed in their own way. Our cities are just making sort of bumblings of real estate and patriotism which have nothing to do with the real expression of making these estates out of an architecture which is just learning to be expressed in all directions. It is a much more wonderful architecture than any I've ever seen in any of the books. All of the things that have been so much are really not adequate for what really can be the expression that is possible.

Now I just want to touch the difference between design and composition. I think architects should be composers and not designers. They should be composers of elements. The elements are things that are entities in themselves. I was just speaking today about why it was that when you see these buildings at Harvard that are these colonial and Georgian buildings they look good. The things that we do somehow don't quite reach the serenity, the simplicity, and the modesty of those buildings.

I really think it's because we are not looking at things elementally. When a real Georgian architect, not the ones at Harvard, took in his hand what was the fireplace before he placed it on the plan, he knew everything about it. It was part of the way of life, and every element of it was known to him. And he composed it around the knowledge of the meaning, let's say of the roof, that had something to do with water and snow. And when he put a dormer in, he made it out of permissions of the roof—he asked the roof first, "I don't want to spoil you, I want to make something there so can you give me permission?" He doesn't make the whole roof over, he simply makes a modest thing for which he makes light, and if he is very ingenious he convinces the roof to put in more. But the point is that it is an element that is related to something in the same way as scraping your feet of snow when you enter the doorway and fumble with the key. There is this relationship of the door which is . . . elemental. This is the same as the walk, and the same as the fireplace because you know it so well.

Now of course, you know very well how anyone wants to be responsible and when it comes to putting it above the roof you really stop and say, "Why did we have to adhere to the building laws?" "Why don't we have little chimneys instead of high chimneys, and why can't we make the roof high enough so you hide the chimney?" All of these things come to your mind because it is not elementally considered. Composition is dealing with elements, and design is a matter of working within them so it becomes perfection. Composition is to me a big attitude and it has to do with the recognition of elements.

I would think that if you are dealing with a column you must give it a beam. You cannot have a column without a beam. It is an elemental thing. You can't have a column and a slab. If you have a column and a slab, you know the slab has a beam inside of it. That consciousness will cause less serious errors in the making of architecture, because how many times do you frame a beam into the side of the column instead of above it? All of those things which are in my opinion very poor acts of architecture.

With this introduction, I would like to show you a few slides and tell you in what way I tried to capture things in the commissions that I have gotten. This is the Salk project. You know this is the laboratory space. The studies are here, and they are in the garden away from the laboratories. I purposely took them away out of the realization that the study was not in the laboratory. Now if the laboratory wanted a study, that is all right. There is nothing wrong with that, but by providing the opportunity to move away from it out of the realizations that this needed space is taken over by the laboratory space which is so very well equipped. There is nothing mandatory about it, but it sets the framework.

The meeting house also is where even the rooms are made so. There is no great dining hall to eat in, but there are little places where you might meet people that you want to meet; rather than try to make some sort of dodge for those you don't want to meet. That is also true of the library and the director's house. They are spaced in the middle where you have my mark which is named nothing, but is a place where actually you can have a banquet.[7] Because there, an unknown space which is big enough for a banquet has little to do with the everyday use of a place that you eat. With a religious place here, a meeting hall there, I set up these elements and this is a little village for those who want to be very close to the laboratories. Many want to practically live in the laboratories themselves. They have to for biological experiments where many of them have to be very close. So it is their nature to have this; it is not just a cute idea to make people comfortable. The scientists do want everything including a "double-tendor"[8] or something like that. Now I have two schemes for the laboratories, and the first one I fought for very strongly. I lost the battle, and I'm very glad I did because the next scheme was so much more resourceful.

This shows the upper and lower levels of the garden. Dr. Salk thought of the idea that there should be no study opposite a laboratory, but there should be a garden opposite a laboratory. So the study should not be visible to the scientist. And one scientist should not feel the feet of another over him. So therefore, the portico separates one study below from the study above. That is how sensitive he became to the premises which I myself set. I was always sliding away, because our society makes us slide away. But he didn't let me when he said, "Spend money" (which I certainly did!).

It shows the laboratories are made so that the laboratory is one here, but the actual surface of the laboratory was in itself a laboratory where you can go in and store many of the experiments which are really refrigerator storage of an endless number of experiments. This clears the laboratory and you are guaranteed by this way always a clearing where you can make changes. And here you can serve and

7. When he could, Kahn designed unnamed, undesignated spaces that lent themselves to whatever activity might arise. An example of this is the atrium at Phillips Exeter Academy Library (1965–72) in Exeter, New Hampshire. Ostensibly a distribution point upon entry to the building, it has been used for concerts, receptions, exhibitions, parties, and informal gatherings.
8. Kahn may have been jokingly referring to a tendour, a heated table common to East Asia.

also store. You see, there the study is opposite the pipe space, but there it's opposite the portico, and opposite the kind of runway and the garden below. This is purely Salk's insistence. I was going to give him capacity. Three studies with one over the other. How economical! He said no, "How wrong!" And he was certainly right.

This shows the relation of the laboratory to the studies. The studies have one idea which I am not sure was such a good idea, but every study had to look out to the sea. Now this idea of Salk's I tried to work out with the garden between it. This teak has become much grayer, not so violent as it is now. It looks like some walnut color; grayish-brown.

These are the studies, and this is the plaza. It contains no trees, it just connects both. I always had trees here and I said it had to be the garden—a main garden just obsessed me. I could never draw it with gardens, I could never make a model where I put a garden in. But still my mind said garden, garden, garden. I invited Barragan,[9] because I was so impressed with his gardens to come and see this place. And he turned to me after he saw the place, and touching the concrete which he loved very much, "You are going to hate me, but there should be no tree here." And he was so right. He released you from the bondage of the tree, so much that I couldn't see it any other way. And so now I say it has no trees, and it is not going to have any. Even the irrigation which I had here ready for the trees, now has to be justified as a drainage system of the plaza. And I think I have a pretty good scheme for it, so it looks just fine. The color of the concrete right through here is a kind of almost cerise color. It is a color of rose.

These are the back buildings where all the turrets and services are. This again does not interfere with the laboratory space. It is completely clear, and has nothing to obstruct it. This stair goes down into the lower garden.

This . . . shows the stair as it continues from the upper stair to the lower garden and its edges to get to the lower garden.

These are travertine walks which with concrete look extremely

9. Barragan advised Kahn not to divide the two laboratory buildings with a garden but rather with a plaza. There is some disagreement about whether the bisecting rill was Barragan's idea or Kahn's.

Lecture to the Boston Society of Architects

well. I had in fact intended to make it slate, because it would look well as a contrast. I couldn't afford slate. It cost more than travertine in California, and luckily concrete is much more the material. The judgment was bad and the economy was right.

This shows the entrance into the lower garden, and these are pools which are not yet filled with water that cascade down to this little sitting place here. This I intended of course to landscape, and this portion will be landscaped and so will this plowed part here. But the plaza now, in my mind is completely blank. It was a very good lesson that Barragan taught me. He said the reason why the plaza should be there is because it adds another façade; the façade that looks to the sky. I thought that was beautiful, he was so convincing!

This ... shows the character of concrete which has been untouched and some will show also that the concrete should bleed out in every joint. All the forms are made out of four by twelve plywood, and at the joints the concrete bleeds out. This gives the opportunity for the concrete to be relaxed in its forming itself; not to be restrained in any way at the points where it cannot be restrained anyway causing bad trammel at those points. Allowing it to go through actually perfected the concrete at the joints, and all corners were made specially, so that they made all three sides removable. The corners were never raw, they were always straight.

These are some of the examples of mechanical space which leads into the laboratory and are some pipe spaces. These are all air-intake areas. And these are the studies in front. I think the tone now, the concrete and the wood, blends together much as this black and white photograph does.

These are the studies.

Some of the character of the concrete. All of the places which allow water to come out were done in lead. All these holes were plugged with lead. . . . All, I think are sympathetic to each other.

Every bit of the formwork was designed; nothing left to the contractor. Here it shows what the effect of the bleeding the concrete can do. In a certain light, these are all accentuated. The corners are quite true. This is a pipe space, and below are the laboratories.

Here is a meeting place which has not yet been started, and is hoped to. I just wanted to demonstrate a thought. It came to me in Africa.[10] It is that of a building within a building which you see there above here and there. Also in other places where the light is protected and which refutes, in my opinion, the need for a *brise-soleil* which is too close to the building and causes heat to enter the building. Whereas, if you have a building outside of a building and it has no roof, then the interior which is the round thing has a chance to look out. And because it has light on the interior of the wall the glare is eliminated because there is no contrast.

This . . . illustrates the principle of this. This is the exterior wall around a lot of paper-thin concrete which flanges to express and also to make a very thin nonsupporting structure. And behind this are the windows of the dining halls which are on three levels.

This shows the effect of the interior with these walls in light. The interior looking out to a modified lighted wall and a glare outside. This, I'm sure, will cause the room not to need curtains or any other such devices. It's architectural, and not brought in, as an appurtenance is, that can be later defiled and possibly misused.

There, of course, shows the interior space I've mentioned as an overall kind of use area unnamed. And here is the beginning of the architecture of the enclosures of the walls within walls.

This shows the general effect of the architecture. This is an old model, and I've since that time changed many of [the] shapes. No glass is present; the buildings are without glass.

This shows the synagogue which I'm going to build in Philadelphia,[11] and in this case the windows are actually twenty feet in diameter. The exterior is glazed with two or three windows. The interior is

10. While designing the unbuilt United States Consulate and Residence (1959–62) in Luanda, Angola (see selection 6), Kahn conceived of a second wall placed a few feet outside the actual space-containing wall. He thought this an improvement on the *brise-soleil* (literally, sunlight breaker), which in Le Corbusier's Unité d'Habitation (1945–52) in Marseilles consisted of a network of beams and low walls sheltering narrow terraces, behind which the apartments were recessed.
11. The unbuilt Mikveh Israel Synagogue (1961–72).

Lecture to the Boston Society of Architects

open and has no glass. The chamber can look out to the light, but not be in the glare. And also, the spaces are used as stairways and also galleries for the women (this is an orthodox synagogue). Even the chapel and the community building which is a rather modest building has a principle of chorus which copies the idea of the synagogue chambers.

This next one is a model of the chamber showing the interior light and the exterior windows which are glazed. Again, the light and the modification of the light are considered as a major architectural element which you compose with. These windows do not do any supporting. What does the supporting is that which is next to the window, but not the window. This is because only one point of the window could do that.

Again, elementally thinking, because you can ... support it on one edge of the round chamber. But still, in the way of composing elementally, you cannot except it.

This is an old drawing of the exterior showing the exterior windows. Here I have some idea also of windows on the outside which I've changed. Taking these other ones and learning from them to make something new.

That is the way I am considering it now. As being a sort of great overcoat which these windows really are. They are not anything that supports anything, they are self-supporting. And these windows on the exterior will be glazed. Incidentally, this door is pivoting on the top and bottom and is a triangular door which opens to allow free movement in, and then has doors within it to allow in bad weather entrance through the door itself. But I thought the scale of a door like that is appropriate to the chamber itself. This is the side of the chapel, and that's the synagogue.

Now here is the Plain of Dacca,[12] and what I've showed you here is changed from the hostels which were supposed to be hotel rooms for ministers, secretaries, members of the assembly, and judges, to studies in a garden on a lake. And I flanked the assembly by the lake. The mosque was here, and at that time it was rather a big thing. And the

12. Now Dhaka, Bangladesh.

Supreme Court was near the other buildings. And this was the center of the institutions, because I felt that an assembly really produces the institutions of man. These were just basic institutions which are placed across. This is the legislative center of the capital of Pakistan. And that is in Dacca in East Pakistan. This is a village which will be turned over for a house that is included in this thousand-acre sight.

This shows the present state of development with the hostels here and the assembly (some buildings here). Now I've changed the Supreme Court to this location, and here is the library, and here is the secretariat, also are the hostels, garden, square, and other institutions. There is a hospital, and house along here, which are still not started.

This shows the general configurations of the assembly. The requirements are numerous. The search for the light causes these shapes to exist. The center area is also fitted out with the means of keeping light inward on the interior areas. Here is a lake, and there are the hostels, and this is the Presidential Garden.

It indicates the light search. Even these buildings have a wall in front to shield the light off the office wings. It isn't, in my opinion, the best scheme with just the wall added. But if it can only be made so that it is an integral part, it is indestructible. Of course, in this case you can take the wall away and say you can not afford it, but if you can make it so that it is tied in with the structure you must be able to afford it. Again it is a weakness in my opinion.

The plan of the assembly is a mosque here which turns slightly to the west. I made it differently that way so that you could, in fact, express this differently. The office spaces are on the sides, and here are some lounges and other requirements. This is another entrance which is the people's entrance on the gardens here. Here is the mosque which is a common entrance so you can walk through the mosque. The assembly is in the middle. These light wells that come down are really the elements, you might say, that puts anything left over into the other spaces. This is elementally thought out.

This is one of the elements I speak about. This is crossed by stairways and other requirements. This makes the opening and the wall to ease themselves into repose. But that is the general idea. And then the stiffening is made also by stairways and other ways that come across on the interior. This concrete is made in five-foot pours with a marble insert every five feet, and this covers the point of termination of the pour, and also acts as a wash on the outside (there is three hundred inches of rain there) every five feet on the building. This is so the building does not get damp throughout from the water that is above. Every five feet determines its own water stop. That is the general theory behind the making of the concrete. It also works with their economy and their way of pouring concrete because they have no machines. They just have a swarm of bees, people, and you don't see what the work has been during the day until they leave. For this reason they are also using sticks instead of vibrators.[13] The idea of controlling the length of pour was part of the design.

This shows . . . below the Presidential Square. There is brick construction, arches, here. And they also face west which is the center mosque below the square. It is inspired by the mosque at [Cordoba], which is such a beautiful mosque. There it gave heart, talking about tradition, and the work was very inspiring.

This shows the structure of [the] square covering this area I just showed you where there could be some gathering with the steps going down into the garden. And these are the interior spaces which lead to the people's entrances and beyond to a lounge which is above. Here are the big openings of the interior. These openings are thirty-five feet across. I've changed this design to something which I think is better. Though changing too often has ill effects.

Here is a drawing of the mosque which shows the position of the five-foot marble strips. The mosque has no windows, and gets its light from drums which are to the side of it. Rain pours down, but it is free of rain on the interior. The light is gotten by the reflection on the walls in the interior. This keeps the mosque cool. . . .

This is a general aspect and an early drawing of the architecture of the hostels. The hostels are in brick and the assembly is in concrete.

Here is the plan of Ahmedabad School of Business Management

13. To help the concrete settle evenly.

which is patterned school-wise after the School of Business Management at Harvard.[14] Here is the school, here are the dormitories, here is the lake, the teachers' houses and the servant houses. Most of these are existing trees that are just groves of mango. The dormitories are really houses which have no corridors. They have an entrance with other facilities in a little corner there. They enter a triangular place which is a tea room, and from the tea room you enter your room. It's studying the principle of the school being case-study minded; no lectures, the lectures are just inspired out of case studies. All the dormitories are also places where people can meet.

So the dormitories and the school are really one; they are not separated. It is within the University of Ridgeerat, which is around this place.[15] Everything is relentlessly adhered to the direction of the wind. Nothing is given in to that importance.

Shows again a picture of it, this is that utility thing. Here you can visualize this little triangular area here which is quite large which enters these spaces and the separation between them. The difference in level between this and that is ten feet. This is also somewhat higher than these dormitories along here. So at the water edge, since you do not enter on the level at this point, but you enter at the level above, you have three stories of building but two stories of dormitory. At this point you have four stories of building and two stories of dormitory, and below is a club room at each point. Each house can have a kind of relationship this way, and it is the club room which is also a place of invitation for everyone in the campus. They have their own kitchen and they have everything of their own. There are many kinds of Indian cultures which are represented here. The idea is to cross any class consciousness here, and I hope that they certainly are successful.

This is from early sketches I have made which show the possible lakefront details. I have since changed them, but they are drawings I still like to look at even though it is far from what I am going to do.

This shows another one, much more elaborate, in which I've tried

---

14. The Indian Institute of Management (1962–74), Ahmedabad.
15. Kahn was referring to Gujarat University in Ahmedabad.

to make a kind of miscellaneous scene here which I've soon abandoned in favor of something a little stronger than just the cutting up into little pieces and making little doilies out of architecture.

Here is what it looks like. I want to introduce to you an idea here. This is a brick and concrete order. It is a composite order[16] in which the brick and the concrete are acting together not only in the floors but also I am making flat arches which are restrained by concrete members. It more extends the idea of concrete entering the brickwork. I understand today there is much work on walls and concrete combining to make structures. It is more consciously done, and I think there could be a composite brick and concrete order established, and I tried to do it here with these restraining members. I have some sketches which show more about this. Now these buttress areas are back of arches, and this is the water. All of this will be water on which these buildings will stand. You see this double space is a club room, and the dormitories are here. Each dormitory room is actually distinguished by its own construction.

It is my belief that structure is the beginning of life, and that structure is already a decision in life. When the walls were thick, and an opening was made through the wall for the first time, the wall cried and said, "What are you doing to me. I am a wall and I am protecting you. Why are you making an opening?" The man hesitatingly complained about this complaint and said, "I must look out. I feel as though I've got enough protection." And the wall was very dissatisfied until the opening was made to discern them, and became part of the order of the wall. The stones were more discerningly made, and the windows were placed over it. The wall was very happy that it could have something other than just itself included in what its powers were. And then came the column. The column was really the beginning of architecture in my opinion, because it made a very distinct picture of what is light, and what is not light. And so, the rhythm of light and no

16. Kahn claimed to have invented a brick-and-concrete composite "order"—brick in the form of arches with concrete beams and footings acting as buttresses—while working on the Indian Institute of Management.

light given by the column gave also birth to the arch, the vault, and all other devices which came out of the realization that you can have a support which is designated, instead of something that you rob or just simply modify by some aesthetic notion at the moment.

It is with this feeling too, that I believe that you can't make a big space and then divide it into little pieces. You make a big space when you have a big space, and the effort of the big space calls for a big effort. And a small space only calls for a little effort. I am not so sure that I hold to the law of space. I think it really is not truly architecture. And I am not so sure that the architects' duty really is not to build all the buildings in the world, but just build their fifty percent if they can do that effectively, and I don't think they can. I think the effective part of it is probably one percent, and they are the guides to what builders should do. Whatever the architect indicates should be the inspiration for the builder. An architect who has too much work proves to himself that he is unable to do it. It takes too much thought, and there are too few of us. Going back to this, I would like to extend the idea of the order which is behind this which was a brick and concrete order.

This is unfortunately very black, and you can see they are made from photographs. There are large openings here. I made these large openings because there are earthquake conditions, and actually the arch below is just as important as the arch above. You have a gravity force, but you also have a force this way. I thought that was expressed. I tried to carry it out, and I think I showed many weaknesses in places where I couldn't find the answer.

These are houses. This shows this opening. That's fairly big, and it is about eighteen feet across.

That is a central area. Here are some of the interior areas which shows the beginning of the buttresses. These are the club rooms which just come out actually of structural necessity. The shape of it is almost made sort of naturally out of that above.

This shows the outer view of where the stairway is and this is included, but it is not in the room itself. It does open into the space— here is the round opening again.

Here it shows the houses on one side across the water which seems very close but actually is some distance. Some of these arches of experimentation I've left in the gardens of these houses so that one can use them as playgrounds. And there are quite a number of experiments I had to make because the attitude towards brickwork was very low in India. It is really a mud attitude; it was mud to begin with and had to end up so. And believe me the brick is quite good if only you put one brick over the other. It is quite as simple as this. So I sat around with a great big hat and learned to chew words like "aurgoo-do" to mean "that is good."

This shows the houses, and again these restraining members across here. You may criticize as being unnecessary, and the ones on the end as being necessary. But this makes the possibility of being a very flat arch and no need of brickwork behind it. Because the thrust, you see, is taken care of by the restraining member. In this way it gives a large opening which you need, and takes it away from brickwork of old. It is a realization of this that carries on.

Water will be here, and the houses are here.

I think this shows the area of the tea rooms. There is that utility tower. The stairway which is up on the roof. Some of these arches you see the way the building is made is manifested on the exterior. This arch is actually the way you build this exterior wall. I could have chosen to have a wall just to take over as a wall, but no, I chose to show the arch, and then fill the arch. It was the teacher working and made me not to argue with the teacher.

This shows fairly clearly the workmanship which is rough, but I think very acceptable. These are all cast in place. I wanted a brick cast, but they couldn't do it. You can't lift one of those things, and must be placed in position.

These are all porches which are necessary. Here is the school. The school has a court, and the court has a library to the side, and here are all the classrooms around which are sort of seminars. Here are the offices along here, and over here is a dining room. And then are the residual spaces of course slyly chosen. These also become a stage which I made to relate to a little outdoor sitting place which would have a canopy over it. The next drawing indicates it more clearly.

There are the classrooms, and here are the offices. Here is that theater in here. I modified this considerably because it is rather complex, and is unnecessarily so.

These are some of the models of the architecture extending the idea of the arches and the restraining members and what can be done with it. And it just rather automatically comes about.

These are the offices, these are the classes. There are seminar rooms and gardens above. The seminar rooms are tucked in here.

I have this because I thought it would remind you of a Greek temple, which is a good thing to be reminded of. I have every feeling that Corbusier really wanted to build a new Parthenon. I feel at least also that he thinks in terms of the Greek architecture. He thinks in terms of material. I would never have thought of material first. I'd think of the nature of something, see the emergence of what kind of institution it would be. But how right it is to think about material! How right to have found that the material inspires. Certainly a monument that is thought of in concrete and then thought of also as carving names in concrete is a man completely insensitive. You would have chips of pebbles flying in your face when you carve the statements of a great president. Then also if you'd asked the president if he would like to carve it he would say certainly no I want to think it over and maybe write it differently.

I show this one Cruikshank[17] because I think that it is a very wonderful indication of something very elemental as well. (I was thinking of something totally different.) What I was thinking of was the idea that a stroke is that where the light is not. And everywhere where the light is, the stroke is not. And how religiously the direction of the light also directs to the direction of the stroke to express this. Where you are released from this by movement which tends to disturb it are the lines which subtly change. And where the light is not you have freedom. How religious the thing is.

---

17. George Cruikshank (1792–1878) was an immensely popular nineteenth-century etcher, caricaturist, and illustrator of innumerable English magazines and books.

The same is true of this drawing. Where everything that moves with the wind seems be done in the same direction. What is stable, is not. And where there is a flame where no detail should exist, there is no detail whatsoever except the direction of the flame.

Here are some arches which I'm dealing with a four-story structure which is next to the two-story structure in the hostels now. Again the play of arches are released by the mere realization that there is a composite order of concrete and brick.

Shows again in the hostels I have stairs which go in between walls. And here the underside. I think this could have been less up here, and more here.

The next slide indicates something of the reversed arch. Because Leonardo in his sketchbook says, "In the remedy for earthquakes if you reverse the arches." I found this book, I must say, after I thought of this, but nevertheless it was very heartwarming to see this wonderful page.

Here is the one that shows the arches much deeper than the ones above.

14 Space and the Inspirations (1967)

• •

Architecture, Kahn said, is "the thoughtful making of spaces" and that "what man makes, nature cannot." Humanity's creations originate in "the desire to be, to express a prevalence of spirit enveloping the Universe." In a sense, therefore, a work of art is not exclusively its maker's because it also belongs to the "in-common-ness" of humanity—that is, to humanity's omnipresent desire to understand itself. So when Kahn writes "Bach is/Thus music is," he means that human creativity simply *is;* where it came from and why matters not at all. Thus art *is,* and though inspired by the temporal and spatial circumstances conditioning its creation, over time it enters the "golden dust" of tradition as an offering to the human spirit.

Following is a transcript of a speech (with minor corrections) given at the New England Conservatory of Music (Boston) symposium on "The Conservatory Redefined."

I sense that this conference is dedicated to the wonders of expression and to the inspirations which bring the urges to express. Inspiration is the feeling of beginning at the threshold where Silence and Light meet: Silence, with its desire to be, and Light, the giver of all presences. This, I believe, is in all living things; in the tree, in the rose, in the microbe. To live is to express. All inspirations serve it. The inspiration to learn comes from the story etched in us of how we were made; and urges us to discover its wonders which encompass unmeasurable desire and measurable law. Institutions of learning must have begun from a commonness of urge that they be established. Here the minds

• •

From "LIK Lectures 1969 [*sic*]" folder, Box LIK 53, Kahn Collection.

are gathered to offer each singular sense of beginning, one to the other. Expression is honored only as Art, the transcendent language.

He who sees another walk with grace, and aspires to that beauty, feels the commonness of spirit in Art. He feels its validity, yet recognizes its unmeasurableness. Physical validity invites measurement by nature's unconscious unchangeable laws. The record of the rock is in the rock. Each grain of sand is in its exact place, is of the exact size and color. Conscious rule invites constant change to new comprehensive levels of Rule. The laws of nature are in the making of all things. Man's indefinable desire to make a house or to shape a stone or to compose a sonata still must obey the laws of nature in their making.

I think of Form as the realization of a nature, made up of inseparable elements. Form has no presence. Its existence is in the mind. If one of its elements were removed its form would have to change. There are those who believe the machine will eventually take the place of the mind. There would have to be as many machines as there are individuals. Form precedes Design. It guides its direction for it holds the relation of its elements. Design gives the elements their shape, taking them from their existence in the mind to their tangible presence. In composing, I feel that the elements of the form are always intact, though they may be constantly undergoing the trials of design in giving each its most sympathetic shape. Form is not concluded in presence, for its existence is of psychological nature. Each composer interprets Form singularly. Form, when realized, does not belong to its realizer. Only its interpretation belongs to the artist. Form is like order. Oxygen does not belong to its discoverer. It is my feeling that living things and nonliving things are dichotomous. Yet Nature, the giver of all presences, without question or choice, can anticipate desire by the fathomless marvel of its laws. It has given us the instruments to play the song of the soul. But I feel that if all living plants and creatures were to disappear, the sun would still shine and rain still fall. We need Nature, but Nature doesn't need us.

Architecture has no presence, Music has no presence—I mean of course, the spirit of architecture and the spirit of music. Music in this sense, as in Architecture, favors no style, no method, no technology—

this spirit is recognized as Truth. What does exist is a work of architecture or a work of music which the artist offers to his art in the sanctuary of all expression, which I like to call the Treasury of the Shadows, lying in that ambiance, Light to Silence, Silence to Light. Light, the giver of presence, casts its shadow which belongs to Light. What is made belongs to Light and to Desire.

In the teaching of Architecture I feel there are three aspects: Professional, Personal, Inspirational. Practice relates to professional responsibilities requiring knowledge, experience, business, regulations, science and technology to make a workable design. The person as an individual looks for the signs of dedication to his art and its nature. He looks for the nature in the painter, the sculptor and the musician, in the movie maker, the printer and in the typist. Here the teacher is distinguished from the instructor. He looks for the expressive powers of his art: Art as the making of a life. It comes from Life.

When a great composition again presents itself, it is as though someone you know well entered the room, someone you still had to see again to know. Because of its unmeasurable qualities, it must be heard and again heard. This, I believe, is the part of education where a man's work should not be judged. And if it is to be criticized, it should inspire constructive criticism. For example, I was asked to write a comment on the work of two 18th-century architects, Ledoux and Boullée.[1] When their drawings were shown to me for the first time (I mean the original drawings), I was struck by two impressions: of the enormous desire shown by their drawings to express the inspirational motivations of architecture, and of how outrageously out of scale they were with human use. But still they were highly inspiring. They were not projected to satisfy function or living in, but belonged to the challenge against narrow limits. For instance, a library by Boullée showed a room 150 feet high, books stacked high along its walls. The idea was to hand a book down to the man below, and so on,

1. Kahn's poem on Claude-Nicolas Ledoux and Étienne-Louis Boullée was published as "Twelve Lines" in *Visionary Architects: Boullée, Ledoux, Lequeu* (1967), the catalogue for an exhibition at the University of St. Thomas in Houston, Texas. Kahn discusses Boullée's "Project for a Public Library . . ." (c. 1785).

down to the reader, in a space without a table or chair. It would be very difficult, I think, to turn the first page in such a library. But still it was stupendous as a kind of audacity belonging to architecture. I wrote an introduction to the catalogue:

Spirit in will to express
can make the great sun seem small.
The sun is
Thus the Universe.
Did we need Bach
Bach is
Thus music is.
Did we need Boullée
Did we need Ledoux
Boullée is
Ledoux is
Thus Architecture is.

I walked up a high flight of stairs to my studio which I share with Le Ricolais and Norman Rice at the University of Pennsylvania.[2] I often stop at the intermediate landing where plates are hung showing architecture, painting and sculpture. Here I met one of the fine teachers of sculpture, Bob Engman, out of Yale, where I too began my teaching. He was standing with his back to me, very sturdy figure indeed—you know him—and I put my elbow on his shoulder and said "What do you see in this old stuff?"—(pointing to a display of Egyptian sculpture)—and he turned to me with a knowing grin expressing without words its wonder. Then with words "Isn't it marvelous . . . such beauty . . . what insight," all words less than his expression. And then I said to him, "Bob, I gave thought to two words: Existence and Presence." Art embodies both. The one speaks of the spirit, the other of the tangible.

Architecture can be said to be the thoughtful making of spaces.

2. Robert Le Ricolais and Norman Rice were colleagues at the University of Pennsylvania.

The Pantheon is a marvelous example of a space projected out of desire to give a place for all worship. It is expressed beautifully as a nondirectional space, where only inspired worship can take place. Ordained ritual would have no place. The ocular opening in the top of the dome is the only light. The light is so strong as to feel its cut.

The domain of Architecture has limit. Within its walls of limit all other activities of man exist, but the emphasis is on Architecture. The domain Business within the walls of its limit has also architecture but the emphasis is on Business. All buildings, therefore, do not belong to Architecture. The Pantheon is an example of what is made in the domain Architecture and not in the domain Market Place. It expresses uninfluenced directions toward the making of its space as an institution of man, as it would direct the making of a place of learning, a place of government, a place of the home, places of well-being, giving them each the space environment aspiring to their dedications. They are places which express what man desires to establish, and give form to a way of life. The inspiration to learn gives rise to all the institutions of learning. The inspirations to express give rise to all places of religion, in which Art is probably the greatest of its languages.

You in music, as we in architecture, are interested in structure. To me the structure is the maker of the light. When I choose an order of structure which calls for column alongside of column, it presents a rhythm of no light, light, no light, light, no light, light. A vault, a dome, is also a choice of a character of light. To make a square room, is to give it the light which reveals the square in its infinite moods. To get light is not just making a hole in a wall, nor is it the selection of a beam here and there to frame the roof. Architecture creates a feeling of a world within a world, which it gives to the room. Try to think of the outside world when you're in a good room with a good person. All your senses of outside leave you. I'm reminded of a beautiful poem by Rumi, the great Persian who lived in the early 13th century.[3] He tells of a priestess walking through her garden. It is spring. She

3. Jalal ad-Din Rumi was a thirteenth-century Islamic mystic poet, storyteller and teacher. Kahn may have read portions of his six-volume *Mathnawi*.

stops at the threshold of her house and stands transfixed at the entrance chamber. Her maid-in-waiting comes to her excitedly, saying "Look without, look without, Priestess, and see the wonders God has made." The priestess answered "Look within and see God." It's marvelous to realize that a room was ever made. What man makes, nature cannot make, though man uses all the laws of nature to make it. What guides it to be made, the desire to make it, is not in universal nature. Dare I say that it is of Silence, of lightless, darkless desire to be, to express a prevalence of spirit enveloping the Universe.

When I see a plan before me, I see it for the character of the spaces, and their relations. I see it as the structure of the spaces in their light. A musician seeing a work must have immediate sense of its Art. He knows the concept from its design, and from his own sense of psychological order. He senses the inspirations from his own desires.

I feel fusion of the senses. To hear a sound is to see its space. Space has tonality, and I imagine myself composing a space lofty, vaulted, or under a dome, attributing to it a sound character alternating with the tones of a space, narrow and high, with graduating silver, light to darkness. The spaces of architecture in their light make me want to compose a kind of music, imagining a truth from the sense of a fusion of the disciplines and their orders. No space, architecturally, is a space unless it has natural light. Natural light has varied mood of the time of the day and the season of the year. A room in architecture, a space in architecture, needs that life-giving light—Light from which we were made. So the silver light and the gold light and the green light and the yellow light are qualities of changeable scale or rule. This quality must inspire music.

I am designing an art museum in Texas.[4] Here I felt that the light in the rooms structured in concrete will have the luminosity of silver. I know that rooms for the paintings and objects that fade should only most modestly be given natural light. The scheme of enclosure of the museum is a succession of cycloid vaults each of a single span 150 feet long and 20 feet wide, each forming the rooms with a narrow slit to

4. Kimbell Art Museum (1966–72), Fort Worth, Texas.

the sky, with a mirrored glass shaped to spread natural light on the side of the vault. This light will give a glow of silver to the room without touching the objects directly, yet give the comforting feeling of knowing the time of day. Added to the skylight from the slit over the exhibit rooms, I cut across the vaults, at a right angle, a counterpoint of courts, open to the sky, of calculated dimensions and character, making them Green Court, Yellow Court, Blue Court, named for the kind of light that I anticipate their proportions, their foliation, or their sky reflections on surfaces, or on water will give.

A student of mine came to my room, which is, by the way, everybody's room, and asked me a question: "How would you describe this era?" I was terribly interested. Reflecting, I said to him, "What is the shadow of white light?" Repeating and reflecting on what I said, "White light, white light, the shadow of white light" (he whispered), "I don't know." I answered, "It's black. But really there is no such thing as white light, black shadow. I was brought up, of course, when light was 'yellow' and shadow was 'blue.' White light is a way of saying that even the sun is on trial, and certainly all our institutions are on trial."

I feel that in the present revolt against our institutions and ways, that there is no Wonder. Without Wonder the revolt looks only to equality. Wonder motivates Desire toward Need. Demands for equality of means can rise only to the trade of old lamps for new without the genii. I feel when Wonder is, the light will become a brighter yellow and the shadow a brighter blue.

I am trying to find new expressions of old institutions. The institutions of learning, let us say, with which we are so concerned today, probably began with a man under a tree, and around him the listeners to the words of his mind. The marvel of the first classroom never leaves me, and now I approach a problem with the desire for the sense of beginnings. I think we need in all schools reverence for the marvels of the beginnings. At this conference we are to speak on the learning of art. The professional, personal and spiritual facets of its realms will be presented to us. I feel that ideas presented based on new realizations must be free of the influences of the circumstantial.

And now, I must tell you the last story which is about meeting a

Space and the Inspirations

man, a wonderful architect of Mexico.[5] As I walked through his house I felt the character of "House"—good for him and good for anyone at any time during its lifetime. It tells you that the artist only seeks truth and that what is traditional or contemporary has no meaning to the artist. His gardens are conceived as personal places not to be duplicated. It gives one the sense that when a garden is made that all drawings for its making must be destroyed. The garden itself survives as the only authentic reality, which must wait for its maturity to realize the spirit of its creation. Later we gathered in good company and he asked me the question: "What is tradition?" This point was brought up earlier today. For the moment I didn't know how to answer except that I had the desire to answer his question, because his outstanding singularity induced a generative sense. I said, "Yes, my mind goes to the Globe Theatre in London. Shakespeare had just written *Much Ado About Nothing*, which was to be performed there. I imagined myself looking at the play through a hole in the wall of the structure, and was surprised to see that the first actor attempting his part fell as a heap of dust and bones under his costume. To the second actor the same happened, and so to the third and fourth, and the audience reacting also fell as a heap of dust. I realized that circumstance can never be recalled, that what I was seeing then was what I could not see now. And I realized that an old Etruscan mirror out of the sea, in which once a beautiful head was reflected had still with all its encrustation the strength to evoke the image of that beauty. It's what man makes, what he writes, his painting, his music, that remains indestructible. The circumstances of their making is but the mold for casting. This led me to realize what may be Tradition. Whatever happens in the circumstantial course of man's life, he leaves as the most valuable, a golden dust which is the essence of his nature. This dust, if you know this dust, and trust in it, and not in circumstance, then you are really in touch with the spirit of tradition. Maybe then one can say that tradition is what gives you the powers of anticipation from which you know what will last when you create.

5. Luis Barragan, whose residence and studio in Mexico City Kahn visited.

15 Silence and Light
(1968, 1969)

Once again, two quite different speeches with the same name and complementary themes. Kahn discussed "silence" and "light" in "Space and the Inspirations" (selection 14), but here he elaborates. Silence is a void, not a place but the desire—a "commonality," he calls it in these texts—of every person to create, which for Kahn was the same thing as being alive. Light was "the giver of all presences," themselves "spent light." He meant, quite literally, that light enabled people to see and experience space and structure: No light meant no architecture. Shadow is not the absence of light but the result of its interplay with material, hence "the shadow belongs to the light." On a more figurative level Kahn was thinking of the sun, the source of all life, thus the ultimate creator. To the silence of humanity's innate urge to create comes the sun's life-supporting power, giving to silence the ability to act. It is no accident that Kahn's libraries, institutions of learning, art musuems, government and religious facilities—all places of contemplation, social intercourse, and creative achievement—were so saturated with natural light.

The December 3, 1968, version of "Silence and Light" was delivered at the Solomon R. Guggenheim Museum in New York. Slightly modified, it was published in 1970 in the museum's *On the Future of Art*. The February 12, 1969, version was delivered at Eidgenössiche Technische Hochschule, Zurich. Under the same or similar titles and in different forms, this talk was published in whole or in part in several countries and languages, becoming one of Kahn's most widely disseminated texts.

First text from "LIK Lectures 1969 [sic]" folder, Box LIK 53, Kahn Collection; second text from Heinz Ronner and Sharad Jhaveri, Louis I. Kahn: *Complete Works, 1935–1974*, 2d rev. ed. (Basel: Birkhäuser, 1987), 6–9.

228

SILENCE AND LIGHT I

Let us go back in time to the building of the pyramids. Hear the din of industry in a cloud of dust marking their place. Now we see the pyramids in full presence. There prevails the feeling "Silence," from which is felt Man's desire to express. This before the first stone was laid.

I note when a building is being made, free of servitude, that the spirit to be is high allowing not a blade of grass in its wake. When it stands complete and in use it seems like it wants to tell you about the adventure of its making. But all parts locked to serve makes this story of little interest. When its use is spent and it becomes a ruin, the wonder of its beginning appears again. It feels well to have itself entwined in foliage, once more high in spirit and free of servitude.

I sense Light as the giver of all presences, and material as spent light. What Light makes casts a shadow and the shadow belongs to Light. The mountain is of Light, its shadow belongs to Light. I sense Threshold, Light to Silence, Silence to Light, the ambiance—Inspiration, wherein the desire to be, to express, crosses with the possible. The rock, the stream, the wind inspires the will to express, to seek the means of imparting presence. The beautiful in the material is transformed from wonder to knowing which in turn is transformed to the expression of beauty that lies in the desire to express. Light to Silence, Silence to Light cross in the ambient sanctuary Art. Its Treasury knows no favorite, knows no style. Truth and rule out of Commonness, Law out of Order, are the offerings within.

Architecture without presence exists as the realization of a spirit. A work of architecture is made as an offering touching its nature. So also one can say that the realms Painting, Sculpture, Literature, exist in spirit, their natures revealed more by works unfamiliar. The mention of the unfamiliar is the recognition of the singularity of every individual in attitude and talent. But above all the phenomena of realizations of a nature from a singular point of view reveals new images of the same nature. So it is in Nature that diversity of forms evolve from universal order.

Form is the recognition of an integrity of inseparable elements. This is true of Art and Nature. In Nature validity is nonconscious. Every grain of sand on the beach is its natural color and shape, is of natural weight and in its only position. It is part of the constant play of equilibria solely governed by the laws of nature. What man makes, yes, must answer to the laws of nature but is governed in his concepts by rules and choice. The one is measurable. The one is completely unmeasurable. What nature makes it makes without man, and what man makes nature cannot make without him. Nature does not make a house. It cannot make a room. How marvelous that when in a room with another soon the mountains, trees, wind and the rain leave us for the mind and the room becomes a world in itself. With only another person one feels generative. The meeting becomes an event. The actor throws aside his lines of performance. The residue from all his thoughts and experiences meets the other on the equal terms. Even now, though I feel I am saying things differently than I have said before, I have thought about them and is therefore not essentially generative. The room is then a marvelous thing.

Architecture primarily deals with the making of spaces which serve the institutions of Man. In the aura Silence to Light, the desire to be, to make, to express, feels the laws that confirm the possible. Avid then is the desire to know, heralding the beginning of the Institutions of Learning, dedicated really to discover how we were made. In Man is the record of Man. Man through his consciousness feels this record sparking his desire to learn that which Nature has given him and what choices he made to protect his desires and self-preservation in the Odyssey of his emergence.

I feel that consciousness is in all life. It is in the rose, in the microbe, in the leaf. Their consciousness is not understandable to us. How much more would we comprehend if he were to uncover their secrets, for then a wider sense of Commonness would enter expressions in Art giving the artist greater insight in presenting his offerings answering to the prevalence of Order, the prevalence of Commonness.

Dissension is in the open. I do not feel that its roots come from need alone. Dissension down deep stems from desire—desire for the yet not made, yet not expressed. Need comes from the known. Giving what is lacking brings no lasting joy. Did the world need the Fifth Symphony before Beethoven wrote it? Did Beethoven need it? He desired it and the world needs it. Desire brings the new need.

I look at the glancing light, which is such a meaningful light on the side of the mountain bringing every tiny natural detail to the eye and teaches about the material and choice in making a building. But do I get less delight out of seeing a brick wall with all its attempts at regularity, disclosing its delightful imperfections in natural light? A wall is built in hope that a light once observed may strike it even for but a rare moment in time. How can anyone think of a building of spaces not in natural light? Schools are being built with little and without natural light, the reasons given of savings in conditioning costs and pupils greater attention to the teacher. The most wonderful aspects of the indoors are the moods that light gives to space. The electric bulb fights the sun. Think of it.

I am reminded of Tolstoy who deviated from faithlessness to Faith without question. In his latter state he deplored the miracles saying that Christ has radiance without them. They were like holding a candle to the Sun to see the Sun better.

Structure is the maker of light. A column and a column brings light between. It is darkness—light, darkness—light, darkness—light. From the column we realize a simple and beautiful evolvement of rhythmic beauty from the primitive wall and its openings. Walls were thick. They protected man. He felt the desire for freedom and the promises of the outside. He made at first a rude opening. He explained to the unhappy wall his realizations that a wall in accepting an opening must follow a greater order bringing arches and piers to it as new and worthy elements. These are realizations in the nature Architecture of Light and Structure. The choice of a square room is also the choice of its light as distinguished from other shapes and their light. I should like to say that even a room which must be dark must have at least a crack of light to know how dark it is. But Architects in planning rooms today have forgotten the faith in natural light depending on the touch of a finger on a switch satisfied with only static light compared to the endlessly changing qualities of natural light in which a room is a different room every second of the day.

I spoke of Form as the realizations of a nature. A shape is derived as an expression of Form. Form follows Desire as a realization of a dream or a belief. Form tells of inseparable elements. Design is the infighting to develop these elements into shapes compatible with each other reaching for a wholeness, for a name. Form in the mind of one is not the same as it is in an other. Realizations of a nature, to Form, to shape is not a process of design manipulation. In design there are wonderful realizations. The order of structure, the order of construction, the order of time, the order of spaces come into play.

As I see a sheet of music, I realize that the musician sees it to hear. To an architect the plan is a sheet on which appears the order of the structure of spaces in their light.

The institutions of learning give a program of requirement to the architect. These requirements are derived from previous plans answering momentary needs. Farther and farther are these needs from the beginning spirit School. The architect must consider the program only as a measurable guide. The spirit in the sense of its conceived Commonness, School, should be considered as though it is coming to realization for the first time.

Recently our class agreed to speculate on what is a University. There was no program. We thought of its nature. The minds were empty of knowing and full of adventure. One student gave emphasis to the central library as the place of the dedication of the mind. It was felt also that the libraries of the professions should be related to the main library by a conscious Architecture of Connection. The University's most direct service to the community is the sanctioning of the professions. But we were distressed because we realized that the University was gradually falling into the sphere of the market place competing with other schools for specific research money and the invention of composite degrees to attract students. Architecture was being isolated from Urban Design and City Planning which discounted students with broad natural talents in architecture, who refuse to accept such distinctions for their profession.

In the marketplace the professions tend toward business which suppresses individual talent whose leadership has always been followed. The architect can only keep realizing the spirit of his art and realize the emerging orders when the problems before him are all-comprising. Relegated to niches of specialization he will become part of a team, design parts, and give the world nothing but solutions of the needs, never free or experienced to guide prevailing desires to inspirations. Though I feel that unique talent cannot be overthrown, it is hurt by being retarded. Talent has to be recognized early to do good work.

The architecture of connection, Library to Library, developed thoughts about significant places found in its path. The garden became inseparable from the room, the court, the entrance place of invitation, the green or the great court as the place of the happening.

Dissension made us think of a place or a structure yet not named but needed as a place of the teacher, student and the directors. Like the Stoa it would not be partitioned and its position on the campus would be on a great lawn with not a path crossing it. Later division would be agreed upon and the lawn modified by the use it evokes.

Then it was thought that a University has much to gain from the city which in turn may consider the University as one of its most important institutions. Professional practice is in the marketplace. The University in sanctioning the professions should be free of it. This brought to mind the role of the city planner. We realized that there must be a place free of the University and free of the marketplace in a forum where both could meet. The visions of planners meet the political economy of the city. This should be recognized as a new institution of man equal to the Institutions of Government, of Learning, and of Health.

The city is measured by its institutions. The growth is felt through the works of its leaders sensitive to the desires of the people and to serve their desire of expression. The studies leading to the emergence of new institutions become the points of departure for planning. Movement plans and redevelopment schemes are merely corrective projects. The known institutions need new vitality, conscious recognition. As an example of current deterioration think of City Hall evolved from the early meeting place. It is probably the most dishonored building in the city. A place associated with taxes, fees, courts and jails where nobody meets. Since the meeting houses the interests of people have become greatly extended and diversified but they have no place to air their interests. A place of auditoria, meeting rooms and seminars would revive the spirit of representation and give every man a place which he feels is his own city house.

The inspirations assist us when we clear our senses of known solutions and methods. The realization of a yet unthought of nature and the elements of its form can stimulate an entirely new point of view about everything. Today we talk about technology as though our minds will be surrendered to the machine. Surely the machine is merely a brain which we get as potluck from nature. But a mind capable of realization can inspire a technology, and humiliate the current one.

Teaching is a work. The beginning is dear to the teacher for he senses what man is from what he accepts and is willing to support. The code of the teacher is often remote from the other man. He seeks therefore, because of his desire to tell about his mind, words that are as close to his code as he can think of yet not to lose their generativeness. I have used "Commonness" instead of "Spirit" for that very reason. Spirit is immediately assumed as understood. Commonness makes one think.

Art is the making of a life, when we hear the strains of a familiar musical masterpiece it is though one familiar entered the room. But still as you must see him again to believe his presence, so must the music be played again to remember all that touched you before.

In Mexico, I met Barragan.[1] I was impressed by his work because of its closeness to nature. His garden is framed by a high private wall, the land and foliage remaining untouched as he found it. In it is a fountain made by a water source lightly playing over a jagged splinter and drop for drop falling in a great native bowl of rhinoceros gray

1. Luis Barragan, whose 1947–50 house and studio in Mexico City Kahn visited.

black stone filled to the brim. Each drop was like a slash of silver making rings of silver reaching for the edge and falling to the ground. The water in the black container was a choice from the path of water as a mountain stream in light, over rocks, and then in deep seclusion where its silver was revealed. He learned about water and selected what he loved most.

His house is not merely a house but House itself. Anyone could feel at home. Its material is traditional; its character eternal. We talked about traditions as though they were mounds of the golden dust of man's nature and from which circumstances were distilled out. As man takes his path through experience he learns about man. The learning falls as golden dust, which if touched gives the power of anticipation. The artist has this power and knows the world even before it began. He expresses himself in terms of validities physiological.

A student asked, "What is the intuitive sense?" Robert Le Ricolais,[2] mathematician, engineer, and scientist, said: "What made man venture to make the first thing? Surely it was not his knowledge but his sense of validity. But intuition must be fed." I might say that everything must begin with poetry.

SILENCE AND LIGHT II

I'm going to put on the blackboard here what may seem at first to be very esoteric. But I believe that I must do it in order to prime myself. Don't forget that I'm also listening and I have really no prepared talk except that I put a few notes down just to get the scaredness out of me because, you know, this is like a blank piece of paper on which I've got to make a drawing. And so, the drawing is a talk this time, you see. It is wonderful to consider, you know, that you must see so well that you hear too. And sometimes it is well to hear so well that you see too. The senses really can be considered one thing. It all comes together. It is the reason why I constantly refer to music in referring to architec-

2. Kahn's colleague at the University of Pennsylvania.

ture, because to me there is no great difference—when you dig deep enough in the realm of not doing things but simply thinking what you want to do—that all the various ways of expression come to fore. To me, when I see a plan I must see the plan as though it were a symphony, of the realm of spaces in the construction and light. I sort of care less, you see, for the moment whether it works or not. Just so I know that the principles are respected which somehow are eternal about the plan. As soon as I see a plan which tries to sell me spaces without light, I simply reject it with such ease, as though it were not even thoughtfully rejected, because I know that it is wrong. And so, false prophets, like schools that have no natural light, are definitely unarchitectural. Those are what I like to call—belong to the marketplace of architecture but not to architecture itself.

So I must put on the board something which I thought on only recently which could be a key to my point of view in regard to all works of art including architecture.

And so, I put this on the board: Silence and Light. Silence is not very, very quiet. It is something which you may say is lightless, darkless. These are all invented words. Darkless—there is no such a word. But why not? Lightless, darkless. Desire to be, to express. Some can say this is the ambient soul—if you go back beyond and think of something in which light and silence were together, and maybe are still together, and separated only for the convenience of argument.

I turn to light, the giver of all Presences, by will, by law. You can say the light, the giver of all presences, is the maker of a material, and the material was made to cast a shadow, and the shadow belongs to the light.

I did not say things yet made here, desire being that quality, that force, unmeasurable force, everything here stems from the unmeasurable. Everything here promises the measurable. Is there a threshold where they meet? Can a threshold be thin enough to be called a threshold in the light of these forces, these phenomena? Everything you make is already too thick. I would even think that a thought is also too thick. But one can say, light to silence, silence to light, has to be a kind of ambient threshold and when this is realized, sensed, there is inspiration.

Inspiration must already have something of a promise of being able to express that which is only a desire to express, because the evidence of the material making of light gives already a feeling of inspiration. In this inspiration, beside inspiration, there is a place, the Sanctuary of Art, Art being the language of man before French, you know, or German. It says the language of man is art. It stems from something which grows out of the needing, of the desire to be, to express, and the evidence of the promise of the material to do it. The means somehow are there. The Sanctuary of Art—sort of the ambience of a man's expressiveness—has an outlet, you might say. It is my belief that we live to express. The whole motivation of presence is to express. And what nature gives us is the instrument of expression which we all know as ourselves, which is like giving the instrument upon which the song of the soul can be played. The sanctuary of art—I'm taking this little lesson to say that it is the treasury of the shadows.

I'm sure there is no such separation. I'm sure that everything began at the same time. There wasn't a time when it was good for one thing or another. It was simply something that began at the same time. And I would say the desire to be, to express, exists in the flowers, in the tree, in the microbe, in the crocodile, in man. Only we don't know how to fathom the consciousness of a rose. Maybe the consciousness of a tree is its feeling of its bending before the wind. I don't know. But I have definite trust that everything that's living has a consciousness of some kind, be it as primitive. I only wish that the first really worthwhile discovery of science would be that it recognizes that the unmeasurable, you see, is what they're really fighting to understand, and the measurable is only a servant of the unmeasurable, that everything that man makes must be fundamentally unmeasurable.

Now, of course if you see that, you wonder how you can make a dime—we call it a dime—but I'll say a franc. It certainly doesn't look to me as though you could make a franc out of that, unless you sell it to *Zodiac*,[3] you know. Well, maybe you can do it; but it is just part of

3. *Zodiac* was an architectural magazine published in Zurich.

an inner belief that you cannot evaluate a Giotto painting. It defies any analyzation, it defies measurement, because after all, Giotto gave us the prerogatives of painting. He said that to a painter, a doorway can be smaller than a person. But the architect must use a doorway that is bigger than a person. Is he less in art than the other? No. He just recognizes his realm of expression. The painter can paint people upside down, as Chagall does, as you know, but he has this prerogative because he's a painter. He's representing nothing; he's presenting everything. It's a presentation of the wide realm of expression which exists in man. A sculptor can make square wheels on a cannon to express the futility of war. Unfortunately, the architect must use round wheels if he wants to bring his stone from place to place. From this, you get the sense of that which tends to be in the marketplace, and that which never reaches the marketplace.

And this is, you might say, the crossroad, the place of realization; the place where one sort of senses, how much there, how much here, is the content. Giotto vibrates in this area, defies time. No time will ever say it's old-fashioned. Tremendous discoveries of expression lie in such a great man, as it did in other great men. The essential quality which I admire most in Einstein is that he was a fiddler. From this he derived much of his sense of the universal—or rather, you might say universal order was something that came to him from his sense of eternity, not from just his mathematical knowledge or the knowledge of science. Why didn't it reach the other fellow if knowledge was there, because it filters through everybody? Knowledge is available. It just happened to be in him, the knowledge of something else, and so it is in every one of us. Knowledge is very specifically something that belongs to each individual in his own way. The book of knowledge has never been written, nor will it ever be written for man. Certainly nature doesn't need it. It's already written for nature.

So let's talk a little bit about a problem that comes to a man as an architect. Suppose you were assigned to say—and what a wonderful commission it would be—what is a university. And, instead of being given a program—saying that a university should be for so many people, the library must have so many books, you have to have so many classrooms, you got to have a student center, and you have to have schools for the professions—think in terms of university as though it never happened, as though it isn't here. You have nothing to refer to, just the sense of a place of learning, an undeniable need: an *undeniable desire on the part of all of us that a place be for learning;* something which comes specially to someone who is willing to convey to others what is so special in him, and what becomes special in those who learn—in their own way special—as though a singularity taught singularities, because we're all singularities, and none of us are like the other. So consider a university. I gave this problem to the University of Pennsylvania, to my students. There was no program—well, I said, yes, consider the University of Pennsylvania as probably the seat, because somebody has to have something to put their hat on, so that was the only indication. Now one student—he was a German student—who in a very halting and most modest way said he believes the core of the University is the library, but a specific library. He said it was the central library. He said that the library of the university is like the Acropolis. It is the offering of the mind. And he considered that when you go into the library, and you see these books, you judge them as offerings of the mind. A man motivated not by profit of any kind—just a sense of offering—he writes a book, hoping that it will be published. He's trying to—he's motivated by the sense that he has somewhere in there, whether it is deep, deep in the silence, or whether it is already on the threshold of inspiration. He must be there to write it, and what he draws from here, and what he draws from there, somehow, he motivates his writing a book. And he gets it also from another, beautiful source, and that is through the experience or the Odyssey of a life that goes through the circumstances of living and what falls as important are not the dates or what happened, but in what way he discovered man through the circumstance. It's a golden dust that falls which, if you can put your fingers through, you have the powers of anticipation. The artist feels this when he makes something. He knows that he does it now, but he knows also that it has eternal value. He's not taking circumstances as it happens. He's extracting circumstances from whatever fell which revealed man to him. Tradition is just mounds of these circumstances, you see, the record of which also is a golden dust from which you can extract the nature of man, which is tremendously important if you can anticipate in your work that which will last—that which has the sense of commonness about it. And by commonness, I mean really, the essence of silence is commonness. That's the essence of it. When you see the pyramids now, what you feel is silence. As though the original inspiration of it may have been whatever it is, but the motivation that started that which made the pyramids, is nothing but simply remarkable. To have thought of this shape personifying a kind of perfection, the shape of which is not in nature at all, and striving with all this effort, beating people, slaves to the point of death to make this thing. We see it now with all the circumstances gone, and we see that when the dust is cleared, we see really silence again. So it is with a great work. I see a Giotto painting also with a feeling of silence—as though it came from here, you see—as though it didn't come from any sense of the marketplace. Like, I will make a painting that's worth so much money, you see, or anything of that nature. It came from there.

Going back to the university, then this was a center; it was something about the humanities that was really the university. Another part of it was that of the professions. This was the engagement of man in the various avenues of expression be he a doctor, or a lawyer, or an architect, or a bookkeeper, or a nurse because you want to, you have something that tells you to be a nurse, or something that tells you to be an architect. And the university position has nothing to do with the marketplace. The marketplace has to do with the way that which personifies this profession is practiced by the individual; this is something the university should not be concerned with, except to inspire him in the nature of his profession, and in what way he will, in the end, be the happiest in the exercise of this expression. Problems of the marketplace really do not belong there, because no matter how much you teach it, the tendency will be for the person to find his own way, *because a man does not really learn anything that's not part of himself.* He might try very hard. He may even pass examinations, but he'll never really be a chemist, even if he studies chemistry, unless he's a chemist from the very, very start. And so, therefore knowledge per se is to me very doubtful, you see. But knowledge taken to prime your way of expression is not; to develop a person's talent is not. Very good. Very wonderful. The place, the realm, within which the talent of people can be exercised.

So the university has nothing to do with the marketplace. It doesn't disdain it, because it gets its support from the marketplace; but it still doesn't teach it, because it's useless to teach it. To prepare you for nature's way yes. The laws of nature must be known, because there are three aspects in the teaching. There is a teaching of the professional position: responsibility to other people which includes the differentiation between science and technology, which are completely different things. And your specific knowledge that you need in statics or acoustics, those are all very necessary things and belong definitely in the realm of teaching, to prepare you for your responsibilities, conducting your office as a responsibility to society—yes, all these things—but there is another responsibility, and that is to teach the man to be himself, which is delving into the various talents which can be employed in the profession, not all having to do with design, not all with specification writing, but it somehow—all belongs to it. You're not teaching geniuses, you're just teaching, you know, actually; the nature of the profession, the many facets, you see, among which self-expression can come about. But the most important thing to teach is to know that architecture has no presence. You can't get a hold of architecture. It just has no presence. *Only a work of architecture has presence,* and a work of architecture is presented as an offering to architecture. Architecture has no favorites; it has no preferences in design; it has no preferences for materials; it has no preferences for technology. It just sits there waiting for a work to indicate again, to revive the spirit of architecture by its nature, from which people can live for many years.

And so the university is a sanction. The library of the sanction place, then, the places of the professions, the library of these professions are there, hooked up because there is also an offering of the mind, and this is somehow connected with the unit—with the more objective offering of the mind—which is the offering of the sanctuary, the Acropolis. You might say objective or subjective—it doesn't really matter. It's just offering. Now if you consider this, it must be put in mind differentiations of a wonderful kind. It brings in mind the difference between the garden, the court, and a piazza. Because your connections are not going to be just colonnades and that sort of thing, it's going to be mental—the connection. You're going to feed it in some way. But the consciousness of a planner that there is an association, a kind of interrespect between the two is already, guides the hand, you know, in saying it should be here, it should be there, it should be there, you see. Otherwise it becomes merely landscraping, I call it, you see. Not landscaping: landscraping. It is really a consciousness, not drawing around trees here and there or stamping them on your plan, you see—I hate that—really I do. So, the connection, then, is the realization of what is a garden, what is a court, what is an avenue, what is a piazza. A garden is a very private thing. You would say that the landscape architect, or the architect, or the gardener, who makes a plan for a garden with his fountains and places to sit, and the trees chosen in relation to porticos and so forth, should make the plan as an instruction for something that will grow into being, and once everything is established that will grow into being and it's full, after that he takes this plan and throws it into the fireplace and doesn't keep it as a record, because the next garden he makes must be completely different, because that garden is very, very private and belongs to the individual. It's not a place of invitation, it's a place of part of the expression of living. The court is different. The court is the boy's place. The court is already a place of invitation. I would like to call it the outside-inside space. It is a place which one feels that if he comes to, he can make a choice as to where he goes from there. And a piazza is man's place, much more impersonal, defined like a court. Playing with this so-called architecture of connection, which happens to have no rules, is a consciousness of the involvement of the land and the buildings, their association with the library. Now there are many things absent. It wasn't sufficient, just the connection. The class was very excited about one aspect which I hinted at, that there must be a place of happening. A place of happening, and you say why can't things happen the way they will. They don't have to. The Agora, for instance, was a place of happening—Agora, the Stoa. The Stoa was made most marvelously. It was made like this. No partitions, just columns, just protection. Things grew in it. Shops became. People met, meet, there. It's shaded. You present a quality, architectural, no purpose. Just a recognition of something which you can't define, but must be built. Today, the general unrest among students should call for this kind of space. You shouldn't try to fight a battle as to who's right and who's wrong, but should create the architectural interpretation of this, which is a place without partitions which will form themselves into partitions some day. So it is a recognition of a place where possibly the student, the administration, and the teacher would meet. It's a club of the university, not the student center, so to speak, but everybody's center, and it sits probably in a green area like this without paths whatsoever, because who knows where you're going. But that's a definite architectural quality. It has the same quality as all religious places, which also just by simple quality of knowing that a stone stands free, that it has something more than just simply singing at random or going through a forest and trying to jump. What is the feeling? It is something in the way of a mysterious decision to make Stonehenge. It's terrific. It's the beginning of architecture. It isn't made out of a handbook, you see. It doesn't start from practical issues. It starts from a kind of feeling that there must be a world within a world. The world where man's mind, you see, somehow becomes sharp. Have you ever said anything significant when you were outside waiting for a bus? Never. You said something significant inside a building, never outside a building. Did you ever say anything significant at a picnic? No. Well, you had a hell of a good time—I realize that, but you didn't say anything that was the mind saying. It was really quiet functioning as humans in the most sparkling, beautiful, amusing way, which is definitely a part of our lives, but it is not necessarily how buildings start. Buildings start as a kind of recognition that there must be a place of concentration where the mind, somehow, is given play. And I make a distinction between mind—and this might be put here too, because it doesn't belong here, but I'll put it here anyway—Mind and Brain. Brain is an instrument given by that fellow over there. Mind is this and the instrument. Somewhere in here is Mind. Mind is the instrument and the soul, Brain. Now this is Mind. Brain is—I would say the machines we make now, you see, for calculating, for putting into; I don't know what you call them, these computers—these are brains—never the mind. The mind makes it but it never will really give you anything that brain can do. And the men who really know the instrument, will tell you that themselves. It's the men who don't know it will tell you otherwise. It's like putting a penny in a slot and getting a very wonderful answer worth more than a penny. I'm afraid not.

So they discovered that this was a place of meeting of everyone, a very necessary thing. From this you recognize also that a school of architecture probably starts with a court, surrounded by shops, in which you build and tear down at will. It's a closed court because nobody really likes to show how badly he does things, so it becomes something which amongst your confrères is okay. Outside, not. It's not an exhibition place. There is no admission set for this thing—it's not this: it's closed. From this grows other things, spaces high and low, but it is a kind of area undetermined, spaces undetermined in their light, in various light, in various heights, and that you move around with a sense of discovering the spaces rather than being named for certain reasons. Actually they're just there and you feel it is a school of architecture because of how much concentration you put into the primitiveness, the fundamentalness with which you made these spaces. These are all, I think, indication of the tremendous opportunities that exist today in architecture. The discovery of the elements of our institutions which need revival, which need to be bolstered up, which need to be redefined.

Now, in the Congress Building in Venice I built,[4] I am thinking of building a place which is the meeting of the mind and a place where expressions of the meeting of the mind can take place. It is also a

4. It may be that Kahn was so intensely involved with his work that a project in design was, in his mind, already constructed. He labored over the Palazzo dei Congressi for two different Venetian sites from 1968 to 1974, but it was never built.

place of happening. I don't believe in inviting shows for the Biennale, saying, You come with your exhibit, bring your big packages, bring the things you've done, but rather say, Come here, meet other people, and by meeting them something will happen to you—and it will. Here in the Palazzo dei Congressi they meet to sense each other's mind. In the Biennale they meet to express something—actually, tangibly. It is somehow a place of existence, which I might put here. I'll put it here, existence here, and presence. You see presence is here, existence is here. It exists. You can feel the thought, but it doesn't have presence. When you describe, when you will say, "Oh! It's marvelous! It's beautiful! It's terrific! It's—it's immense!" you are saying words which no university professor understands at all. But when you say, when you see a thing, you say, "Oh, I don't like stone. I think it should be taller. I think it ought to be wider," you are dealing with the measurable, because it is made. So in the work of art there is the measurable and the unmeasurable. When you say, "It's terrific," you're talking about the unmeasurable and nobody understands you—and they shouldn't because it is fundamentally unmeasurable.

Now, from this grew other things. It wasn't just the university and the buildings there, which are not yet, have not been made in the university. And there were other buildings—I don't want to mention the whole story. But what grew in it: a realization of the marketplace and the university; and it so turned out that, the university here, the marketplace, there was place between—it happened to be in Philadelphia, the Schuylkill River. City-planning couldn't be here, because it is too politically infested. City-planning could also not be here because it is too theoretically oriented. So there had to be a place of happening, a place where the marketplace goes to, where the university goes to, both represented—but they are not here and they're not particularly here—and this was a place of happening right here, that was designed by one of the students as a bridge crossing the Schuylkill, and it was a kind of place of auditoria, a place where there were many auditoriums, many that would be the proper ones that selected for the kind of discussion which is a generator of the sense of the institutions of man, which a city planner should be most conscious of—not the traffic, not housing particularly, not any of these things—but fundamentally first, the sense of the institutions of man which yet have not been made and those which are here, but they're very badly in need of change. From this is the true generator of planning, not the other things like traffic. To me it's childplay. Traffic—we can really put it into a machine and find the answer. In a certain way you can. At least a help. Not the real answer, but at least a temporary one.

So there must be found in every city really, a place free of the marketplace, free of the school, which is, in a sense, the nerve-center of worthiness, you know; of that which can make a city great, really, because you measure the city, really, not by the excellence of its traffic system, but *why* it has a traffic system because there is worthiness to serve. And this architecture of connection between, let's say, of the whole city, takes direction. The university, you see, and the other schools take direction by the reason of their courts, their gardens, and their avenues, and so forth. The connection is both mental and physical. This institution I think, is necessary everywhere, because otherwise, nothing will progress, really. The marketplace won't progress, nor will this progress. There must be a ground here which is a kind of—it's a freedom ground at this point. This came out of no program, simply as speculations on the power of architecture to set down that which commands technology, which really writes the program, because after all, if an architect gets a program from a client, he gets an area program. He has to change the areas into spaces, because he's not dealing only with areas. They're spaces: It isn't just feelings. They are feeling, ambience. They are places where you feel something—different. As I said you don't say the same thing in a small space, you see. So a school must have small spaces as well as large spaces, and all classes need not be the same. There's something like a place of learning. Felt so. Taken out of the very essence of your feeling as a person, the various other people to a sense of commonness, which is a tremendous guide to a person's mind.

You say the institutions of man. I don't mean institutions like the establishment. I mean, really, institution being that it's an undeniable desire to have the recognition that man cannot proceed in a society

Silence and Light

of other men without having certain inspirations that they have—be given a place for their exercise. Actually, the institutions of learning stem from the way we were made. Because nature, in what it makes, it records how it was made. In the rock is the record of the rock, and in man is the record of man. Man, through his consciousness, senses inside of him all the laws of nature, except that his instrument is usually very poor, which he gets from nature, in the way of a brain, and when he mixes it up with his sense, you see, and desire, he finds that there are plenty of obstructions, and he takes years before he senses this himself. But regardless, the quality which he inherited, that part which I say is the golden dust which he does inherit, that which is the nature of man, he inherits, just like his physical being, in this he senses the desire to learn to express. So all learning, you see, stems from the way we were made, only to find out the laws of the universe because it's in you. And so it is with other inspirations which are in us. The sense of physical well-being comes from the desire to live forever: to express. The highest form of expression is art because it's the least definable.

Desire to live—to express. The institutions, therefore, are established, because there is this sense of wanting to learn, and the wanting to learn makes you pay a tax to see that a school is established. Nobody resists this tax because it is in the nature of man that he wants to learn. Sometimes he's beaten out of it because of certain things, like he's scared to be in front of a class, he loses his courage because he's slower in becoming free of this thing. That's why I believe that no marking should exist at any school because it's destructive of man. And it's very difficult, well I say, I know it is, but really, if you didn't mark anybody, I think you'd find that your class would become brighter. Actually, it is so because people don't grow equally. I have good experience in this because I was a very poor student, and I somehow managed to get past, but I only learned the things that were taught to me after I got out of school and not during the time, because I was naturally bashful. I didn't want to assert myself, and also I made my lessons three days afterward instead of the day I should. So all these things are just part of the person.

Now another example, let's say, of searching for the nature of the problem: A boy's club, I gave one time as a problem. And the speculation was: What would be the first room that one would make, which would present a boy's club. If I were to take the programs issued by the Association of Boy's Clubs, which has a standard program, or what it is, I would meet this kind of a situation: I would come to the entrance, and then there would be a supervisor who would see to it that you're a boy or a girl. Then you would go through, you see, and then you would be hit by a room that is ping-pong—noise—absolute stress and strain, because it is good to feel, as they said, that the boy must feel that he's now amongst others, you see. And then there are some guidance rooms, so to speak, and also where the older boys can be. Well, it just continues. There is, of course, a swimming pool; there is a gymnasium. But I tell you that many people would never join because of that shock, you see, of being supervised from the start, and they go into a place where you're likely to be pushed. When a boy is delicate and frail and not a fighting sort of person he walks into a gang of enemies. So, the problem was given: What is the first room. One thought that it should be a room with a fireplace: a generous one with much seating around it, and one can take a seat, hopefully that someone would come, you see, and sit by him, or that he had at least a choice not with any strain attached to it. But during the course of the development of the problem, it was found that the best place was a court. You open the door and you're in a court with an arcade around it, but the promise of the kind of room that you'd want to go to all around it. So the man chooses—the boy chooses what room he wants to go into because he's just entering life, so to speak, you see, with others, and the sensitiveness of this is certainly far greater than knowing exactly how a boy's club works. You don't know. And so you make a plan which you don't know, and it's a far superior plan.

I'll now talk about functionalism. I think you can talk about machines being functional, bicycles being functional, beer plants being functional, but not all buildings are functional. Now, they must function, but they function psychologically. There is a psychological function which is a paramount function whether it's a factory or otherwise. Just so people are involved, there must be a place for people. Even an atom-cracking plant must consider that there are people involved in this thing, and there are places for everything, but there is something which has to do with the association of people with it. And that sense, I think, brings about a new era in architecture which doesn't try to make everything be accountable. So, when you are given, as I said, a program by a client in which he gives you how much square-foot area he needs, let's say, for a lobby which he measures by square-foot area, you usually won't have more than three or four people at a time, or maybe ten or twenty. That's where the elevators are, where the stairways are, from which you go upstairs. Now measure, if this were also an entry for a school of architecture, you see how it would fail. But the program reads just the same for a school of architecture as it does for an office building—pretty much the same. It's measured by so many square feet per person; three and a half people per acre—that kind of thing. But actually, you translate the lobby into a place of entrance, and it becomes a very different thing. It is a space of entrance, not a lobby. You change it. You change corridors into galleries because you know their value, you know their tremendous association value when they are a gallery instead of a corridor, and the first thing that must be done of great importance is to make the budget economical, which means worthwhile; which means that you may spend the same amount of money, but the attitude shouldn't be that the money rules what you do. You must find that which is worthy within what is considered for the moment to be a limit, but your duty is also to portray what may increase this limit, in order to bring a worthwhile thing to the client—depending on just how you are made, whether you give in to certain things. But the going through this exercise of portraying what seems to be the nature of something is a very essential thing, I feel, to your eventual powers, which will bring about a new architecture.

Now, I have some other things here, but I cannot speak enough about light because light is so important, because, actually structure is the maker of light. When you decide on the structure, you're deciding on light. In the old buildings, the columns were an expression of light, no light, light, no light, light, no light, light, you see. The module is also light–no light. The vault stems from it. The dome stems from it, and the same realization that you are releasing light. The orders which you think about when you are, in a sense, determining the elements of design—that is to say, the elements, and how you are considering them in design to be perfected. There is in the design the consideration of the difference between the order of structure and the order of construction. They're two different things. There is an order to construction which brings in the orders of time. They're very much married to each other. The order of structure can make conscious the crane. The crane that can lift twenty-five tons should appear in a specification of present-day architecture which does not appear now. The architect says "Oh! They're using a crane on my building. Isn't that nice—so they can pick it up more easily," never realizing that the crane is a designer; that you can make something that's twenty-five tons coming to something that's twenty-five tons, and you can make a joint that's so magnificent, because that joint is no little thing. In fact, if you'd put gold into it, you wouldn't be spending too much money, because it's so big. So the realization that joint-making, which is the beginning of ornament—because I do believe that the joint is the beginning of ornament—comes into being again, you see. What you can lift as one thing should be something that motivates the whole idea of making a single thing which comes together with another single thing. So in the order of structure you make this decision like I did in Ahmedabad[5] when I said that a beam needs a column. A beam needs a column; a column needs a beam. There is no such thing as a beam on a wall. And if you make the decision which I made, saying that the beam of brick is an arch, therefore, since I did not want to use any concrete beams, and since I was not going to use any columns, it became so natural to use an arch, because it was only part of the wall construction which is characteristic of brick, and I placed everything supported under arches, and invented many things about arches, like big arches which stretch

5. The Indian Institute of Management (1962–74).

as much as twenty feet, let us say, with a very low thing using restraining members in concrete like this to take the thrust away, bringing the wall very close together, giving a space with that much opening because I made a composite order in which the concrete and the brick will work together. This is a composite order. A sort of sense of structure, a sense of the order of brick, sense of the order of structure, which made this possible. The design goes on and on; speculation of the ways you can do this thing in the most characteristic fantastic ways, because you recognize that structure has an order; that the material has an order; that the construction has an order; the space has an order in the way of the servant spaces and the spaces served; that the light has an order because it has an order in the sense that it is given by structure, and that the consciousness of the orders be felt.

I just remind you in closing, the story of Rumi,[6] a very famous Persian poet, who lived in 1200 or so, who writes of a poet; I'm not going to write the poetic language, because I don't read Persian, and also, it's far from me, the words that I read. There was a priestess who was going through her garden in spring, and of course it was a glorious day. As she went through her garden, observing everything, and came to the threshold of her house, and there she stopped in admiration— standing at the threshold, looking within. And her servant-in-waiting, came over to her, saying "Mistress, Mistress. Look without, and see the wonders that god has created." And the mistress said, "Yes, yes, but look within and see God." In other words, what man has made is very, very manifestation of God.

6. See selection 14, note 3 (page 224).

16 The Room, the Street, and Human Agreement (1971)

● ●

This is the speech Kahn gave in Detroit when he accepted the American Institute of Architects Gold Medal for lifetime achievement, a much-coveted prize awarded to one person annually. There are more preliminary drafts of this text in the Kahn archives than of any other speech he gave, indicating the determination with which he labored so as not to be misunderstood, for the occasion represented the culmination of his career and the summit of peer recognition.

In many ways, this speech also represents the culmination of Kahn's thinking, bringing together all the elements of his mature thought. "The room is the beginning of architecture," he said, and "the plan is a society of rooms"; "a long street is a succession of rooms," and the city a place of "assembled institutions." All these—room and plan, street and city, which is to say *all* architectural spaces—were also "institutions" based upon "human agreement."

But in 1971 Kahn thought "these institutions [were] on trial," operating "as matter of course" because the "inspirations" that had called them into being were "no longer felt." He saw "dissension" all around him, a "mad outburst of frustration" and "hopelessness" stemming from "the far-awayness of human agreement." Nevertheless, he was confident that "a new sense of human agreement," when it arrived, would yield "new spaces"—renewed institutions—because he was certain that "human agreement has always been and will always be."

● ●

From "Draft—AIA National Gold Medal—1971" folder, Box LIK 52, Kahn Collection.

have some thoughts about the spirit of architecture. I have chosen to talk about the room, the street and human agreement.

The room is the beginning of architecture. It is the place of the mind. You in the room with its dimensions, its structure, its light respond to its character, its spiritual aura, recognizing that whatever the human proposes and makes becomes a life.

The structure of the room must be evident in the room itself. Structure, I believe, is the giver of light. A square room asks for its own light to read the square. It would expect the light either from above or from its four sides as windows or entrances.

Sensitive is the Pantheon. This nondirectional room dedicated to all religions has its light only from the oculus above, placed to invest the room with inspired ritual without favoritism. The entrance door is its only impurity. So powerful was this realization of appropriate space that even now the room seems to ask for its release to its original freedom.

Of the elements of a room, the window is the most marvelous. The great American poet Wallace Stevens prodded the architect, asking, "What slice of the sun does your building have?" To paraphrase: What slice of the sun enters your room? What range of mood does the light offer from morning to night, from day to day, from season to season and all through the years?

Gratifying and unpredictable are the permissions that the architect has given to the chosen opening on which patches of sunlight play on the jamb and sill and that enter, move and disappear.

Stevens seems to tell us that the sun was not aware of its wonder until it struck the side of a building.

Enter your room and know how personal it is, how much you feel its life. In a small room with just another person, what you say may never have been said before. It is different when there is more than just another person. Then, in this little room, the singularity of each is so sensitive that the vectors do not resolve. The meeting becomes a performance instead of an event with everyone saying his lines, saying what has been said many times before.

Still, in a large room, the event is of commonality. Rapport would take the place of thought. This room we are in now is big, without distinction. The walls are far away. Yet I know if I were to address myself to a chosen person, the walls of the room would come together and the room would become intimate. If I were now reading, the concern would be diction.

If this room were the Baptistry of Florence, its image would have inspired thoughts in the same way as person to person, architect to architect. So sensitive is a room.

The plan is a society of rooms. The rooms relate to each other to strengthen their own unique nature. The auditorium wants to be a violin. Its envelope is the violin case. The society of rooms is the place where it is good to learn, good to work, good to live.

Open before us is the architect's plan. Next to it is a sheet of music. The architect fleetingly reads his composition as a structure of elements and spaces in their light.

The musician reads with the same overallness. His composition is a structure of inseparable elements and spaces in sound. A great musical composition is of such entity that when played it conveys the feeling that all that was heard was assembled in a cloud over us. Nothing is gone, as though time and sound have become a single image.

The corridor has no position except as a private passage. In a school, the boy walks across a hall as in his own classroom where he is his own teacher, observing others as others do. The hall asks for equal position with the library.

The society of rooms is knit together with the elements of connection which have their own characteristics.

The stair is the same for the child, the adult and the old. It is thought of as precise in its measures, particularly for the young boy who aspires to do the floors in no time flat, both up and down. It is good also to consider the stair landing as a place to sit near a window with possibly a shelf for a few books. The old man ascending with the young boy can stop here, showing his interest in a certain book, and avoid the explanations of infirmity. The landing wants to be a room.

A bay window can be the private room within a room. A closet with a window becomes a room ready to be rearranged. The lightless corridor, never a room, aspires to the hall overlooking the garden.

The library, the work court, the rooms of study, the place of meeting want to group themselves in a composition that evokes architecture. The libraries of all university schools sit well in a court entrance available to all its students as a place of invitation. The entrance courts and their libraries and the gardens and paths knitting them together form an architecture of connection. The book is an offering of the mind.

The work court of a school of architecture is an inner space encircled by workshops available to construct building experiments. The rooms of study and criticism are of a variety of dimension and spaces in their light, small for the intimate talk and work, and large for the making of fullsize drawings and group work.

Rooms must suggest their use without name. To an architect, a school of architecture would be the most honored commission.

The street is a room of agreement. The street is dedicated by each house owner to the city in exchange for common services.

Dead-end streets in cities today still retain this room character. Through-streets, since the advent of the automobile, have entirely lost their room quality. I believe that city planning can start with realization of this loss by directing the drive to reinstate the street where people live, learn, shop and work as the room out of commonality.

Today, we can begin by planting trees on all existing residential streets, by redefining the order of movement which would give these streets back to more intimate use which would stimulate the feelings of well-being and inspire unique street expression.

The street is a community room.

The meeting house is a community room under a roof. It seems as though one came naturally out of the other.

A long street is a succession of rooms given their distinction, room for room, by their meeting of crossing streets. The intersecting street brings from afar its own developed nature which infiltrates any opening it meets. One block in a stream of blocks can be more preferred because of its particular life. One realizes the deadliness of uninterested movement through our streets which erases all delicacy of character and blots out its sensitive nature given to it of human agreement.

Human agreement is a sense of rapport, of commonness, of all bells ringing in unison—not needing to be understood by example but felt as an undeniable inner demand for a presence. It is an inspiration with the promise of the possible.

Dissension does not stem from need but from the mad outburst of frustration, from the hopelessness of the far-awayness of human agreement. Desire, not need, the forerunner of the new need, out of the yet not said and the yet not made seems to be the roots of hope in dissension.

How inspiring would be the time when the sense of human agreement is felt as the force which brings new images. Such images reflecting inspirations and put into being by inspired technology. Basing our challenges on present-day programming and existing technologies can only bring new facets of old work.

The city from a simple settlement became the place of the assembled institutions. The settlement was the first institution. The talents found their places. The carpenter directed building. The thoughtful man became the teacher, the strong one the leader.

When one thinks of simple beginnings which inspired our present institutions, it is evident that some drastic changes must be made which will inspire the re-creation of the meaning, *city,* as primarily an assembly of those places vested with the care to uphold the sense of a way of life.

Human agreement has always been and will always be. It does not belong to measurable qualities and is, therefore, eternal. The opportunities which present its nature depend on circumstances and on events from which human nature realizes itself.

A city is measured by the character of its institutions. The street is one of its first institutions. Today, these institutions are on trial. I believe it is so because they have lost the inspirations of their beginning. The institutions of learning must stem from the undeniable feeling in all of us of a desire to learn. I have often thought that this feeling came from the way we were made, that nature records in everything it makes how it was made. This record is also in man and it is this within us that urges us to seek its story involving the laws of the universe, the source of all material and means, and the psyche which is the source of all expression. Art.

The desire to learn made the first school room. It was of human agreement. The institution became the modus operandi. The agreement has the immediacy of rapport, the inspiring force which recognizes its communality and that it must be part of the human way of life supported by all people.

The institution will die when its inspirations are no longer felt and when it operates as a matter of course. Human agreement, however, once it presents itself as a realization is indestructible. For the same reason a man is unable to work below his level of comprehension. To explain inspiration, I like to believe that it is the moment of possibility when what to do meets the means of doing it.

City planning must begin to be cognizant of the strength and character of our present institutions and be sensitive to the pulse of human relationship which senses the new inspirations which would bring about new and meaningful institutions. Traffic systems, sociological speculations, new materials, new technologies are servants to the pulse of human rapport which promises revelations yet not felt but in the very core of human desires.

New spaces will come only from a new sense of human agreements —new agreements which will affirm a promise of life and will reveal new availabilities and point to human support for their establishment.

I realized in India and Pakistan that a great majority of the people are without ambition because there is no way in which they are able to elevate themselves beyond living from hand to mouth, and what is worse, talents have no outlets. To express is the reason for living. The institution of learning, of work, of health, of recreation should be made available to all people. All realms of expression will be opened. Each singularity will express in his way. Availabilities to all can be the source of a tremendous release of the values locked in us of the unmeasurable in living: the art of living.

One city can distinguish itself from the other by just the inspirational qualities that exist in sensing natural agreements as the only true source of new realizations. In that sense the spaces where it is good to learn, to work and to live may remain unexpressed if their nature is not redefined. It is not just enough to solve the problem. To imbue the spaces with newfound self-quality is a different question entirely. Solution is a "how" design problem, the realization of "what" precedes it.

Now a word about inspired technology. The wall enclosed us for a long time until the man behind it, feeling a new freedom, wanted to look out. He hammered away to make an opening. The wall cried, "I have protected you." And the man said, "I appreciate your faithfulness but I feel time has brought change."

The wall was sad: The man realized something good. He visualized the opening as gracefully arched, glorifying the wall. The wall was pleased with its arch and carefully made jamb. The opening became part of the order of the wall.

The world with its many people, each one a singularity, each group of different experiences revealing the nature of the human in varied aspects, is full of the possibility of more richly sensing human agreement from which new architecture will come. The world cannot be expected to come from the exercise of present technology alone to find the realms of new expression. I believe that technology should be inspired. A good plan demands it.

A word about silence and light. A building being built is not yet in servitude. It is so anxious to be that no grass can grow under its feet, so high is the spirit of wanting to be. When it is in service and finished, the building wants to say, "Look, I want to tell you about the way I was made." Nobody listens. Everybody is busy going from room to room.

But when the building is a ruin and free of servitude, the spirit emerges telling of the marvel that a building was made.

When we think of great buildings of the past that had no precedent, we always refer to the Parthenon. We say that it is a building that grew out of the wall with opening. We can say that in the Parthenon light is the space between the columns—a rhythm of light, no-light, light, no-light which tells the tremendous story of light in architecture that came from the opening in a wall.

We are simply extending what happened long ago: The beginning may be considered the most marvelous—without precedent, yet its making was as sure as life.

Light is material life. The mountains, the streams, the atmosphere are spent light.

Material, nonconscious, moving to desire; desire to express, conscious, moving to light meet at an aura threshold where the will senses the possible. The first feeling was of beauty, the first sense was of harmony, of man undefinable, unmeasurable and measurable material, the maker of all things.

At the threshold, the crossing of silence and light, lies the sanctuary of art, the only language of man. It is the treasury of the shadows. Whatever is made of light casts a shadow. Our work is of shadow; it belongs to light.

When the astronauts went through space, the earth presented itself as a marvelous ball, blue and rose, in space. Since I followed it and saw it that way, all knowledge left me as being unimportant. Truly, knowledge is an incomplete book outside of us. You take from it to know something, but knowing cannot be imparted to the next man. Knowing is private. It gives singularity the means for self-expression.

I believe that the greatest work of man is that part which does not belong to him alone. If he discovers a principle, only his design way of interpreting belongs to him alone. The discovery of oxygen does not belong to the discoverer.

I invented a story about Mozart. Somebody dropped a dish in his kitchen, and it made a hell of a noise. The servants jumped, and Mozart said, "Ah! Dissonance." And immediately dissonance belonged to music, and the way Mozart wrote interpreting it belonged to him.

Architects must not accept the commercial divisions of their profession into urban design, city planning and architecture as though they were three different professions. The architect can turn from the smallest house to the greatest complex, or the city. Specializing ruins the essence of the revelation of the form with its inseparable parts realized only as an entity.

A word about beauty. Beauty is an all-prevailing sense of harmony, giving rise to wonder; from it, revelation. Poetry. Is it in beauty? Is it in wonder? Is it revelation?

It is in the beginning, in first thought, in the first sense of the means of expression.

A poet is in thought of beauty and existence. Yet a poem is only an offering, which to the poet is less.

A work of architecture is but an offering to the spirit architecture and its poetic beginning.

17

Address to
Naturalized Citizens
(1971)

This talk—which was given in the United States District Court for the Eastern District of Pennsylvania in Philadelphia at the request of Kahn's friend, the Honorable Edward R. Becker, Jr. (the "judge" to whom he refers), presiding—is noteworthy for two reasons. First, it demonstrates Kahn's increasing inclination to refer to "institutions" as "availabilities," meaning their potential for human betterment if they remain true to, while improving upon, their "beginnings" in "human agreement." Second, it reveals his patriotism—his belief that despite its "terrible mistakes," the United States was more "a country of availability" than any other. Kahn, himself an immigrant whose parents struggled financially after their arrival in the United States, ended up famous and comparatively well-off. This in itself was proof to Kahn of his adopted country's availability.

It is wonderful to speak in chambers where you can hear without all kinds of contraptions, and it is nice. I am going to speak about human agreement. It is different from legal agreement in that it is based on rules growing out of human experience. But human agreement is a kind of sense that everyone has. It is a soul sense—what is true and what is false and what one can readily agree to support. I would say the basis of all our institutions stems from human agree-

From "Edward R. Becker, Jr." Box LIK 52, Kahn Collection.

ment. It is an inspiring sense in man. The institution is the modus operandi. It is the way that human agreement is exercised, put into support; but it is always in a way on trial, because whatever we establish rule-wise is subject to change, whereas the laws of nature never change. They are all part of a great, enormous order, and in the order no things turn from one thing to another.

But a rule is made to be changed. It is very natural to look for the next rule which is more powerful than the one you established before, because it stems from the depths of the unmeasurable qualities of men; whereas law is set, only to be discovered. It is already here. But everything that man makes is not here. The artist's work is the work completely unique. It takes man to make a work of art. Nature does not make works of art. But that is great beauty and this inspires works of arts. I think that a nation is measured by the character of its institutions. And I believe this country is the richest in institutions. And what it means and what it has meant to me is availability, when one has the feeling that he wants to express himself a certain way: He wants to be a doctor, a lawyer, a writer, an architect. It should be like it is in this country. There is the sense that it is possible to attain this form of expression. I worked in India; I worked in Pakistan. And I know that more than 98 percent of the people cannot dare to have any desires whatsoever as to what they might want to be. And it never crosses their mind because the sense of availability is not there.

My mother was 200 percent American because she came and recognized immediately this was a country of availability; that one could by simply feeling strongly how they wanted to be, their sense of expression in their life, that one could avail themselves of the means of making this possible.

There are people in this world who can't even dare, as I said before, to think about it. When I gave my views on what the bicentennial should be like,[1] which is the celebration of the Declaration of Inde-

---

1. A talk about how Philadelphia might organize its 1976 bicentennial celebration, published in *Thursday's Drummer* (Philadelphia), 25 February 1971.

Address to Naturalized Citizens

pendence, I said that it should be the meeting of people who will discuss the possibility of broader availabilities in all countries to make a child be able to say that I want to be a doctor, I want to be one who writes, one that does beautiful bits of carpentry. I think it is the greatest catastrophe in the world when people live their lives only from hand to mouth and never cross in their minds that there is such a thing as personal expression, which is the real reason for living. If you stop to think, the real reason for living is to express, and it is just like death if you are unable to express.

Now, I think our institutions are on trial, and that is natural because every institution falls away from its original inspiration. And in the operation of an institution there are many managers who are not really good managers. There are people who don't interpret very deeply what is meant by an original inspiration. Certainly, all schools started probably with a man who didn't know he was a teacher talking to children who didn't know they were pupils. But everyone agreed in a human agreement way that there must be a classroom when it rains. And from this simple experience grew the institutions of learning because it was a non-deniable force in the mind, in the human agreement mind that the school just had to be. And it is still in my opinion the greatest institution of all. It hasn't even been tried to be expressed as yet as to the potentiality of that sense of human agreement which makes school possible.

It is that which gives you the instrumentation from which you can learn, and that means you can express more eloquently than you can without it.

I thought it was particularly appropriate to state about this following the remarks of his Honor, the Judge, who has just almost taken the words out of my mouth in expressing the inspirational qualities of this country. We are making terrible mistakes, but only because of the sense of freedom in this country, which is so marvelous that even some people think that when you make a law, you get a lawyer; you don't follow the law because it is only human-made and therefore considered rather tentative. But that is only an indication of the sense of freedom which is expressed beautifully by [Edmund] Burke before the revolution. Burke appealed to Parliament and said, "Be careful about the people of America. Don't sell them short."

Surely the sense of freedom was given to the Americans by the British who had a tremendous sense of freedom. To prove this point he warned that though the sense of freedom was gotten from England, the chapel of freedom is in America. And that chapel was meant to be the vast frontiers. The sense of freedom which is much more encompassing, which made a kind of judgment, which was beyond just circumstantial judgment; it was real inspiration quality that filtered in everyone that things are possible, that things are available. And the trees beyond and the mountains beyond and the adventure made freedom very strong. And I can say that the Constitution, that the Declaration of Independence and our Constitution is an inspiring document based on human agreement. It's gotten from the sense of broad freedom, the kind of freedom that Burke actually defined in his very beautiful words—a young man, he was like even those who wrote the document that we are speaking about, but he had a sense of human agreement which could penetrate deeply into the nature of man and knows what can stand up, what is temporary and what has eternal quality which never can be erased.

Now, I as an architect look for this quality in my work. Every building that I do, I know must answer some institution of man. When I build a school, I don't look at the fear about schools. I try to sense, as if no school has ever been made, the sense of school. When I do that, I eliminate all corridors, and I build halls, because halls become a classroom of the student. He sees in front of him people who are different. And he learns in these halls, which is a transformation from corridor, which is just circulation, to a place where students meet students and don't feel the harsh obligation of teacher and student and judgment of man, and here he feels free, and he can learn to know himself through others. Just how far do we have to go to change all our buildings to be truer than they are now, just schools? Certainly we have many schools. But we must consider that schools are a growing sense in us. And we must eventually have schools of talent, natural talent, not just the drudgery of learning which is not part of learning. I don't believe anybody learns anything that is not part of himself. Eventually with all the examinations we pass, your human quality, your sense of human agreement is what comes out for most, and from this you learn also very rapidly. I even believe that a person who knows how to dance beautifully, naturally, should be taught through dancing to learn that. So much could be learned quickly because the natural talent of a person is deep and it sets kind of a natural source of learning as well.

We've got a long way to go. And that makes it exciting because when you have no way to go it is not exciting.

I say we must go back to the original inspirations that caused our institutions to be institutions, because the original inspirations are completely indestructible. While our institutions can be said to be better, every day we must think of how we can recapture in the exercise of our institutions the original inspirations which made it.

18

Lecture at
Pratt Institute (1973)

In Kahn's second-to-last major speech, given to students at Pratt Institute in Brooklyn, he discussed humanity's unending search for the unmeasurable—the relentless probing of possibility. When he said, as he had on many other occasions, that "what was has always been, what is has always been, and what will be has always been," he was simply reaffirming the continuity of social institutions and of humanity's relentless pursuit of self-knowledge. Kahn often spoke about "what a building wants to be," which was itself, and "itself" was a design that was nearly as possible its ideal type, that Platonic-like form that had existed in the beginning but would always remain unknowable. Design exists now as "what is," as a contemporary attempt to state "what has always been," and as an endless search for form.

The architect's job, Kahn says in the last paragraph, "is to find those spaces" in which the possibilities of form might be realized, an impossibility that is nevertheless an "offering of man to [the] next man," which he defined as joy. "If you don't feel joy in what you're doing, then you're not really operating." You will live through miserable moments, "but really," he concluded, "joy will prevail."

I discovered something one day. I was in Maryland getting another sort of honorary degree, and I had some prepared speech, which of course I wasn't going to read. I knew what I was going to say. They had a new building, the architects did. They had built a new building

From *Perspecta* 19 (1982): 89–100. Reprinted with permission.

and it was there—I think the room was in the center—where the celebration, the degree-giving, was held. The room was about a hundred and twenty feet or so long and maybe fifty feet wide and had a balcony. On two ends of the balcony there were musicians—brass instrument musicians on either end—and they played some baroque music of Venetian origin, and it was absolutely wonderful. Nobody played excellently. I heard little sounds that weren't really too good: But altogether, in the way it occupied the hall, this thing made me think of something to say which was not what I had intended, and I think that seeing you all puts me in the same frame of mind.

I was going to show slides, but I'm not going to show any slides because I am bored with them, you see, myself. Maybe this is because I really don't think that telling you how I do things means very much.

I believe that a man's greatest worth is in the area where he can claim no ownership. The way I do things is private really, and when you copy you really die twenty deaths because you know that you wouldn't even go so far as to copy yourself, you see, because anything you do is quite incomplete. But the part that you do which doesn't belong to you is the most precious for you and it's the kind of thing that you really can offer, because it is a better part of you, actually. The premises anyone can use. Though you may be someone who thinks about them, you only think about them because they are part of a general commonality which really belongs to everybody.

And in getting up to speak, I had to say—after the music had been played, this great music—that it told me something that was terribly important to me. I felt, first of all, very joyous. I felt that which joy is made of. And I began to realize that joy itself must have been the impelling force that was there before we were there. That somehow joy was in every ingredient of our making. That which was the ooze, you see, without any kind of shape or direction. There must have been this force of joy, which prevailed everywhere within the context, that was reaching out to express. Somehow that word joy became the most unmeasurable word. It was the essence of creativity, the force of creativity. I realize that, if I were a painter and I were to paint a canvas of a great catastrophe, I couldn't put the first stroke on the canvas without thinking first of joy in doing it. You cannot make a drawing unless you are joyously engaged. And somehow, when I thought that art was a kind of oracle, a kind of aura, which had to be satisfied by the artist, and that the artist made something and he dedicated it to the art, an offering to the art as though it were something that preceded the work, I began to realize that art cannot be art unless it is a work, and not something absolutely there that is in the blue somewhere.

I thought then that the first feeling must have been touch. When you think of it, it probably is the first feeling. Our whole sense of procreation has to do with touch. Touch desired to be so much in touch that eyesight came from touch. To see was only to touch more accurately. And then I thought that these forces within us are beautiful things, which you still can feel although they come from the most primordial, unformed kind of existence. It still is retained in you.

I was writing a statement of appreciation for someone who helped me in doing work on the Roosevelt Memorial in New York, which I am now engaged in doing.[1] I had this thought that a memorial should be a room and a garden. That's all I had. Why did I want a room and a garden? I just chose it to be the point of departure. The garden is somehow a personal nature, a personal kind of control of nature, a gathering of nature. And the room was the beginning of architecture. I had this sense, you see, and the room wasn't just architecture, but was an extension of self. I'll explain this because I think it has qualities that don't belong to me at all. It has qualities which bring architecture to you. It has nothing to do with the practice of architecture, which is a different thing entirely. Architecture really has nothing to do with practice. That's the operational aspect of it. But there is something about the emergence of architecture as an expression of man which is tremendously important because we actually live to express. It is the reason for living.

So there is then this striving, you might say, from touch to "touch," and not just touch. In this sense there is the development of what

1. Kahn worked on this unbuilt Franklin Delano Roosevelt Memorial in 1973 and 1974.

Lecture at Pratt Institute

could be sight. When sight came, the first moment of sight was the realization of beauty. I don't mean beautiful or very beautiful or extremely beautiful—just beauty, which is stronger than any of the adjectives you may put to it. It is the total harmony that you feel without knowing, without choice—just simply beauty itself, the feeling of total harmony. It is like meeting your maker, in a way, because nature, the maker, is the maker of all that is made. You cannot design anything without nature helping you. And there is a great difference between design and form and shape. And that's what we'll talk about.

This sight then came about, and sight immediately felt the total harmony—beauty—without reservation, without criticism, without choice. And art, which was immediately felt, was the first word. One can say the first line, but I think it was the first word. The first utterance could have been "Ah"—just that. What a powerful word that is; it expresses so much, you see, with just a few letters. Now from beauty came wonder. Wonder has nothing to do with knowledge. It's just a kind of first response to the intuitive, the intuitive being the odyssey or the record of the odyssey of our making through the billions, the untold billions, of years in making. I don't believe one thing started at one time, another thing at another time. Everything was started in one way at the same time. It was at no time, either: It just simply was there. Then came wonder. This is the same feeling that the astronauts must have felt when they saw the earth at a great distance. Of course I followed them, and I felt what they felt: this great ball in space, pink or rose and blue and white. Somehow all the things on it—even the great achievements like, let us say, Paris, a great achievement, or London—they all sort of disappeared and became circumstantial works. Yet, somehow the toccata and fugue did not disappear, because they are the most unmeasurable and therefore the closest to that which cannot disappear.

The more deeply a thing is engaged in the unmeasurable, the more deeply lasting is its value. So the toccata and fugue you could not deny. You couldn't deny some of the great works of art, because they are really born out of the unmeasurable. And so I think that what you felt was, again, just wonder, not knowledge or knowing. You felt that knowledge was really not as important as your sense of wonder, which was a great feeling—without reservation, without obligation, without accounting for yourself, just the closest in-touchness with your intuitive wonder. From wonder must come realization, because in the record of your making you have gone through every law of nature. It is part of you. Recorded in your intuitive are all the great steps and momentous decisions of the making. Intuition is your most exacting sense. It is the most reliable sense. It is the most personal sense that a singularity has, and it, not knowledge, must be considered your greatest gift. If it isn't in wonder you needn't bother about it.

This must be considered when knowledge, which is a tremendously valuable thing, comes to you. It is valuable because from knowledge you get knowing, which is private. The only thing valuable to you is knowing, and knowing must never be imparted because it is very singular, very impure: It has to do with you. But knowing can give you in-touchness with your intuitive, and therefore the life of knowing is very real, but personal. Just think how much the schools must learn before they can honor the mind of a person. Within lodges the spirit; in the brain, it doesn't lodge. The brain is simply a mechanism. So the mind is different from the brain. The mind is the seat of the intuitive and brain is an instrument: You get them potluck from nature. That's why each one is a singularity.

The instrument can bring to the fore that which, if it is a good instrument, would bring the spirit within you out and put it in touch; the brain makes the mind the mind. The singularity, however, is the mind, not the brain. So, with the sense of wonder comes realization—realization, somehow born out of the intuitive, that something must be so. It has definite existence though you can't see it. Nobody can see your mind, but in it lies existence. You strive because existence makes you think of what you want to express because the expression is a drive: to express is to drive. You then make the distinction between existence and presence, and when you want to give something presence you have to consult nature.

This is where design comes in. The realization is realization in form, which means nature. You realize that something has a certain nature. When you think of the making of a school, the school has a certain nature. In making it you must consult the laws of nature, and the consultation and approval of nature are absolutely necessary. There you will find, discover, the order of water, the order of wind, the order of light, the order of certain materials. If you think of brick, for instance, and you consult the orders, you consider the nature of brick. This is a natural thing. You say to brick, "What do you want, brick?" And brick says to you, "I like an arch." And you say to brick, "Look, I want one too, but arches are expensive and I can use a concrete lintel over you, over an opening." And then you say, "What do you think of that, brick?" Brick says, "I like an arch."

It's important, you see, that you honor the material that you use. You don't bandy it around as though to say, "Well, we have a lot of material around. We can do it one way. We can do it another way." It's not true. You can only do it if you honor the brick and glorify the brick instead of just shortchanging it or giving it an inferior job to do, where it loses its character. When you use it as infill material, for instance—which I have done, you have done—the brick feels like a servant. Brick is a beautiful material and it has done beautiful work in many places; it still does because it's a completely live material. In three-quarters of the world the brick is the only logical material to use because concrete is a highly sophisticated material and not as readily available as you think. And so you can talk to nature about many other things.

When I talk to students, the one feeling I always have is that everyone can surpass me in my work. They don't, but that's my attitude. I feel that being in school is like being in a chapel, and my duty is to write psalms. I come much more refreshed and challenged from the classes. I learn more from the students than I probably teach. This is not an idle thing; it is only learning, but I learn it in my own way. It isn't what they teach me, but what I teach myself in the presence of those who I think are singularities. Therefore, teaching is the art of singularity to singularity. It is not talking to a group; a group is just a matter of so many and so many singularities. They teach you your own singularity because only a singularity can teach a singularity.

Lecture at Pratt Institute

Design from form is a realization of the nature of something which is in here. It's completely inaudible, unseeable, and you turn to nature to make it actually present from existence in the mind. I turn to what I said before about a room. And I would not like to feel that I have forgotten, nor you as I speak to you, about the stream of joy which must be felt. Otherwise you don't really feel anything. If what I say somehow activates it I'd be, of course, terribly pleased and honored. But back to the room as the beginning of architecture.

If you think about it, you realize that you don't say the same thing in a small room as you do in a large room. If I were to speak in the Sheraton Hotel I would have to pick one person who smiles at me in order to be able to speak at all, especially extemporaneously, without notes in front of me. It's an event and you treat it as an event, and therefore the room is different. Three people can make you say your lines that you've always said before because already you're somehow performing and not just thinking in terms of them.

Also, what's marvelous about a room is that the light that comes through the windows of that room belongs to the room. And the sun somehow doesn't realize how wonderful it is until after a room is made. So somehow man's creation, the making of a room, is nothing short of the making of a miracle. To think that a man can claim a slice of the sun. Now when you get an order from the school board which says: "We have a great idea! We should not put windows in schools because, after all, the darlings, you see, in the class need wall space for their paintings. And after all, also, a window could distract the teacher." But what teacher deserves that much attention? I'd like to know. After all, the bird outside, the person scurrying for shelter, the rain and you inside, the leaves falling from the tree, the clouds passing by, the sun penetrating are all great things. They're lessons in themselves. The windows are essential to the school. You were made from light and therefore you must live with the sense that light is important. It isn't just a direction from a school board, an educator, so to speak, telling you what life is all about. This must be resisted. Without light there is no architecture.

Then the room is a terribly important thing. And if you realize also

Lecture at Pratt Institute

that a plan is a society of rooms, then the large room and the small room become a kind of great thing that you can employ. The tall room, the low room, the one with the fireplace, and the one without, become a great event in your mind and you begin to think, not of the requirements but of the nature of the architectural elements that you can employ to make the environment a place where it is good to learn or good to live or good to work. Then you are really in the midst of architecture and not in the operational atmosphere of the professional man.

You're highly protected as a professional man. There isn't a person who can even say he's not as good a professional as the other fellow. You can't especially if you join the A.I.A. Everybody's completely equal. That is not so; they're not equal. They're marvelous, yes, but not equal. And not everybody is equally talented. There's no question that talent prevails anywhere. There's no person without talent. That's ridiculous. They all have talent. It's only a question, you see, of which way your singularity can blossom, because you cannot learn anything that's not part of yourself. It's impossible.

You've learned physics, I'm sure, many of you, and you don't know a word of it, yet you passed the examination. That happened to me. I copied the notes of the guy next to me, who could listen and write. If I listened, I couldn't write; if I wrote, I didn't listen. And so I had to copy his notes because he could do both things. He knew what the professor was talking about before he said it, and I had to listen to every word. Now if the teacher had said to me, "Louie Kahn, it's important for you to learn physics because you're going to be an architect," I knew that a long time, so he was right. But he says, "I know what you are. You'll be examined but I'll ask you to *draw* physics for me. That's all. Don't just write what I said." And I would surprise him. It would be my forte, my way, and therefore must not be disturbed. You lose the sense of your worth by putting yourself in—crowding yourself—with that which doesn't belong to you at all. You'll just forget it. It will never be with you. I don't know any more than one or two principles of physics.

The plan is a society of rooms. When you realize that you don't say the same thing in a small room that you do in a large room you realize that a school should be a kind of environment of rooms which would be ready for, would be offerings to school. And in doing this you become inventive in the way that is applicable to school. You would eliminate every corridor, I'm sure, and turn the corridors into halls. The halls would be the pupils' spaces that belong to them as the classroom of the students. There, the little boy can speak to the other little boys and say, "What did the teacher say?" The other boy listens and records. When the boy gets the lesson from a person of the same age, somehow the lesson becomes understandable.

How many things must happen and where does the architect sit? He sits right there. He is the man who conveys the beauty of space, which is the very meaning of spaces, of meaningful spaces. They're all meaningful. You invent an environment, and it can be your own invention. It doesn't have to be a prototype. It simply has to be the way you see the environment for learning, and not taken from all the directions that may be gotten from your books of standards. Therein lies the architect. He is not defined by being able, let's say, to gather sufficient information to operate as a professional. Now these can be harsh words and they don't seem to be applicable to everybody. But I think it is true. I think it is applicable. That's putting up an argument and solving it yourself, right?

Now then, the society of rooms is plan. You can say it is the structure of the spaces in light. And you can relate it also to an assignment that I gave myself to draw, a picture that demonstrated light. Now if you assign yourself a theme like that, the first thing you do is escape somewhere, because it is impossible to do this, you say. The white piece of paper is the illustration. If I illustrate light, I have a white paper, and that is light. What else can I do? I thought that was the only thing to do. But I realized that I wasn't right at all. When I put a stroke on the paper, a couple of strokes in ink, I realized that the black was where the light was not. And then I really could make a drawing. I would only be discerning as to where I put the black, where the light is not, and this made the picture come out.

I have some drawings and some slides with me, which I'll show to you some other time, which indicate this very clearly. The drawing is by Cruikshank, you know, an English illustrator of great importance to everyone.[2] He made a drawing of a man sitting by a fire with a swaying female sort of next to him. Through a doorway in the night was a horse. The walls were receiving the light from the fire. A fireplace, out of the picture, radiated light, which caught on the folds of the undulating female and on the man sitting on his chair; the horse behind did not receive the light, but just little sparks of it. Every pen was subservient to the sense that where the stroke was, the light was not. And the thing became absolutely luminous. Closer to the fire it was practically white paper, and then it shaded away. It was a beautiful illustration of the realizations of the expresser to find the means of making evident this fact.

Now this came from the realizations I had about light and I said that all material in nature—it being, as I said before, the mountains and the streams and the air and we—are made of light which has been spent. And all material is light which has become exhausted. And this crumpled mass called material casts a shadow. And the shadow belongs to light. So light is really the source of all being. And I said to myself, the existence will be to express in this ooze, which you might say was just completely infiltrated with joy. To be, from touch to sight to hearing that one becomes manifest and the experience of this has become ingrained. And the will, the desire, was somehow a solid front to make sight possible.

Now, you say, where is the significance in all this? It is the movement from silence, which is somewhat the seat of the measurable, which is the will to express, moving toward the means to express, which is material made of light. And light comes to you because actually it is not divided. It is simply something that's become manifest and that which desires to be manifest coming together. And that movement to light and the movement from light to a desire to be, to express, which meet at a point which may be called your singularity. There are as many meetings as there are people, and there must, in a way, almost be as

2. George Cruikshank (1792–1878).

many meetings as there are leaves on a tree, because I believe that sense must be in a tree or in a microbe equally as much as it is in every living creature. And this meeting spells your singularity.

So where's the scientist and where's the poet? The poet is one who goes from the seat of the unmeasurable and travels toward the measurable but keeps the force of the unmeasurable with him all the time, disdaining almost to write a word, which is the means. Art, the first word. And he goes toward the measurable but holds the unmeasurable and at the last moment he must write a word because, although he desires not to say anything, words propel his poetry. He has to succumb to the word after all. But he's traveled a great distance before he used any of the means. Just a smidgeon, if you will, you see. And it was enough. The scientist, who has the unmeasurable qualities, which after all are all he has as a man, holds his line, does not go away or travel with the unmeasurable because he's interested in knowing. He's interested in the laws of nature. He allows nature to come to him. Which means he has so many degrees, you know. And it comes to him. And he at that point must grab it because it's as long as he can stand the difficulty of holding back. And so he receives knowledge in full. And he works with this and you call that being objective. But Einstein traveled with the poet. He holds the unmeasurable because he's a fiddle player. And so he holds the unmeasurable for a long, long time. And he also reaches nature or light at the very, very doorstep, because he only needs a smidgeon of knowledge, because from that smidgeon he can reconstruct the universe, because he deals with order and not knowing.

No piece of knowing, you see, which is always fragmentary, is enough for a man who is truly visionary like Einstein. And he would not accept knowledge unless it belonged to all knowledge. Therefore he can so easily write his beautiful formula of relativity. It was just the way in which he just simply gave you that which can lead you to a greater sense of awe of order which all knowledge is really answerable to. One does not consider knowledge as belonging to anything human. Knowledge belongs only to that which has to do with nature.

It belongs to the universe, but doesn't it belong to eternity? And there's a big difference.

When you're making something you must consult nature, like the conversation with the brick. And you can make the same conversation with concrete. And you can make the same conversation with paper, or with papier maché, or with plastic, or with marble, or any material that has its nature. And it's the beauty of what you create that you honor—the material for what it really is. And never say that you use it in a kind of subsidiary way which makes the material itself wonder when the next man will come who will honor its character, you see.

How much can be learned, and it's not how much you learn, but it is really how much you honor, you see, the position of learning in connection with what you're doing. Because you must really . . . you must know to feed your intuitive, but you must not trust the knowing as being something that may be imparted to someone else. You translate it into the work you do, and that is your best character because your singularity will make that which is unfamiliar if you will just trust it for what it is. It will be unfamiliar in your own way. And the various expressive arts will be, will bring forward, something which had you in it as a kind of offering to the art which you are in the middle of.

So, now turning let's say—so far I think I haven't talked about architecture at all—we talk simply about, let's say, the plan, and what is a room, and a plan being a society of rooms. You can do the same thing when you're dealing, see, with plans, with city plans. There's no difference to a person who sees this in the light of its nature. What is the nature of what you are doing? Then, a plan as big as a whole city is no more complex than a house. Not at all. It's just realizing that it isn't a bag of tricks or something to do with a traffic system or things like that, because a traffic system and all the other operational systems of a city are merely operational problems. You can get people with different singularities to help you with this.

The great symphony of all the forces which make a city, I think, belongs to the mind of the architect. He is the best trained to bring it all into some symphonic character. And that has nothing to do with making a kind of beautiful-looking plan. Not at all. It must be very true to its nature. So when you're dealing with a traffic problem, and you forget the helicopters, you forget the planes, you forget the parking, you forget all these things, you're only dealing with little things. Now the force of a road is one whose objective is to come somewhere. And this coming somewhere must be considered an event which serves you very well. If at that point you spend hours trying to find a parking space you have no plan. So you consider the movement as being rewarded, you consider the tall building on the street must surrender the six stories on the street for the street's purpose, and you have an elevator reach the sixth story, which exactly is what the person living in the tall building wants. He doesn't want to live on the first level. And you just consider everything as though it had its nature.

Most of all we mustn't forget that in a city the street must be supreme. It is actually the first institution of the city. It is a decision out of commonality that you choose a place out of all places to build a place where others can settle. It's a very important decision. It's of the same importance as the positioning of the Greek temple in Greek days amongst the hills. Of all the hills, this hill is chosen for the temple. And then all the other hills sort of beckon to it as though bowing to this decision, because you do not see the hills. No, you see them as only respecting the decision of the placing of this eulogizing kind of building which, you might say, is remarkable in that it has never been there before.

I honor beginnings. Of all things, I honor beginnings. I believe that what was has always been, and what is has always been, and what will be has always been. I don't think the circumstantial play from year to year and era to era means anything, but what has become available to you from time to time as expressive instinct does. The man of old had the same brilliance of mind as we assume we have only now. And that which made a thing become manifest for the first time is our great, great moment of creative happening. I have books in my place. I like

English history. I like the bloodiness of it somehow—you know it's horribly bloody—but out of it came something. It's really just a miscuing of how things are made, and if you were to write a history of fear, I think you would write the most true of history books. And I have one of eight volumes, and I only read the first volume and only the first chapter, because every time I read it I also read something else into it. And the reason is that I'm really interested in reading volume zero. And maybe, when I get through with that, volume minus-one. History could not have started at those places. History was much, much preceded. It just isn't recorded.

And that is the beauty of our work in that it deals with the recesses of the mind from which what is not yet said and what is not yet made comes. And I think it's important to everybody, because desire is infinitely more important than need. And it's disgraceful not to be able to supply the need. It mustn't be considered an achievement if the country gives us our needs. It must be something that is a foregone conclusion if you're brought upon this world. But desire, to stymie that, to stymie the qualities of the not yet said and the not yet made, desire is the very reason for living. It is the core of the expressive instinct that has to be given play.

In cities, probably the measure of a city is the degree or the quality of the availabilities. We are living in a country which is the richest of all in availabilities, if we were to speak up. And I'm glad we don't, because as soon as we become conscious of it, it'll be just as ruinous as McCarthy, who spoiled our true consciousness, our sense of democracy.[3] He tried to define it and called for sides to be held, to be counted, and therefore destroyed the beauty of what democracy could be. And we're suffering to this day because of the attempt to isolate, you know, the qualities of democracy. I believe that the availabilities are really in this country. And we don't really appreciate them because they are there to be had. We want more of it because it's the very nature of us. It's possible to avail yourself of something. And so

3. Joseph R. McCarthy, Republican senator from Wisconsin in the 1950s, infamous for his destructive anti-Communist crusade.

availability is the hallmark of America. And it's been bandied around, it's been kept from certain people, but I think it's just there. You're about to assert yourself, and you find that it also comes your way. And I think that in the city, if I were to say, if I were to make a city plan, I think I would say, "In what way can I make the architecture of connection which would enliven the mind as to how the availabilities can be even more enriched than they are?" Put them into focus. They lose their character in course of the operations because the original inspirations are gone. Other people take over and you do not sense, you see, those inspirational moments which made those intuitions possible. And there are many still that are, in the air, completely possible.

The architect's job, in my opinion, and I must close on this, is to find those spaces, those areas of study, where the availabilities, not yet here, and those that are already here, can have better environments for their maturing into those which talk and say things to you and really make evident that the spaces that you make that are the seat of a certain offering of man to next man. It is not an operational thing. You can leave that to the builders and to the operators. They already build eighty-five percent of the architecture, so give them another five percent if they're so stingy, so very selfish about it, and take only ten percent or five percent and be really an architect and not just a professional. A professional will bury you. You'll become so comfortable. You'll become so praised, equally to someone else, that you'll never recognize yourself after a while. You get yourself a good business character, you can really play golf all day and your buildings will be built anyway. But what the devil is that? What joy is there if joy is buried? I think joy is the key word in our work. It must be felt. If you don't feel joy in what you're doing, then you're not really operating. And there are miserable moments which you've got to live through. But really, joy will prevail.

Lecture at Pratt Institute

For Further Reading

There are numerous books about Louis Kahn's work, although no comprehensive biography yet. Most are monographs or photographic studies of individual buildings, short anthologies of his texts, or reproductions of single speeches. The major books on Kahn include the following two collections of his texts, now out of print:

Wurman, Richard Saul, ed. *What Will Be Has Always Been: The Words of Louis I. Kahn.* New York: Access Press and Rizzoli International Publications, 1986. This book is wide-ranging but poorly organized, with excerpts and complete speeches not identified as such, beginnings and endings of texts not clearly indicated, and chronology neglected.

Latour, Allesandra, ed. *Louis I. Kahn: Writings, Lectures, Interviews.* New York: Rizzoli International Publications, 1991. This volume is user-friendly but does not draw upon unpublished material from the Kahn archives.

Three excellent books illustrate Kahn's best-known projects:

Brownlee, David B., and David G. De Long. *Louis I. Kahn: In the Realm of Architecture.* New York: Rizzoli International Publications, 1991. (Accompanied a major traveling exhibition.)

Larsen, Ken. *Louis I. Kahn: Unbuilt Masterworks.* New York: The Monacelli Press, 2000. (Contains computer-generated plates of eight unrealized projects.)

Rykwert, Joseph, and Roberto Schezen. *Louis I. Kahn.* New York: Harry N. Abrams, 2001. (On fifteen completed works.)

Brownlee and De Long's *Louis I. Kahn* is the best overview of Kahn's career, but Kahn's daughter wrote a more personal treatment:

Tyng, Alexandra. *Beginnings: Louis I. Kahn's Philosophy of Architecture.* New York: John Wiley & Sons, 1984. (Also contains a selection of his texts.)

For a discussion of eight commissions in the context of Kahn's relationship to modern architecture, consult:

Goldhagen, Sarah Williams. *Louis Kahn's Situated Modernism.* New Haven and London: Yale University Press, 2001.

For the first compilation of Kahn's drawings and plans, see:

Ronner, Heinz, and Sharad Jhaveri. *Louis I. Kahn: Complete Work, 1934-1974.* 1977. Rev. and expanded ed., Basel, Switzerland, and Boston, Mass.: Birkhauser, 1987. (Lists every project for the years it covers but does not illustrate them all.)

Gast, Klaus-Peter. *Louis I. Kahn: Complete Works.* New York: Prestel, 2001. (Lists all Kahn projects beginning with the first in 1925.)

Index

283

285